THE
PRACTICE AND PROCEDURE
OF THE
COMMERCIAL COURT

THE
PRACTICE AND PROCEDURE
OF THE
COMMERCIAL COURT

By

ANTHONY D. COLMAN

One of Her Majesty's Counsel, of Gray's Inn and
sometime Scholar of Trinity Hall,
Cambridge

LONDON

LLOYD'S OF LONDON PRESS LTD.

26–30 Artillery Lane, Bishopsgate,
London E1 7LX

1983

©

ANTHONY D. COLMAN

1983

ISBN 0-907432-58-1

PRINTED IN GREAT BRITAIN BY
The Eastern Press Limited
SPECIALIST LAW BOOK
AND JOURNAL PRINTERS
LONDON AND READING

PREFACE

The last ten years have seen changes of major importance in the work, practice and procedure of the Commercial Court. From being a fairly minor side street in the 1950s the Court had, by 1980, become a central thoroughfare accommodating an ever-increasing volume of traffic. A forum in which one judge was intermittently employed in hearing all the commercial summonses and all the actions and special cases stated by arbitrators had become what Sir John Donaldson, M.R., has recently described as "the curia franca"—the busiest commercial tribunal in the world, frequently sitting in five divisions and in the course of a year disposing of as much interlocutory work as the whole of the rest of the Queen's Bench Division.

It is not only in the volume of the Court's work that great changes have occurred, but also in the nature of the work. What might with justification be described as the most far-reaching judge-made change in the common law in recent times—the *Mareva* injunction—owes its development in large measure to the work of the judges of the Commercial Court. The administration of the *Mareva* jurisdiction has occupied a large part of the time of the Court during the last eight years and uniform principles of practice have been developed. A very substantial body of case-law has emerged; much of it not previously collected and considered in a convenient form.

The second major development in the work of the Court in recent years has been the creation and subsequent administration of the Arbitration Act 1979. Born out of the Report on Arbitration of the Commercial Court Committee published in 1978, the Act has brought about considerable changes in the work of the Court. The hearing of special cases stated by arbitrators under the Arbitration Act 1950 has declined and will shortly disappear entirely but has been replaced by the deluge of applications for leave to appeal against arbitration awards under the 1979 Act. A practice has been developed for dealing with these applications and a substantial section of this book has been devoted to a discussion of the principles set out in the large number of recently decided cases.

Apart from dealing in detail with these two major areas of the Court's work— the *Mareva* injunction and the Arbitration Act 1979—this book sets out to help the overworked practitioner in his day-to-day work in dealing with commercial actions and arbitration work in the Commercial Court by attempting to supply him with what, it is hoped, will be most of the answers to most of the questions on practice and procedure which he may need to answer at short notice, particularly on a Friday afternoon. Inevitably though, some of the answers will have to wait for future editions of this book.

By the very nature of the topics covered by this book, it has been necessary to set out procedural steps in considerable detail. The descriptions of the administrative operations involved in commercial litigation would have been quite impossible without the ample and enthusiastic help of David Bird, the Listing Officer of the Commercial Court, whose interest in this book and constant encouragement have been of immense assistance and support. I am also most grateful to Sir John Donaldson, M.R., Lord Justice Goff and Mr Justice Mustill, all of whom have given up valuable time to discuss this book and its contents.

In connection with the precedents of orders, summonses, originating summonses and motions which are to be found in the chapters on *Mareva* injunctions and on the Commercial Court and Arbitration proceedings, the work of Victor Lyon has been of the utmost assistance and is greatly appreciated.

Finally, the physical task of putting into legible form the author's disparate, random and often barely comprehensible thoughts has been skilfully accomplished by Jan Campbell, Gillian Beard, Karen Woodall and Shirley Rodriguez.

I am also most grateful to Philip Littler and Paul Vivian of my publishers for their enthusiastic help and suggestions on lay-out and presentation and not least for their tolerant acquiescence in the delays and late alterations of which this author has been substantially guilty.

A. D. C.

Temple, London, EC4.
10 May 1983.

TABLE OF CONTENTS

TABLE OF CASES

TABLE OF STATUTES

TABLE OF RULES OF THE SUPREME COURT

THE ORIGIN AND DEVELOPMENT OF THE COMMERCIAL COURT

The foundations of much of English mercantile law were laid in the latter half of the eighteenth century. Trials of commercial actions were frequently held in the Court of King's Bench, one of whose judges would sit at *nisi prius* in the Guildhall in the heart of the City of London. It was there that Lord Mansfield often sat during the 32 years from 1756 to 1788 during which he was Chief Justice of the Court of King's Bench. It was there that under his influence there were developed consistent principles of mercantile law, particularly in relation to bills of exchange, insurance and shipping. The incorporation into English law of mercantile usage and the consequent consistent application of those usages to the cases which came before the Court was brought about by Lord Mansfield's practice of empanelling a body of jurymen who were experienced merchants from the City conversant with mercantile usage. He would leave to the jury specific questions as to mercantile usage and then incorporate their verdict on such questions into his judgment. The same jurymen served over a number of years and Lord Mansfield was thus able to conduct the trials at the Guildhall in such a way as to encourage City merchants to feel that their disputes would be decided by a tribunal closely conversant with trade practice and mercantile law.

After the era of Lord Mansfield commercial cases continued to be tried at the *nisi prius* sittings at the Guildhall but the popularity of this forum with the City merchants seems to have diminished during the nineteenth century. In 1865 the Guildhall sittings were discontinued. The City business houses were obliged to litigate their disputes in the Common Law Courts. This was not an attractive forum. Judges tended to disappear on circuit, dates for trial were uncertain and often not maintained and more often than not the cases came before judges who knew little or nothing about mercantile law or commercial disputes.

There was at this time a strong feeling amongst those trading in the City that the Courts were not a satisfactory forum for the resolution of commercial disputes. Litigation was regarded as too slow and too expensive. The widely-held view was that the judges and the juries before whom most commercial actions were tried were out of touch with the world of international commerce and were unfamiliar with everyday commercial activity. There was nothing new about this complaint.

1

Two hundred years earlier Samuel Pepys commented on hearing a case on a policy of marine insurance argued in the Court of King's Bench that "to hear how the counsel and judge would speak as to the terms necessary in the matter would make one laugh". There was a considerable increase in the popularity of commercial arbitration. When the Judicature Commission was sitting in the years 1869 to 1874 the City made great efforts to persuade it to recommend the establishment of tribunals of commerce or a system of judicial arbitration. One witness before the Commission put it thus:

> "To guard myself against the possibility of litigation, this is the clause which I have inserted in my form of charter-party: 'Should any difference arise between the owners and the charterers as to the meaning and intention of the charter-party, the same shall be referred to three parties in London, one to be appointed by each of the parties hereto, and the third by the two so chosen, and their decision, or any two of them, shall be final and binding; and this agreement may, for enforcing the same, be made a rule of Court'. Now we regard this between two respectable persons as a great safeguard. We know, of course, that litigation may be forced upon us, but between two fair men our differences in nine cases out of ten, or in a greater proportion of cases, are settled by this arbitration reference. I may state that with regard to many articles, especially corn, and sugar, and seed, and so on, there is a clause to a similar effect inserted, particularly in cost, freight, and insurance transactions. There is generally a clause to this effect,
> 'If any dispute arises out of this contract it is to be referred to two parties, one to be chosen by each, with power to select a referee'. These disputes, which are generally questions either of quality or of condition of the cargo, or of some minor detail, arise daily. The number of arbitrations that take place daily in London is extremely numerous, and there is, both in the Baltic Coffee House and in other large centres of trade, a regular system of arbitration. At Mark Lane there is a system of the kind".[1]

The Judicature Commission rejected the suggestion that there should be tribunals of commerce or judicial arbitration. Its Report dated 21st January 1874[2] considered the subject of special tribunals for the trial of commercial disputes in some detail:

> "We find that those by whom legislation on this subject has been promoted (although generally desiring that some provision should be made for more summary proceedings in many commercial cases), are not agreed as to the character of the tribunals which they wish to establish, or the class of cases that should come within their cognizance. Indeed, there is no unanimity of opinion as to whether the judges should be wholly commercial, or partly commercial and partly legal; whether the commercial members of the tribunals should be

---

1. Statement by C. M. Norward, M.P., Judicature Commission: Parly Papers, 1874, Vol. 24, Reports from Commissioners, xiii, p. 146.
2. Parly Papers, 1874, Vol. 24, Reports from Commissioners, xiii, p. 7.

judges having an equal voice in the decision, or assessors or advisers only to a legal judge, who would in that case be president of the Court; whether the commercial members should be paid or not for their services; whether the tribunals should observe the ordinary rules of evidence, or be at liberty to admit anything as evidence which they may consider material to the point in issue; whether they should be guided by the principles laid down by the Superior Courts of Law, or decide irrespectively of precedent and according to their own views of what is just or proper in each particular case; whether the parties should be allowed to be represented by counsel or solicitors; whether there should be any appeal, and in what cases, and to what Courts. Upon all these points there appears to be the greatest diversity of opinion.

"We find moreover that, even in the countries in which tribunals of commerce are established, great diversity exists with regard to the constitution of these Courts. Thus, in France, in Belgium, and in some other countries, all the members of the Court are merchants, except the greffier or registrar, and he has technically no voice in the decision. On the other hand, in many of the German States, the Court is presided over by a lawyer. In Dantzig, the tribunal consists of a legal president, four other legal judges, and four merchants, but the merchant judges do not attend unless required. In Konigsberg, the commercial members have no vote, only a deliberative voice, the decision resting entirely with the legal members of the Court. In Prussia, generally, it is in contemplation to substitute a paid lawyer for an unpaid merchant as president. There is, in fact, no uniformity in the constitution of these tribunals; in some countries the mercantile, in others the legal, element prevails, sometimes in the latter case to the exclusion of the commercial altogether.

"We also find that, where the tribunal is composed entirely of mercantile judges, assisted by a greffier who is a lawyer, the latter, although he has no vote, becomes of necessity the most important member of the Court; and thence arises the anomaly, that the person who virtually decides the case is not clothed with the responsibilities of a judge.

"Now, we think that it is of the utmost importance to the commercial community that the decisions of the Courts of Law should on all questions of principle be, as far as possible, uniform, thus affording precedents for the conduct of those engaged in the ordinary transactions of trade. With this in view it is essential that the judges by whom commercial cases are determined, should be guided by the recognised rules of law and by the decisions of the Superior Courts in analogous cases; and only judges who have been trained in the principles and practice of the law can be expected to be so guided. We fear that merchants would be too apt to decide questions that might come before them (as some of the witnesses we examined have suggested they should do), according to their own views of what was just and proper in the particular case, a course which, from the uncertainty attending their decisions, would inevitably multiply litigation, and with the vast and intricate commercial business of this country would sooner or later lead to great confusion. Commercial questions, we think, ought not to be determined without law, or by men without special legal training. For these reasons, we are of opinion that it is not expedient to establish in this country tribunals of commerce, in which commercial men are to be the judges".

The Report recognised the disadvantages of the frequent lack of technical knowledge of commerce displayed by judges and juries and recommended that commercial actions should be tried by a judge assisted by two business assessors. They would be commercially-experienced men and their function would be to sit with the judge and to advise him on technical and practical matters which might arise during the trial and by their presence to "deter skilled witnesses from giving such professional evidence as is often a scandal to the administration of justice".

The Commission was not unanimous in its recommendation and the City was distinctly sceptical as to its usefulness.[3]

The Government did not adopt the Commission's recommendation. The Judicature Acts of 1873 and 1875 hindered rather than helped towards the speedy, efficient and informal resolution of commercial disputes. The fusion of common law and equity made available in commercial actions certain features of the procedure of the old Court of Chancery, such as interrogatories and discovery of documents, which tended to lengthen the interlocutory stages of litigation and thereby greatly increase the cost of having disputes resolved in the Courts.

By 1894 the decline in the volume of commercial litigation had been so pronounced that one of the judges felt able to publish in an article in *The Times* of 10th August 1892 the following comments:–

> "The bulk of the disputes of the commercial world seldom, in these modern days, finds its way into the Courts. Merchants are shy of litigation. No solicitor can tell his client beforehand, even with a moderate degree of certainty, what is the limit of cost to which a man may be put, either in prosecuting or in defending his just rights. Statements of claim and statements of defence, affidavits of documents, and copies of correspondence, interrogatories and further interrogatories, all may furnish materials for learned arguments before master and judge, before Divisional Court, and Court of Appeal. And when at last the exhausted belligerents arrive at the verdict of a jury or the decision of

---

3. In his reasons for declining to sign the Third Report Sir Sydney Waterlow put the view of the City thus:

"I am unable to agree in all the recommendations of this report, and therefore do not sign it. I feel very strongly that in a great commercial country like England tribunals can and ought to be established where suitors might obtain a decision on their differences more promptly, and much less expensively, than in the Supreme Courts as at present constituted and regulated. Those who support the present system of trying mercantile disputes seem to regard them all as hostile litigation, and lose sight of the fact that in the majority of cases when differences arise between merchants or traders, both parties would rejoice to obtain a prompt settlement by a legal tribunal duly constituted, and to continue their friendly commercial relations. The present system too frequently works a denial of justice, or inflicts on the suitors a long-pending, worrying law-suit, the solicitors on either side pleading in their clients' interests every technical point, and thus engendering a bitterness which destroys all future confidence and puts an end to further mercantile dealings.

"It is essential that the procedure of our merchantile Courts (whether called Tribunals of Commerce or by any other name) should be of the simplest and most summary character".

a High Court judge, a year's delay is given even then to the defeated party, during which he may appeal to the Court of Appeal, and one more year within which to begin his luxurious march towards the House of Lords. Two considerations are important to men of business when contemplating the possibilities of litigation. The first is—money. 'How much is it likely at most to cost?' The second is—time. 'How soon at latest will the thing be over?' They want to close their books at the end of the current year, to write off bad and hopeless debts, to know upon what lines next year to deal with similar questions should they arise. For such and other reasons of their own the mercantile public is not fond of law, if law can be avoided.

"They prefer even the hazardous and mysterious chances of arbitration, in which some arbitrator, who knows about as much of law as he does of theology, by the application of a rough and ready moral consciousness, or upon the affable principle of dividing the victory equally between both sides, decides intricate questions of law and fact with equal ease".

It was generally acknowledged that commercial arbitration could be a hazardous adventure. The parties could not disturb an award in the Courts however obvious the arbitrator's error of law if the error were concealed behind the face of the award and if no special case had been requested or ordered under the Common Law Procedure Act 1854, sections 4 or 5 or, latterly, under the Arbitration Act 1889, section 7. A certain disenchantment with commercial arbitration began to emerge.

In an attempt to re-establish the City's confidence in the Courts the Government introduced in Parliament in 1891 a Bill to restore sittings of the judges of the Queen's Bench Division at the Guildhall. In introducing the Bill in the House of Lords, the Lord Chancellor, Lord Halsbury, observed that his attention had been called by a great variety of persons to the diminution of City causes due to the inconvenience caused by existing arrangements to businessmen in the City. Businessmen, he was informed, would not go out of the City in business hours. Therefore sittings at the Guildhall were to be tried as an experiment,[4] The Bill became the Judicature (London Causes) Act 1891. The new sittings were inaugurated by the Lord Chief Justice, Lord Coleridge, and Mr Justice Willes. But they were not a success. Not a great deal of Court business emerged. The City and legal profession regarded the mere transfer of the trial venue as quite inadequate. They wanted a new tribunal which could freely depart from the excessively formal procedures of the High Court.

In a report published in January 1892 by a joint committee set up by the Bar and the Law Society, whose members included such experienced leaders as

---

4. Hansard, Parliamentary Debates, Vol. 352, p. 1583.

Channell and Kennedy,[5] it was stated that if the High Court of Justice was to regain the confidence of the commercial community or even retain its present share in the settlement of mercantile disputes, it was essential that a separate list should be established for the entry of commercial actions in London and that this list should be operated separately from all other work of the Queen's Bench Division.[6]

Lord Coleridge, the Lord Chief Justice, did not favour this suggestion. Efforts to persuade him to agree to the setting up of a separate list to be manned by judges who had commercial experience, such as Mr Justice Mathew and Mr Justice Willes, failed. He felt that anything which involved the suggestion that all the judges of the Queen's Bench Division were not equally fit and sufficiently experienced to try all civil disputes was undesirable. In late 1891 Lord Justice Bowen and Mr Justice Mathew addressed to him a letter which invited the summoning of a council of judges under section 75 of the Judicature Act 1873. In 1893 the council issued a report recommending that a list of commercial causes should be created in London which would be separate from the general list of causes. The parties to a mercantile cause were to be free to enter their action in the mercantile list and the associate was to determine whether the cause was of a mercantile character. Two judges were to be selected by the judges of the Queen's Bench Division at their first meeting in the legal year to try mercantile causes for the ensuing year. There were to be two parallel lists and the two judges would try the cases entered in their respective lists unless they were engaged on circuit. The two judges were to have power to advance a case in the list and to fix a date for its trial. This recommendation was, however, blocked by Lord Coleridge.

On 24th May 1894 the Queen's Bench judges made a further recommendation "that it is desirable that a list should be made of commercial causes to be tried at the Royal Courts of Justice by a judge alone or by jurors summoned from the City, and that a Commercial Court should be constituted of judges to be named by the judges of the Queen's Bench Division". In June 1894 the main obstacle to the foundation of the Commercial Court disappeared with the death of Lord Coleridge. His successor as Lord Chief Justice, Lord Russell of Killowen, gave strong support to the movement.

There were, however, still considerable difficulties in founding the Court. Many held the view that nothing could be done without legislation. Others said that the Government was unlikely to find time for a Bill and that great delays would occur if that course was adopted. It was thought that the Rule Committee had power to

---

5. For the composition of the Committee see Mathew, *Practice of the Commercial Court*, 2nd edn., p. 7.

6. *Law Times*, Vol. xcii, p. 198.

sanction the proposed change. It started to work on the matter but found the task of defining what was a commercial cause one of almost insuperable difficulty. Eventually the judges of the Queen's Bench Division met and appointed a committee from themselves to consider whether it was possible to establish a Commercial Court relying simply on existing Rules of the Supreme Court on the assumption that the Queen's Bench judges had inherent power to make such changes in procedure and administration as they considered necessary for the better administration of justice.

In February 1895 the fruits of the committee's work emerged in the form of the famous "Notice as to Commercial Causes":

HIGH COURT OF JUSTICE

QUEEN'S BENCH DIVISION

COMMERCIAL CAUSES

NOTICE

The judges of the Queen's Bench Division desire to make in accordance with the existing rules and orders, further provision for the dispatch of commercial business as herein provided:

1. Commercial causes include causes arising out of the ordinary transactions of merchants and traders; amongst others, those relating to the construction of mercantile documents, export or import of merchandise, affreightment, insurance, banking and mercantile agency, and mercantile usages.

2. A separate list of summonses in commercial causes will be kept at chambers. A separate list will also be kept for the entry of such causes for trial, but no cause shall be entered in such list which has not been dealt with by a judge charged with commercial business, upon application by either party for that purpose or upon summons for directions or otherwise.

Commercial causes may be transferred from the Chancery Division to the Queen's Bench Division in accordance with the existing practice.

3. With respect to town commercial causes it is considered desirable, with a view to dispatch and the saving of expense, that all applications shall be made direct to the judge charged with commercial business, and with respect to country commercial causes applications may, by consent of the parties, be made to him in like manner.

4. As to commercial causes already entered for trial, application may be made to such judge by either party to enter the same in the commercial cause list.

5. Applications in commercial causes under Order 14 shall be made as heretofore, but where leave to defend has been given, such causes may be dealt with like other commercial causes.

6. Application may be made to such judge under the provisions of the Judicature Act 1894, and the rules thereunder, or by consent, to dispense with the technical rules of evidence for the avoidance of expense and delay, which might arise from commissions to take evidence and otherwise.

7. Application may also be made to such judge, after writ or originating summons, for his judgment on any point of law.

8. Such judge may at any time after appearance and without pleadings make such order as he thinks fit for the speedy determination, in accordance with existing rules, of the questions really in controversy between the parties.

9. Parties may, if they so desire, agree that the judgment or decision of such judge in any cause or matter shall be final.

10. Application may be made to such judge in urgent cases to fix an early day for the hearing of any cause or matter.

11. Summonses may be entered in the list of commercial summonses on and after Wednesday the 20th day of February next; these will be heard by Mr Justice MATHEW, who, on Friday the 1st day of March next, will sit, and thenceforward will, until further notice, and as far as is practicable, continue to sit *de die in diem* for the dispatch of commercial business. Where necessary, other judges of the Queen's Bench Division will assist in the disposal of commercial business.

12. Country commercial causes will be tried as is usual at the Assizes.

By Order.

The Queen's Bench judges nominated Lord Russell and Mr Justice Collins to sit, in addition to Mr Justice Mathew, if necessary. But more than anyone else it was Mr Justice Mathew who in the first few months of the existence of the new Court set about creating an entirely new approach to the resolution of commercial disputes by the Courts. No doubt Lord Mansfield would strongly have approved. For the first time since his day there was a Court which was being run expressly for the benefit and convenience of the commercial houses of the City and the commercial community at large. Its judges would not be strangers to bills of exchange, policies of marine insurance, charter-parties and bills of lading. In that Court, pleadings, interlocutory applications and the conduct of trials were not to be treated as art-forms in themselves. Instead, the Court was to be run as a brisk, business-like and efficient service to the commercial community. The object was to achieve definition of the real matters in issue as early as possible with as few technicalities and as few interlocutory proceedings as were consistent with an orderly trial.

The hallmark of the Court was procedural innovation aimed at greater efficiency. This is illustrated by the reports of cases in the early volumes of *The Times Reports of Commercial Cases*. The Introduction to Volume I expressed the general approach:

> "The learned judge was guided in the course he adopted by the obvious objections to the existing methods of administering the law. It was clear that, if the legal advisers of the parties were willing to assist the Court, commercial disputes might be settled as promptly by a judge as by an arbitrator. But to attain this end it was necessary that the judge should be made acquainted at the earliest possible stage of the proceedings with the nature of the plaintiff's and the defendant's case. This could only be done effectively if the respective

solicitors made careful enquiry into the facts, and were so enabled to give the judge the fullest information. The commercial litigation of the country being in the hands of solicitors of high character and great professional skill, who were not likely to fail to conduct the cases entrusted to them in the best interests of their clients, they were relied upon to respond to any reforms designed to lead to despatch and prevent useless expense . . . The course of procedure followed in chambers has been to ascertain, upon the making of the order for the transfer of the case to the commercial list, what directions were needed to secure a trial at the earliest convenient date. This has been done without difficulty. Commercial cases present themselves for the most part in similar shapes, and are readily defined. In former times pleadings in such cases generally followed common forms. As the result of this preliminary discussion before the judges many cases have been put in train for settlement. When it has been found that the case must be tried, a note has been made by the judge of the questions which the parties have expressed their intention of raising, and a copy of this note has been furnished to each side, or a direction has been given that notice of the grounds of claim and defence should be exchanged . . . Commercial cases have been tried upon the evidence prescribed by the orders made in chambers without difficulty or delay, and with a great diminution of the cost incidental to actions in which the ordinary modes of litigation are followed. The grasp which the judge obtains of the case in chambers, and the power which he consequently acquires to prevent the taking of steps which will not assist the Court at the trial, have been found to be of extreme value in securing expedition".

Although it was popularly assumed that as a result of the Notice as to commercial causes the "Commercial Court" had been created, there was in form no new Court at all. All that had formally been done was to create a new list as part of the administration of actions to be tried by the Queen's Bench Division. "It is a mere piece of convenience in the arrangement of business", said Lindley, L.J., in *Baerlein* v. *Chartered Mercantile Bank*.[7]

It was not until 1970, by section 3 of the Administration of Justice Act 1970, that the Commercial Court was formally established as such.[8] The Notice of 1895 contained nothing which conflicted in any respect with the existing Rules of the Supreme Court.[9] Even the provisions for the commercial judge to hear all interlocutory applications was not inconsistent with the Rules. Until 1867 interlocutory applications in the Court of Queen's Bench had been heard by the judges. It was only in that year that Masters were given power to sit in chambers to determine interlocutory matters.[10] But the judges did not thereby lose their jurisdiction in chambers and this jurisdiction was confirmed by section 39 of the Judicature Act 1873.

---

7. (1855) 2 Ch.D 488, at p. 491.
8. See p. 13 below. Since repealed and replaced by section 6 of the Supreme Court Act 1981.
9. See the remarks of Lord Esher, M.R., in *Barrie* v. *Peruvian Corporation* (1896) 1 Com.Cas. 269.
10. Judges' Chambers Act 1867.

Following the establishment of the Commercial Court the commercial judges from time to time regulated the practice and administration of the Court by issuing Practice Directions. Those issued before 1962 are now of no more than historical interest.[11] Their objective is almost always the more efficient disposal of the actions before the Court and the more efficient use of the Court's time.

Although the business-like atmosphere of the Commercial Court initiated by Mathew, J., survived for many years, the original momentum seems to have been largely lost by the time of the Second World War. There was a loss of speed, a loss of informality of procedure and a loss of efficiency. Orders for trial without pleadings became infrequent. The pleadings which in the early days of the Court were in extremely brief form became long and elaborate. The commercial judges latterly took a much less positive line on the summons for transfer to the Commercial List than that adopted by the commercial judges in the early days of the Court. Parties who set out to prolong commercial litigation by taking technical points were succeeding in doing so. By 1960 the Commercial Court had faded in popularity with the commercial community. In 1958 only 27 actions were set down for trial and only 21 actions were actually tried in the Court. The previous year only 15 actions had been tried.

Commercial Court Users' Conference 1960

In response to this great decline in the business of the Commercial Court the Lord Chancellor, Viscount Kilmuir, appointed in 1960 a Commercial Court Users' Conference under the chairmanship of Lord Pearson to enquire into this decline and to report as to the views of the commercial community upon any reforms of the constitution, practice and procedure of the Commercial Court which might improve its service. The Report of the Conference was published in 1962.[12]

The Conference attributed the decline in the work of the Court to the fact that, trading organisations having increased in size and become fewer in number, only those disputes involving relatively large amounts would be litigated; that foreign trading organisations preferred arbitration to a decision by an English Court; that the accumulation of case law contained in past decisions of the Court had removed doubts as to the law and thereby discouraged litigation; that the commercial community had an "inherent dislike of publicity and especially of the system of oral examination and cross-examination"; that costs and delays had increased; that it was more difficult to enforce a judgment of the Court abroad than it was an arbitral award, by reason of the Geneva Convention 1927 on the reciprocal

---

11. A summary of the more important Practice Directions can be found in Mathew, *Practice of the Commercial Court*, 2nd edn., pp. 18–19. For the text of these directions see *The Annual Practice*, 1965, Vol. 2, p. 2402 f.
12. 1962 Cmnd. 1616.

enforcement of awards having been signed by many more States than allowed enforcement within their territory of judgments of the Commercial Court. A further special factor was the current practice of resolving claims involving loss of or damage to cargo, not as in the period between the two World Wars by litigation in effect between cargo underwriters and the shipowners' Protection and Indemnity Association, but by compromise which had been assisted by the centralization of settlements in Lloyd's Claims Bureau and by the Gold Clause Agreement.

In spite of the decline in the business of the Commercial Court the Conference considered that its importance to the commercial community had not diminished and that the Court should continue in being, but subject to certain reforms.

The Conference regarded as the Court's most important defect the decline in the significance of the summons for transfer to the Commercial List as the central interlocutory function in commercial actions. In consequence, the commercial judges had lost most of their ability to control the interlocutory stages and thereby to run the Court in the efficient and business-like way in which it had been run at the end of the nineteenth century. Not only had trials without pleadings become a rarity but it had become the practice for counsel practising in the Commercial Court to plead at inordinate length. Much of the delay in bringing commercial cases to trial was due to delays in the preparation and delivery of pleadings. It was recommended that pleadings should be avoided wherever possible and that trials on agreed statements of fact should be encouraged. The Conference also attached great importance to extending the commercial judges' powers to order, without the consent of the parties, informal proof of primary facts and, in particular, that unsworn statements of witnesses should be admissible evidence of their contents. Finally, in order to satisfy the desire of the commercial community for the settlement of disputes in private and to overcome the disadvantages not attaching to arbitration awards that judgments of the Commercial Court were unenforceable or not easily enforceable in most countries outside the Commonwealth, the Report recommended that commercial judges should have power to sit in private as arbitrators.

Consequences of the 1962 Report

Three important consequences flowed from the 1962 Conference Report.

Firstly, in October 1962, Megaw, J., issued a new Practice Direction[13] which stressed the importance of not treating the summons for transfer as a mere formality and emphasized the need to work out on that occasion a full order for directions and also underlined the need to shorten and simplify pleadings if they could not be dispensed with altogether.

---

13. [1962] 1 W.L.R. 1216.

The New Order 72

Secondly, in 1964 there was introduced Order 72 of the Rules of the Supreme Court. This was the first attempt substantially to regulate by the Rules the practice and procedure of the Commercial Court. But with Order 72, rule 4,[14] there was introduced a procedural change which was to have very far-reaching consequences. For the first time it became possible for a plaintiff to commence his action in the Commercial List without the need to apply to the commercial judge for an order for transfer. All he had to do was to mark the writ "Commercial List" in the top left-hand corner and the action was then automatically entered in the Commercial List. Either party could still apply to the commercial judge at any stage in the proceedings before trial by summons for an order to transfer commercial actions pending in the Queen's Bench Division to the Commercial List[15] and there was also provision[16] for the removal of actions from the Commercial List. The effect of this procedural change was very considerable. In practice it was now the legal advisers of plaintiffs who decided whether an action should be entered in the Commercial List. Once the new procedure for automatic entry had been used it was rare for any other party to apply to have the action removed from the List. Since this procedure was introduced the summons for transfer has been much less frequently used than before. This has brought about a substantial saving in time and costs. It has also had the consequence that in commercial actions where there is no particular urgency in bringing the matter to trial the matter has first been brought before the commercial judge for directions after the close of pleadings and often after completion of discovery. The solicitors and counsel involved can therefore normally be reasonably conversant with the real issues in the action and thus able to join in obtaining an order for directions which is likely to be of real help in the efficient conduct of the proceedings. They can say with some confidence when the case is likely to be ready for trial and how long the trial is likely to last.

In the years following the introduction of automatic entry there was a steady overall increase in the number of actions in the Commercial List. The impact of this procedure took a few years to affect the number of cases listed for trial. In 1966 it was only 25 but in 1968 it was 89 and in the period 1970 to 1975 it ranged from 90 to a peak of 130 in 1974.[17]

Introduction of judicial arbitration

The third consequence of the 1962 Report was the introduction of the system of judge-arbitrators by section 4 of the Administration of Justice Act 1970.[18]

---

14. See p. 176 below.   15. RSC Order 72, rule 5.

16. RSC Order 72, rule 6.

17. These aggregate figures include special cases under the Arbitration Act 1950 and the increase in the work of the Court during this period must be attributed in part to an increase in the number of hearings of special cases.

18. Set out at p. 185 below.

Commercial judges have been empowered to accept appointments as sole arbitrator or umpire provided that (1) the dispute appears to be of a commercial character, (2) the commercial judge thinks in all the circumstances that it is fit that he should accept the appointment and (3) the Lord Chief Justice informs the judge concerned that, having regard to the state of business in the High Court and in the Crown Court the judge can be made available to hear the arbitration. The control and supervision which the High Court exercises over ordinary arbitrators is in various respects vested in the Court of Appeal in relation to judge-arbitrators. The procedure and practice relating to judicial arbitrations is fully discussed at pages 149 to 154 below.

It might have been thought that judicial arbitrations would have been widely used by the commercial community, but this has not been so. There have been, until the last two years, remarkably few judicial arbitrations. Recently, the number has increased and it is thought that there are now several appointments each year. The lack of interest in judicial arbitration may be attributable to the fact that it is not widely known that this service is available. It may also be, however, that the parties to commercial disputes often prefer to retain the practice of appointing commercial men rather than lawyers, even as umpire, or merely that they do not generally feel that it is worth paying fees[19] for a judge-arbitrator to hear their disputes in private when they can get their cases tried in public by the Commercial Court without a fee.

The Commercial Court becomes a Court

The Commercial Court was formally created a Court for the first time by section 3 of the Administration of Justice Act 1970, which provided that:

> "(1) There shall be constituted, as part of the Queen's Bench Division of the High Court, a Commercial Court to take such causes and matters as may in accordance with rules of Court be entered in the Commercial List.
>
> "(2) The judges of the Commercial Court shall be such of the puisne judges of the High Court as the Lord Chancellor may from time to time nominate to be Commercial Judges.
>
> "(3) Nothing in this section is to be taken as prejudicing provisions of the said Act of 1925[20] which enable the whole jurisdiction of the High Court to be exercised by any judge of that court".

This provision has recently been repealed and replaced by the Supreme Court Act 1981, of which section 6 provides that:

> "(1) There shall be— . . .
> (b) as parts of the Queen's Bench Division, an Admiralty Court and a Commercial Court.

---

19. For judge-arbitrators' fees, see p. 154 below.
20. Supreme Court of Judicature (Consolidation) Act 1925.

"(2) The judges of . . . the Admiralty Court and of the Commercial Court shall be such of the puisne judges of the High Court as the Lord Chancellor may from time to time nominate to be . . . Admiralty Judges and Commercial Judges respectively".

Expansion in Court business 1975 to 1982

During the period from 1975 to 1982 there has been an enormous increase in the volume of work before the Commercial Court. In 1975 the number of cases listed for trial was 128. This number had increased by 1982 to 431.[21] In 1975, 659 commercial summonses were issued. Yet in 1982 this number had risen to 2,930.[22] Much of the increase in the Court's work during the earlier part of this period was attributable to the great volume of special cases stated by arbitrators relating to the trade in soya beans and other edible products. Statistics showing the number of hearings of trials and summonses and also the number of *ex parte* applications as published in the Commercial Court Committee Annual Report 1982 will be found reproduced at pages 17 to 18 below.

The Arbitration Act 1979

The abolition of the special case procedure by the Arbitration Act 1979[23] has reduced this area of the Court's work as those arbitrations commenced before 1st August 1979 are concluded. Nevertheless, since the Arbitration Act 1979 came into operation and as those arbitrations conducted under that Act were brought to a hearing, there has been a steadily increasing number of applications for leave to appeal under section 1 of the 1979 Act and of hearings of appeals. The practice has developed that appeals are heard at a separate hearing from applications for leave to appeal.[24] This often involves the Court hearing the same point of law argued on two separate occasions—first in outline on the application for leave to appeal and secondly at greater length on the hearing of the appeal. This is a distinctly cumbersome procedure and probably an expensive one for litigants. It may well be that the time has come to reconsider this practice.

Effects of RSC Order 73, rule 6

An additional factor in the increase in the work of the Commercial Court has been the introduction in 1979 of the new Order 73, rule 6[25] This has the effect of

---

21. This compares with 25 cases listed for trial in 1966.
22. This compares with 219 summonses listed for trial in 1966.
23. See p. 123 below.
24. See p. 132 below and *Tor Line A.B.* v. *Alltrans Group of Canada Ltd.* [1982] 1 Lloyd's Rep. 617, at pp. 626–7.
25. See p. 181 below.

bringing before the commercial judge in the first instance all applications arising out of any arbitration which by sections 2 and 3 of the Arbitration Act 1979 have to be heard by a judge. These are applications:—

(1) to remit an award under section 22 of the Arbitration Act 1950;

(2) to remove an arbitrator or umpire under section 23(1) of the Arbitration Act 1950;

(3) to set aside an award under section 23(2) of the Arbitration Act 1950;

(4) for leave to appeal under section 1(2) of the Arbitration Act 1979;

(5) to determine under section 2(1) of the Arbitration Act 1979 any question of law arising in the course of the reference;

(6) for an order under section 1(5) of the Arbitration Act 1979 for an arbitrator or umpire to give reasons for his award;

(7) for an order under section 5 of the Arbitration Act 1979 that an arbitrator should have extended powers in the event of the failure of a party to comply with the arbitrator's order.

The effect of this provision is that the commercial judges have the primary responsibility for operating the Arbitration Act 1979. The circumstances in which the Commercial Court will order such applications to be heard by Queen's Bench judges who are not commercial judges and the practice and procedure applicable to the Arbitration Act 1979 are considered in detail in Chapter 8 of this book at pages 121 to 122. One of the consequences of this provision is that disputes arising out of arbitrations which might not otherwise have come before the Commercial Court have in those cases to be brought before the Court in the first instance.

Increase in number of commercial judges

In order to absorb the great increase in the Commercial Court's business the number of commercial judges now available in London at any one time to try commercial actions and summonses has been raised to five. In 1963 a single commercial judge was only intermittently occupied with the work of the Court. Each year one of the commercial judges takes charge of the Commercial List.

The Commercial Court Office

With the increase in volume of work and of the number of commercial judges it has become necessary to equip the Commercial Court with a permanent administration. Formerly, the Commercial List was in practice administered by the clerk to the commercial judge appointed to be in charge of the Commercial List for that year. The Commercial Court now has its own office—Room 198 in the Royal Courts of Justice, Strand, London, WC2A 2LL—under the management of the Commercial Court Listing Officer, Mr David Bird. He is often popularly referred to as the Commercial Judge's Clerk or the Commercial Court Clerk. Contact with the Commercial Court Office can be made by telephone at London 405-7641, extension 3826, and by telex at 296983 COMM—G. It is the objective of the Office to be as helpful and informative as possible and it is believed that many of the procedural and practical problems which this book does not solve can be resolved by contacting Mr David Bird.

Commercial Court sits during Long Vacation

The Commercial Court, unlike the remainder of the Queen's Bench Division, sits for ordinary business during a period of about four weeks out of the Long Vacation. This period is usually made up of about one week at the beginning of August and about three weeks in September. This system was first introduced in 1977 by a Practice Direction of Mr Justice Kerr.[26] It is not necessary to establish that the matter is Long Vacation business as defined by Order 64, rule 4, but the judge in charge of the Commercial List does exercise a discretion in deciding whether to allow a particular matter to be tried in the Long Vacation, priority being given to urgent matters.

Hearings of commercial summonses

The hearing of practically all commercial summonses, except those expected to take more than half a day, takes place on Fridays.[27] All five of the commercial judges then available in London are normally able to hear such summonses. Trials of actions which are part-heard at the end of Thursdays are normally adjourned until the following Monday, except where great inconvenience or prejudice or unjustifiable extra expenses would thereby be caused to one or both parties involved. Arrangements for the dates for the hearing of summonses and difficulties arising out of the clashing commitments of counsel are considered in Chapter 5 of this book at pages 54 to 55.

Commercial Court Committee

In order to maintain contact between the Commercial Court and those who use it a Users' Liaison Committee was set up in 1967 with the encouragement of Mr Justice Donaldson.[28] There is now a standing committee which was set up by the Lord Chancellor in 1977 so as to provide a direct link between the commercial

26. [1977] 1 All E.R. 912. This is set out at p. 167 below.
27. Practice Direction dated 9th November 1981 of Parker, J., at [1982] 1 Lloyd's Rep. 115.
28. Practice Statement dated 6th November 1967 at [1967] 1 W.L.R. 1545.

users of the Court and the Court itself for the purposes of improving the service of the Court. The committee meets under the chairmanship of the commercial judge for that year in charge of the Commercial List. It is comprised of all the commercial judges, representatives of counsel and solicitors who practise in the Court, and of the commercial users of the Court. Its operation and work is described in detail in Chapter 2 of this book, at pages 19 to 22 below. It has proved a very valuable link between the Court and the commercial community and it is hoped that the existence of this continuing link will prevent in future the kind of departure of business from the Commercial Court which occurred after the Second World War.

The Commercial Court was founded for the purpose of providing for the commercial community—the shipping industry, the banks, the underwriters, the commodity merchants and all the other business houses—a service which was not otherwise available in the High Court and which was, above all, what the commercial community wanted. The continued existence of the Commercial Court depends on its ability to satisfy the needs of its users for an efficient and convenient means of resolving commercial litigation. The Court strongly encourages comments and suggestions from the commercial community and the legal profession aimed at improving the service it provides. These should be addressed to the Secretary to the Commercial Court Committee, Mr P. Denyer, of the Crown Office, Royal Courts of Justice, Strand, London, WC2A 2LL.

COMMERCIAL COURT COMMITTEE ANNUAL REPORT 1982
COMMERCIAL COURT WORK FOR THE TWELVE MONTHS ENDING JULY 1982

HEARINGS
The following table shows the number of cases given trial dates for each of the past five years and the manner of their disposal.

	1978	1979	1980	1981	1982
Cases given trial dates	339	381	416	446	421
Settled	118	152	174	162	189
Adjourned at request of parties	80	94	111	103	71
Stood out by the Court	20	10	6	18	8
Heard and disposed of	110	118	125	157	153

SUMMONSES

	1978	1979	1980	1981	1982
Summonses issued	1590	1909	2536	2898	3022
Summonses heard	1180	1424	1817	2106	1998
Judge/days occupied	115	228	256	277	329

EX PARTE APPLICATIONS
(i) *Injunctions*

1978	1979	1980	1981	1982
119	197	244	280	384

(ii) *Documentary Applications.* (Requests for leave to serve process out of the jurisdiction; approval of consent orders etc.)

1978	1979	1980	1981	1982
Approx 700	734	1011	1015	1092

CHAPTER 2

THE COMMERCIAL COURT COMMITTEE

The chief and most effective means of ensuring that the Commercial Court is aware of and catering for the needs of those who use it is the Commercial Court Committee. This was set up by the Lord Chancellor in 1977[1] under the chairmanship of the judge in charge of the Commercial List, then Mr Justice Kerr. The purpose of the Committee was to provide a direct link between the commercial users of the Court and the Court itself, for the purpose of improving the service which the Court is able to offer. The terms of reference of the Committee, as originally specified, were to consider and keep under review the working of the Commercial Court and the Arbitration Special Case procedure and to make recommendations to the Lord Chancellor as might be necessary *from time to time*. It is thus a standing committee.

The Committee now meets about four times a year. The judge for that year in charge of the Commercial List acts as Chairman and all the other commercial judges are *ex officio* members. There are representatives of the leading and junior counsel in practice at the Commercial Bar and of those solicitors who practise in the Commercial Court. The arbitrators of the City of London are also represented—through the London Maritime Arbitrators' Association and the Chartered Institute of Arbitrators. So also are the clearing banks, the association of the commodity trades and the Protection and Indemnity Clubs. The Department of Trade and Industry has a representative. There is also an American lawyer member to make known transatlantic views on the operation of the Court and also a member from Continental Europe. The composition of the Committee is designed to help the Commercial Court to consult the views of those who use it as to the kind of service which it should try to provide. The fact that the Committee membership includes representatives of foreign legal and commercial interests underlines the fact that the Court is now consciously performing a function which is in substance much wider than that of a mere domestic Court.

---

1. The Committee had a predecessor of great importance to the development of the Commercial Court, namely the Commercial Court Users' Conference set up in 1960 by the Lord Chancellor, Viscount Kilmuir, its terms of reference being to report on the *decline in business* in the Court and upon any reforms in the constitution, practice or procedure which were considered likely to improve the service of the Court. The Report it produced in 1962 (Cmnd. 1616) and its consequences are discussed at p. 10.

Indeed, it is in effect now providing a forum for the litigation of disputes between overseas trading, banking and shipping organizations and corporations which often do not carry on business in London and whose disputes are often wholly unconnected with London or with Britain save for the incorporation of English law or a reference to London arbitration in the underlying contracts. If, as may well be true, this is the only domestic Court in the civilised world whose administration is fashioned in regular consultation with and on the advice of foreign legal and commercial interests that is because the Commercial Court is performing a unique function in providing a venue for the conduct of a very substantial proportion of all the world's mercantile litigation. Indeed, in a recent judgment in *Amin Rasheed Shipping Corporation* v. *Kuwait Insurance Company,*[1a] Sir John Donaldson, M.R., referred to the Commercial Court as "the *curia franca* of international commerce" and as being far more than a national or domestic Court but rather an international commercial Court, most of whose judgments were concerned with the rights and obligations of foreign nationals.

The Committee meets under the auspices of the Lord Chancellor's Department and the Secretary is currently Mr P. Denyer of the Crown Office.[2] Those who litigate in the Commercial Court or who regularly practise in it are strongly encouraged to make known to the Secretary any suggestions they may have as to the administration and operation of the Court, and also with reference to the operation of the Arbitration Act 1979 and the jurisdiction in relation to *Mareva* injunctions.

The Committee has a major function in monitoring the working of the Arbitration Act 1979. Although the Committee's recommendation[3] that an Arbitration Rules Committee should formally be set up with powers similar to those of the Supreme Court Rules Committee has not yet been adopted, the Commercial Court Committee's views on the working of the new provisions of RSC Order 73 introduced for the purpose of operating the Arbitration Act 1979 will no doubt be conveyed to the Supreme Court Rules Committee. In 1981 a small sub-committee was set up under the chairmanship of Mr Justice Mustill to monitor the working of the 1979 Act and to consider amendments to the 1950 and 1975 Acts.

It was partly in consequence of the recommendations of the Committee that the provisions in the Arbitration Act 1979, whereby a party could appeal to the Court of Appeal against the decision of a commercial judge granting or refusing leave to appeal against an arbitration award, were amended by section 148 of the Supreme Court Act 1981.[4]

1a. [1983] 1 W.L.R. 228.
2. Views and suggestions relating to the operation of the Commercial Court may be sent to Mr P. Denyer, Crown Office, Royal Courts of Justice, Strand, London, WC2A 2LL.
3. Report on Arbitration. Cmnd. 7284, para. 55.
4. See p. 139.

A major part of the Committee's work has been related to the efficient administration of the Commercial Court, in particular, the consideration of what steps should be taken to reduce the lead time for the hearing of actions and summonses. Among steps more recently approved by the Committee have been the more rigorous exclusion from the Commercial List by the operation of the judges of RSC Order 72, rule 6 of all actions in which the matters in dispute are not strictly commercial.[5] By a Practice Direction of 9th November 1981[6] an important change was made with the agreement of the Committee in the organisation of the Commercial Court's business. The old system under which the judge in charge of the Commercial List heard as many as possible of the outstanding summonses on Tuesdays and Fridays with other commercial judges who might be available hearing the "overflow" was abolished and for an experimental period all the commercial judges available in London now hear summonses on Fridays. Actions will not normally be heard on Fridays so as to release as many of the judges as possible for the hearing of summonses. This change was introduced in order to deal with the increasingly large backlog of summonses which had been building up for some time in the Commercial List. The Practice Direction made special provision for dealing with the difficulties that might confront solicitors and members of the Bar who were engaged in summonses listed before more than one judge. It also invited the bringing to the attention of the Commercial Court Committee any difficulties encountered in working the new system and suggestions for dealing with them. After the first year of working the new system the Committee Report for the period ending in July 1982 noted a reduction in the lead times for commercial summonses: whereas in July 1981 it would have taken four months to obtain a hearing date for a half day summons, a year later the time had been reduced to four or five weeks.

---

5. For a discussion of the operation of the power to order an action to be removed from the Commercial List, see p. 56 below.

6. This Practice Direction is set out at p. 170 below. The invitation to communicate difficulties in working the new system to the Commercial Court Committee included in that Practice Direction refers to a further practice statement set out in the Supreme Court Practice 1982, Vol. 1, at para.72/8/3. This refers to the setting up in 1967 of a Users Liaison Committee and is in the following terms:—

Suggestions concerning the Commercial Court

The Commercial Court was established at the end of the last century in order to meet the special problems of the commercial community. Since then it has sought periodically to adapt its procedure to the continually changing needs of that community. The success of this process depends in part upon a steady flow of information and constructive suggestions between the Court and those who appear there either as litigants or as their professional advisers. The formation of the Commercial Court Users Liaison Committee will greatly assist this process and it is hoped that all concerned will make the fullest use of this additional channel of communication.

The working of *Mareva* injunctions has also been considered by the Committee, in particular the administrative problems and the expenses of third parties such as the clearing banks in giving effect to such injunctions. Consideration of this matter by the Committee underlay the judgment of Mr Justice Goff in *Searose Ltd.* v. *Seatrain (U.K.) Ltd.*[7] The Committee's July 1982 Report referred in particular to the desirability that undertakings exacted from plaintiffs should include an undertaking to inform any third party upon whom an injunction is served of his right to apply to the Court to discharge or vary the injunction in so far as it affected him.

Amongst other matters considered by the Committee in 1980 and 1981 have been the great delays in the reporting of important commercial cases. The Committee has dealt with the availability of adequate Court accommodation, particularly for the hearing of the increasingly frequent heavy cases which involve many parties, their solicitors and counsel and vast quantities of documents. In January 1982 the Committee recommended that the Commercial Court should have a telex terminal in the Royal Courts of Justice. This has now been installed for an experimental period and its use is encouraged to help increase the administrative efficiency of the Commercial Court.[8]

It is the Committee's practice to publish towards the end of each year a brief report on its work during the previous legal year. These annual reports give a useful account of the progress of the Committee and of the expanding volume of the Commercial Court's work year by year. They also contain interesting statistical information on the number of actions and summonses dealt with each year by the Commercial Court. The statistical information set out in an Appendix to the Committee's 1982 Report is reproduced at pages 17 to 18 above.

---

7. [1981] 1 W.L.R. 894, and see generally p. 101 below.
8. Telex number 296983 COMM-G.

CHAPTER 3

WHAT IS A COMMERCIAL CASE?

It is extremely difficult and almost certainly undesirable to put forward any comprehensive definition of what constitutes a commercial case and is a fit action for the Commercial Court. The commercial judges and those who frequently practise in the Court will, however, normally experience little difficulty in identifying any given case as being fit or unfit to be tried in that forum.[1] Thus it is perhaps most helpful to illustrate the kind of disputes which are likely to give rise to commercial actions fit to be tried by the Court rather than to lay down any all-embracing definition of a commercial action. This is the approach adopted by the Rules of the Supreme Court, Order 72, rule 1(2). It was also the approach of those concerned with the initiation of the Commercial List. In 1892 the Joint Committee appointed by the Bar and the Law Society to consider the trial of commercial cases, in recommending that a separate list of commercial actions in London and Middlesex should be set up and tried separately from the other actions in the Queen's Bench Division, reported[2] that:

> "The Commercial List should be confined to actions related clearly to mercantile, commercial, and shipping matters, such, e.g. as the following:
>
> Fire and marine insurance.
>
> The carriage of goods by land or water and contracts relating thereto.
>
> Negotiable and other mercantile instruments.
>
> Banking, stock exchange, and similar financial business.
>
> Questions between principal and agent in mercantile business.
>
> Contracts between merchants and their clerks or employees.
>
> Dealing with or in relation to mercantile property of any kind, or in relation to the sale, manufacture, or hire of the same.
>
> The construction, alteration, or repair of ships or of buildings, or machinery used, or to be used, for commercial purposes.
>
> Questions relating to patents.
>
> Whilst suggesting the above classification the joint committee do not pretend that it is exhaustive, or that it is not capable of improvement. They believe that

---

1. Like the elephant contemplated by Scrutton, L.J., in *Merchants Marine Insurance Co. Ltd.* v. *North of England Protecting and Indemnity Association* (1926) 26 Ll.L.Rep. 201, at p. 203: "One might possibly take the position of the gentleman who dealt with the elephant by saying he could not define an elephant but he knew what it was when he saw one".

2. January 1892, *Law Times*, Vol. xci, p. 432.

in practice there would be very rarely any difficulty in deciding what is properly
a commercial or mercantile action".

It will be seen that some of the matters illustrated would not now be
considered as lying within the jurisdiction normally exercised by the Commercial Court. Thus disputes under ordinary contracts of employment are not
normally heard. Disputes relating to the construction and repair of buildings[3]
are rarely heard and only then if they raise questions as to the meaning of the
contract or difficult matters of the law of contract. In *Peter Lind & Co. Ltd.* v.
Constable Hart & Co. Ltd.[4] Mr Justice Mustill heard an application under
section 21(1) of the Arbitration Act 1950 where the issue was whether a
building contract had been repudiated and duly ordered the award to be stated
in the form of a special case. In that application, however, there was a major
issue of some general importance, namely whether the issue of repudiation was
in itself a question of law. Actions relating to patents are now assigned to the
Chancery Division and are heard by the Patents Court and not in the Commercial Court.[5]

The question of definition of a commercial cause was further considered by the
Rule Committee in 1895 before the establishment of the Commercial List. In the
event no comprehensive definition was incorporated into the Notice of February
1895, paragraph 1 of which stated that:

> "Commercial causes include causes arising out of the ordinary transactions of
> merchants and traders; amongst others, those relating to the construction of
> mercantile documents, export or import of merchandise, affreightment, insur-
> ance, banking, mercantile agency and mercantile usages".

No more precise or comprehensive definition of a commercial action was thought
to be necessary when in 1964 Order 72, rule 1(2) was introduced. Apart from
minor changes in the wording of the Order of 1895, with one qualification, the
substance of the definition and the examples remain unchanged in Order 72, rule
1(2).[6]

---

3. For a discussion of the possible impact on the area of the Court's jurisdiction of the appeal
procedure set up by the Arbitration Act 1979 and in particular the requirement in RSC Order 73, rule
6 that any matter reserved by Order 73, rules 2 and 3 to be heard by a judge shall in the first instance
come before a commercial judge, see p. 181. It may well be that the Court will now entertain disputes
under R.I.B.A. and civil engineering contracts.
4. [1979] 2 Lloyd's Rep. 248. See also *Modern Engineering (Bristol) Ltd.* v. *C. Miskin & Sons Ltd.*
[1981] 1 Lloyd's Rep. 135—application to remove the sole arbitrator for misconduct in a civil
engineering dispute.
5. RSC Order 104, rule 2(1).
6. RSC Order 72, rule 1(2):
> "In this Order 'commercial action' includes any cause arising out of the ordinary transactions
> of merchants and traders and, without prejudice to the generality of the foregoing words, any
> cause relating to the construction of a mercantile document, the export or import of merchandise,
> affreightment, insurance, banking, mercantile agency and mercantile usage".

One modification in the wording of the original Notice of 1895 which appears in Order 72, rule 1(2) which may prove to be of significance is that commercial actions are now defined as including "any cause arising out of the ordinary transactions of merchants and traders . . ." as distinct from *"causes* arising out of the ordinary transactions of merchants and traders". It is suggested that the effect of the 1964 wording is that all those causes which can be shown to arise out of the ordinary transactions of merchants and traders are *ipso facto* commercial actions and ought to be treated as fit to be tried in the Commercial Court. Before the modified wording was introduced it was probably open to the commercial judge in his discretion to decline to transfer to the Commercial List some actions which, although they arose out of the ordinary transactions of merchants and traders and were therefore on the face of it covered by the Notice, were for some special reason unsuitable for trial in the Commercial List. Whereas it may no longer be open to the commercial judges to decline to try actions which are covered by the definition in Order 72, rule 1(2), they can still of their own motion refer any question or issue of fact arising in a commercial action to an official referee for an inquiry and report.[7] This power of referral may be particularly useful where there are major issues involving accounts, the valuation of goods or other property or complex calculations of damages. However, it is suggested that there is nothing in Order 72 which gives the commercial judges discretionary power to decline to maintain in the Commercial List commercial actions, as defined by Order 72, merely because the only issues are of fact: it is not a prerequisite for trial in the Commercial Court that the action should raise issues of law or construction.

Within the broad guidelines of the definition of "commercial action" in Order 72, rule 1(2), whether any particular action will be treated as fit to be tried in the Commercial Court depends on the practice of the commercial judges developed over the years and in marginal cases on the way in which the commercial judge exercises his discretion.

The definition is not intended to be exhaustive and cases may from time to time arise which may not clearly fall within its scope but which are treated as fit to be tried in the Commercial Court. For example, *Pan-American World Airways Inc.* v. *Department of Trade*[8] was the trial of a summons by an airline for a declaration that the Secretary of State for Trade could not revoke or suspend its operating permit because of the payment by the airline of more than the maximum agency commission agreed by the International Air Transport Association. In *Seaboard World Airlines Inc.* v. *Department of Trade*[9] the Commercial Court heard a dispute

---

7. RSC Order 36, rule 2.
8. [1975] 2 Lloyd's Rep. 395.
9. [1976] 1 Lloyd's Rep. 42.

as to which route and upon what terms the plaintiff airline was obliged to carry
cargo between New York, Paris and London under the terms of its operating
permit and of the Bermuda Agreement 1946. In *Rockwell Machine Tool Co. Ltd.
v. Commissioners of Customs and Excise*[10] the plaintiff company claimed that it
was entitled under the provisions of the Customs (Import Deposits) Act 1968 to
be repaid by the Customs a sum paid as an import deposit in respect of machinery
imported into Britain from the United States. The issue was whether the plaintiffs
themselves or the buyers of the machinery had paid the deposit and whether the
Customs were entitled to repay the deposit to those buyers in accordance with
their own regulations as to documentation and repayment procedures. In *The
Neapolis II*[11] the Commercial Court heard a claim by the owners of a cargo vessel
which had sustained damage by grounding for damages for negligence and breach
of duty under the Occupiers' Liability Act 1957 against the owners of a wharf on
the River Neath where the vessel had been moored. There was also an issue as to
whether the defendants were entitled to limit their liability.

In *N.W.L. Ltd. v. Nelson and Laughton, The Nawala*[12] the plaintiff shipowners
unsuccessfully claimed an injunction against representatives of the International
Transport Federation restraining them from causing the vessel to be blacked by
members of the Federation.

In case of doubt as to whether the Court is likely to regard a particular case as
fit for hearing as a commercial action the best course is to examine for similar
cases the index of *The Times Reports of Commercial Cases,* which contain reports
of the principal cases heard in the Commercial Court up to the Second World
War, and that of *Lloyd's Law Reports* which give a similar coverage from 1919 to
the present.

It can safely be assumed that all disputes relating to the carriage of goods by
sea, air and land will be heard by the Court, as will disputes relating to the sale,
chartering or hire of ships, aircraft and commercial road vehicles, including those
designed to carry passengers rather than goods. The Commercial Court does not
normally hear claims by passengers in respect of their baggage or personal
injuries.[13] Where, however, the case raises an issue of construction of an inter-

---

10. [1970] 2 Lloyd's Rep. 42; [1971] 2 Lloyd's Rep. 298 (C.A.).
11. [1980] 2 Lloyd's Rep. 369. This is a case of a kind much more usually to be found in the
Admiralty Court.
12. [1980] 1 Lloyd's Rep. 1 (H.L.).
13. Claims by the passengers and their dependants arising out of the disastrous fire on board the
Greek liner *Laconia* in 1963 were pursued through their interlocutory stages in the Commercial Court
but were all settled before any were brought to trial. They were perhaps exceptional because they
involved so many claimants and because there were major issues as to the construction of the terms
and conditions of passage on the tickets, as to whether some of the passengers were bound by the
terms and as to the effect of the interposition of travel agents on the binding force of the conditions.

national agreement, such, for example, as the Warsaw Convention, or a statute, such, for example, as the Carriage of Goods by Air and Road Act 1979, it may be heard by the Commercial Court.[14] Disputes in relation to contracts of marine and aircraft insurance and reinsurance and to the insurance of all kinds of commercial property will be heard. Disputes as to matters of construction of other types of insurance policy are also occasionally heard.[15] Contracts for the sale of all types of goods between dealers will be heard, but the Commercial Court will not normally entertain disputes relating to retail sales. Members of the public having retail purchase or private sale disputes should enter their actions in the Queen's Bench Division Non-Jury List. Actions involving such disputes have recently on a number of occasions been removed from the Commercial List by the exercise of the commercial judges' powers of removal under Order 72, rule 6(1).[16] Disputes arising out of shipbuilding contracts are commonly heard and it is not uncommon for disputes relating to contracts for the construction of plant and machinery to be litigated in the Commercial Court. Actions by and against agents and brokers involved in transactions of the kind referred to earlier in this paragraph are normally heard in the Court, notably those affecting shipbrokers, chartering brokers, insurance and reinsurance brokers and agents and freight forwarders. Disputes relating to the warehousing of goods may be brought before the Court.

Banking disputes are frequently heard by the Commercial Court, including actions in tort for negligence.[17] The fact that they involve issues relating to the mortgage of land or goods is not in itself a reason for their being treated as unfit for trial in the Commercial Court. In *Midland Bank* v. *Stamps*,[18] an action in the Queen's Bench Division, in which the bank claimed moneys said to be due on a current account and under a guarantee of the indebtedness of a company of which the defendant was a director, the defendant applied to have the action transferred to the Chancery Division by virtue of Order 88, rule 2, by which there is assigned to the Chancery Division any action in which there is a claim for "payment of

---

14. See, for example, *Fothergill* v. *Monarch Airlines Ltd.* [1980] 1 Lloyd's Rep. 149 and [1980] 2 Lloyd's Rep. 295.

15. See, for example, *Rigby* v. *Sun Alliance & London Insurance Ltd.* [1980] 1 Lloyd's Rep. 359—a case involving the construction of a householders' comprehensive policy, the action being brought by the assured householder against his insurers; *Harker* v. *Caledonian Insurance Co.* [1980] 1 Lloyd's Rep. 556 (H.L.)—a claim by the estate of a soldier killed in a motor accident against the insurers of the driver at fault, involving construction of Colonial legislation.

16. "The judge may, of his own motion or on the application of any party, order an action in the Commercial List to be removed from that list".

17. See, for example, *Box* v. *Midland Bank* [1979] 2 Lloyd's Rep. 391.

18. [1978] 1 W.L.R. 635. See also *Amalgamated Investment & Property Co. Ltd.* v. *Texas Commerce International Bank Ltd.* [1982] Q.B. 84, an action in which the central issue was the construction, scope and application of a guarantee to the defendant bank but where that guarantee was secured by mortgages to the bank of real property.

moneys secured by a mortgage of any real or leasehold property". The defendant had executed a mortgage of real property in favour of the bank to secure all moneys due from him on his current account and under the guarantee. The bank applied for the transfer of the action to the Commercial Court. Donaldson, J., relying on the Lord Chancellor's *Practice Direction (High Court: Divisions)*[19] and section 58, proviso 2, of the Supreme Court of Judicature (Consolidation) Act 1925,[20] held that he had a complete discretion whether to retain the action in the Queen's Bench Division or whether to transfer it to the Chancery Division. He exercised his discretion in favour of retaining the action and transferring it to the Commercial Court. Having observed that the action was a "commercial action" within the definition in Order 72, rule 1(2), he went on:

> "Two specialist Courts thus have grounds for claiming or declining jurisdiction. As it seems to me, I have to consider whether the dispute is primarily a banking dispute or a mortgage dispute. In the present instance it is primarily a banking dispute, although questions as to the conduct of a receiver appointed by the bank may be raised by counterclaim. At this stage at least the matter is, in my judgment, wholly appropriate to decision by a judge of the Commercial Court.
>
> "If it had been clearly a mortgage dispute, turning upon the rights of mortgagors and the remedies of mortgagees, I should have had no hesitation in transferring it to the Chancery Division. If it had been a dispute which raised issues both of banking law and practices and of the law relating to mortgages, I should have considered whether it would be more conveniently heard in the Commercial Court or in the Chancery Division, bearing in mind that each has the same power to grant or refuse the remedies and reliefs sought by the parties and that each would seek to dispose of the matter in precisely the same way as would the other".

---

19. [1973] 1 W.L.R. 627.
20. Supreme Court of Judicature (Consolidation) Act 1925:
   "Subject to rules of Court and to the provisions of this Act, every person by whom any cause or matter is commenced in the High Court shall assign the cause or matter to such division as he thinks fit by marking the document by which the cause or matter is commenced with the name of that division and giving notice thereof to the proper officer: Provided that—(1) All interlocutory and other steps and proceedings in or before the High Court in any cause or matter subsequent to the commencement thereof, shall, subject to rules of Court and to the power of transfer, be taken in the division to which the cause or matter is for the time being attached: and (2) If any plaintiff or petitioner assigns his cause or matter to any division to which, according to rules of Court or the provisions of this Act, it ought not to be assigned, the Court or any judge of that division, on being informed thereof, may, on a summary application at any stage of the cause or matter, direct the cause or matter to be transferred to the division to which, according to those rules or provisions, it ought to have been assigned, or may retain it in the division in which it was commenced; and (3) All steps and proceedings taken by the plaintiff or petitioner or by any other party in any cause or matter and all orders made therein by the court or any judge thereof before any transfer shall be valid and effectual to all intents and purposes in the same manner as if the steps and proceedings had been taken and the orders had been made in the division to which the cause or matter ought to have been assigned . . ."

The observation that if the case had been "clearly a mortgage dispute" it would have been transferred to the Chancery Division must be read in the context of a case involving a mortgage of real or leasehold property. It is suggested that actions involving disputes about mortgages of goods would normally be retained in the Commercial Court.

Actions raising disputes as to letters of credit, bank guarantees and performance bonds often come before the Court. So also do actions relating to cheques.[21] As the use of bills of exchange in the course of international trade declines so do actions raising points on such documents become rarer. The Commercial Court will usually entertain such actions unless they are merely debt-collecting actions between private individuals as distinct from disputes arising in the course of international trade. Actions relating to promissory notes issued in the course of commercial transactions rather than between private individuals will similarly be heard by the Court.

In general, disputes arising out of international loan agreements will be heard by the Commercial Court. In *Lively Ltd.* v. *City of Munich*[22] the Commercial Court had to consider what was the appropriate currency exchange rate applicable on maturity of certain international bonds issued by the City of Munich before the Second World War. For this purpose it was necessary for the Court to investigate by means of expert evidence the working of the International Monetary Fund and its methods of fixing exchange rates.

Cases involving disputes arising out of the practice and procedures of Lloyd's, the Stock Exchange and other market institutions dealing with trading in commodities are normally heard in the Commercial Court.

Disputes relating to company matters are now very rarely heard by the Commercial Court. At one time the practice was quite different. This is clear from the earlier editions of Scrutton's *Charterparties and Bills of Lading,* which contained a chapter on the Commercial Court. In the period after the First World War many company cases were transferred "especially those involving the construction of agreements for promotion, reconstruction and similar matters",[23] although cases involving misrepresentations in prospectuses were less frequently dealt with. While there seems to be no reason in principle why such disputes should not be entertained by the Commercial Court the modern practice is to bring such cases before the Chancery Division. Nevertheless, from time to time

---

21. See, for example, *London Intercontinental Trust Ltd.* v. *Barclays Bank Ltd.* [1980] 1 Lloyd's Rep. 241; *Barclays Bank Ltd.* v. *W. J. Simms Son & Cooke (Southern) Ltd. and Sowman* [1980] 1 Lloyd's Rep. 225.

22. [1976] 1 W.L.R. 1004.

23. See Scrutton, *Charterparties and Bills of Lading* (11th edn., 1923), p. 446.

actions arising out of contracts for the sale of shares or for the take-over of companies are heard by the Court.[24]

Until 1979 it was not the practice of the commercial judges to treat disputes as to the conduct of arbitrations or relating to arbitral hearings as necessarily commercial actions and therefore automatically fit to be tried in the Commercial Court. It was necessary that the arbitration should arise out of or be concerned with disputes which were essentially "commercial" in character. The introduction in 1979 of the new Order 73, rule 6 of the Rules of the Supreme Court reflects the position that most arbitration disputes which come before the Courts do involve commercial matters. The effect of the new rule is that every application to remit an award under section 22 of the Arbitration Act 1950 or to remove an arbitrator or umpire under section 23(1) or to set aside an award under section 23(2) or for leave to appeal under section 1(2) of the Arbitration Act 1979 or to determine any question of law arising in the course of the reference under section 2(1) or for an order that an arbitrator should give reasons for his award under section 1(5) or for an order under section 5 of the Arbitration Act 1979, giving an arbitrator the same powers as a judge where there has been a breach of an interlocutory order must now be heard by a commercial judge, unless such judge otherwise orders. It remains to be seen whether the effect of this change in the rules will be that the Commercial Court tends to adopt the practice of hearing all arbitration matters which come before it under Order 73, rule 6, or only those disputes arising out of commercial arbitrations. Since Order 73, rule 6 expressly envisages that the commercial judge before whom the application comes on for hearing may decline to hear it, the practice which will probably be adopted is that where the subject-matter of the arbitration in question does not have a commercial flavour the commercial judges will decline to hear it and will exercise this power to adjourn the application to a High Court judge not sitting in the Commercial Court.[25] Where, however, the subject-matter of the application involves some important general principle of arbitration law or contract law it is suggested that, even if the arbitration has arisen out of a non-commercial dispute, it would be appropriate in many cases for the application to be retained for hearing in the Commercial Court. This would be consistent with the general responsibility cast upon the commercial judges by Order 73 of supervising the operation of the Arbitration Act 1979, a responsibility reflected in the practice now adopted that all applications for leave to appeal under section 1(2) of that Act are heard by commercial judges notwithstanding that they arise from arbitrations involving non-commercial disputes.[25a]

---

24. See, for example, *Carvalho* v. *Hull Blyth (Angola) Ltd.* [1980] 1 Lloyd's Rep. 172
25. See, generally, p. 122 below.
25a. See p. 132 below, footnote 46, and *F. G. Whitley & Sons Co. Ltd.* v. *Clwyd C.C.* (*The Times*, 6th August 1982).

An appeal to the Court of Appeal will lie with leave of the commercial judge or of the Court of Appeal in the following cases:—

(1) Where the action has not been commenced in the Commercial List by marking the writ in accordance with Order 72, rule 4, and an application is made under Order 72, rule 5 for transfer of the action to the Commercial List, from the order of the commercial judge on that application.

(2) Where the action has been commenced in the Commercial List by marking the writ in accordance with Order 72, rule 4, or has been transferred to the List before entry of appearance and the defendant or a third party applies under Order 72, rule 6 to have the action removed from the Commercial List, from the order of the commercial judge on that application.

(3) Where the action has been commenced in the Commercial List in accordance with Order 72, rule 4, and the commercial judge of his own motion orders that the action be removed from the Commercial List, from that order.

In practice, appeals from a decision of the commercial judge as to whether an action ought to be tried in the Commercial Court are virtually unknown in modern times. The parties are almost always content to accept the decision of the commercial judge as conclusive. Indeed, it is very rarely that application is made for actions to be transferred out of the Commercial List once they have been commenced there. Nor are applications to transfer actions to the Commercial List frequently opposed.

The appeal procedure was first considered by the Court of Appeal in *Barrie* v. *Peruvian Corporation*.[26] In that case Lord Esher, M.R., said:

"Either of the parties is allowed to apply to have a case put in the Commercial List, and when the application is made to the judge he must decide whether it is in fact a commercial cause. I think that the judge may say that a cause is a commercial cause and one which ought to be entered in the Commercial List as soon as the writ is issued; but if the defendant objects that the cause is not commercial he ought to be heard upon his objection . . . If, after the defendant has appeared, he desires to object to the cause being entered in the Commercial List, and to say that it ought to proceed in the ordinary way, he may take out a summons to remove the cause from the Commercial List upon the ground—and only upon the ground—that it is not of a commercial nature. If the judge refuses to remove the cause from the List, the defendant may appeal, but, again, upon that ground alone".

---

26. [1896] 1 Q.B. 209.

In *Sea Insurance Co.* v. *Carr*[27] the Court of Appeal confirmed that an appeal would lie from an order transferring an action to the Commercial List but the Court of Appeal in a later case has made it clear that it will only interfere with the exercise of the commercial judges' discretion on an application to transfer in the most exceptional circumstances.[28] In dismissing an appeal from the refusal of Bailhache, J., to transfer the action to the Commercial List, Bankes, L.J., said:

> "the question of whether permission should be given to enter an action in the Commercial List is a question entirely for the discretion of the Learned Judge for the time being in charge of that List. I can hardly imagine a case in which it would be the duty of the Court of Appeal to interfere with the exercise of the Learned Judge's discretion".[29]

---

27. (1900) 6 Com.Cas. 11.
28. *Hudson's Bay Co.* v. *J. P. Byrne* (1920) 2 Ll.L.Rep. 192.
29. ibid., at p. 192.

CHAPTER 4

WRITS, ORIGINATING SUMMONSES, MOTIONS AND PLEADINGS

The writ

Actions in the Commercial Court may be commenced by a writ of summons indorsed with a statement of the nature of the claim made or the relief or remedy required in the same way as any other action which is commenced in the Queen's Bench Division. The writ may also be indorsed with points of claim in the same way as an ordinary writ may be indorsed with a statement of claim.

If from the outset it is intended that the action should be tried in the Commercial Court the writ should be headed "Queen's Bench Division" and the words "Commercial Court" may be marked in the top left-hand corner. In this way the action automatically begins its life in the Commercial Court without the necessity of a subsequent summons to transfer it to that Court. This procedure is prescribed by Order 72, rule 4(1), and was first introduced in 1964 in order to facilitate the use of the Commercial List and to reduce costs by removing the need to take out a summons for transfer in respect of each case destined for the Commercial Court.[1] This procedure for automatic entry in the Commercial List is only available for actions commenced in London or in the district registries of Liverpool or Manchester. In order to save costs it is important that solicitors and counsel should wherever possible advise clients who have claims of a commercial nature to take advantage of this procedure rather than to commence actions in the ordinary way in the Queen's Bench Division and to issue a formal summons for transfer to the Commercial Court at a later stage. This automatic procedure has the further advantage that once the action is in the Commercial List all interlocutory matters must be brought before the commercial judge. In cases where the interlocutory stages raise or are likely to raise complex disputes this may be of great assistance to the parties. In such cases it is usually possible for the Commercial Court Listing Officer to arrange for the same commercial judge to hear all the interlocutory applications relating to that case, thereby giving some continuity of approach to the progress of the action up to trial.

---

1. This change went some way towards implementing the recommendations of the Commercial Court Users' Conference Report of 1962, Cmnd. 1616.

Originating summons procedure

This is sometimes a very useful procedure and one which at present is not used as often as it might be. Its main function is to bring before the Court issues of law or the construction of contracts or legislation in those cases where such issues are the only substantial matters in dispute between the parties. This procedure is not particularly helpful where there are substantial disputes as to the facts. In that case the writ is to be preferred. In cases where a speedy determination of the matters in dispute is needed it is usually possible to obtain a date for trial of the matters raised by the originating summons at short notice. Pleadings will not usually be required and discovery may often be restricted to the relatively few documents directly relevant to the issues of law or construction to be determined by the Court. The remedy usually claimed by an originating summons is a declaration.[2]

A typical example of the use of this procedure is to be found in *Atlas Levante-Linie Aktiengesellschaft* v. *Gesellschaft Fuer Getriedehandel.*[3] In that case the issue was whether bills of lading issued on behalf of the plaintiff shipowners and of which the defendants were the holders incorporated an arbitration clause in the charter-party under which the vessel had carried the defendants' cargo. The defendants commenced arbitration proceedings and the plaintiff shipowners commenced proceedings in the Commercial Court by originating summons claiming a declaration that the defendants were not entitled to appoint an arbitrator because there was no reference to arbitration binding as between them and the defendant holders of the bill of lading. The declaration was obtained.

The speed and flexibility of the originating summons procedure is illustrated by *Marseille Fret S.A.* v. *D. Oltmann Schiffahrts G.m.b.h. & Co. K.G.*[4] In that case the vessel *Trado* was time-chartered to the plaintiff charterers for six months expiring on 24th November 1981 but subject to charterers' option to extend the period of hire for a further six months, such option "to be declared 60 days in advance 20 days more or less in charterers' option on final period". A dispute arose as to whether the option had been validly exercised. The charterers commenced proceedings by originating summons inviting the Court to declare that the option had been validly exercised, and in view of the fact that there remained only six weeks before the end of the initial six-month period the Commercial Court treated the matter as one of great urgency. The originating summons was issued on 13th October 1981, the matter was brought before the commercial judge on the following day when an order was made that there should be a trial on the

---

2. *Punton* v. *Ministry of Pensions* [1963] 1 W.L.R. 186, *per* Lord Denning, M.R.
3. [1966] 1 Lloyd's Rep. 150.
4. [1982] 1 Lloyd's Rep. 157.

earliest possible date. Consequently judgment was given on 26th October. As Parker, J., commented:[5]

> "In such circumstances . . . whatever the state of the List it is always possible for people engaged in trade and commerce to come to this Court for a quick determination".

All such originating summonses should be in the form set out at Form No. 8 of Appendix A in Part 2 of the Supreme Court Practice. This is known as the General Form.

The originating summons procedure is also used for making those applications under the Arbitration Acts which are not required by the Acts to be commenced by originating motion where there is no existing action in which the applicaton is to be made.[6] These include applications to appoint an arbitrator or umpire under section 10 of the Arbitration Act 1950, all applications under section 12(6) of the 1950 Act for interlocutory relief, under section 24(1) to revoke the authority of an arbitrator or for an order that an arbitration agreement shall cease to have effect in cases involving fraud and under section 27 for an order extending the time for commencing arbitration proceedings. All such applications by originating summons should be made in the form prescribed by Form No. 10 of Appendix A in Part 2 of the Supreme Court Practice.[7] This is known as the Expedited Form.

Just as the action commenced by writ can be commenced in the Commercial Court automatically without a summons for transfer so also can proceedings commenced by originating summons. The originating summons can be marked "Commercial Court" in the top left-hand corner.[8]

Following the issue of the originating summons in the Commercial Court the procedure is that laid down under Order 28. In those cases where the Court is asked to determine a point of law or construction and the summons is therefore in the form of Form No. 8, the General Form, the plaintiff must, before the expiration of 14 days after the defendant has acknowledged service, or, if there are two or more defendants, at least one of them has acknowledged service, file with the Commercial Court and serve on that defendant the affidavit evidence on which he intends to rely in accordance with RSC Order 28, rule 1A which came into effect on 1st January 1983. The defendant, if he wishes to adduce affidavit evidence, must within 28 days after service on him of copies of the plaintiff's affidavit evidence, file his own affidavit evidence in the Commercial Court and

---

5. ibid., at p. 158.
6. RSC Order 73, rule 3(3).
7. RSC Order 7, rule 2.
8. RSC Order 72, rule 4(1).

serve copies on the plaintiff and on any other defendant who is affected thereby.[9] The plaintiff must, within one month of the expiry of the time within which copies of affidavit evidence must be served as set out above in accordance with RSC Order 28, rule 1A,[9a] obtain from the Commercial Court a date for the preliminary hearing of the summons by the commercial judge and not less than four clear days before the date fixed by the Court must serve a copy of the notice fixing it on every other party who has acknowledged service of the summons. The notice must be in Form No. 12 in Appendix A of Part 2 of the Supreme Court Practice,[9b] although the time can be abridged in cases of real urgency.[10]

Where the originating summons is for relief under the Arbitration Acts and is therefore in Form No. 10, the Expedited Form, the plaintiff can obtain a date for the preliminary hearing before the defendant has acknowledged service of the summons.[11] The date for the hearing is then fixed by the Commercial Court and is recorded in a notice in Form No. 12 in Appendix A of Part 2 of the Supreme Court Practice and this must then be served on all defendants who have acknowledged service not less than four clear days before the date fixed for the hearing.[12] If the defendant has applied for a date he must likewise serve the notice on the plaintiff.

The time limits for filing affidavit evidence described above are in the case of the Expedited Form of originating summons that the plaintiff must before the expiration of 14 days after the defendant has acknowledged service file his own affidavit evidence with the Commercial Court but the time for acknowledging service is to be abridged where appropriate to expire on the next day but one before the day fixed for hearing. Similarly, the time for service of the plaintiff's affidavit is to be abridged so as to expire the next day but one before the day fixed for the hearing.[12a]

Service of proceedings outside the jurisdiction

When it is necessary for the plaintiff to commence a commercial action by writ or originating summons against a defendant outside the jurisdiction of the English Court upon whom proceedings must be served abroad and where it is intended that the matter should be tried in the Commercial Court application *ex parte* for

---

9. RSC Order 28, rule 1A; see the Rules of the Supreme Court (Amendment No. 3) 1982, S.I. 1982 No. 1786 (c.32).
9a. RSC Order 28, rule 2(1).
9b. RSC Order 28, rule 3(1).
10. RSC Order 3, rule 5.
11. RSC Order 28, rule 2(2).
12. RSC Order 28, rule 3(1).
12a. RSC Order 28, rule 2(2) as amended by the Rules of the Supreme Court (Amendment No. 3) 1982, *supra*.

leave to issue and serve the writ or originating summons[13] outside the jurisdiction under RSC Order 11, rules 1 or 2 should be made to the commercial judge and not to the Queen's Bench Division Masters.[14] The affidavit in support of the application should state in addition to those matters specified in RSC Order 11, rule 4(1) that the plaintiff intends to mark the writ or originating summons with the words "Commercial Court" in accordance with RSC Order 72, rule 4(1).[15]

The commercial judges do not ordinarily hold oral hearings of *ex parte* applications for leave to serve proceedings outside the jurisdiction. The proposed writ or originating summons, together with the affidavit in support of the application, should be handed in to the Commercial Court Listing Officer at Room 198, Royal Courts of Justice, and they will then be considered by the judge and in due course may be collected from the Listing Officer having been indorsed with the order giving leave or not, as the case may be. There may be occasions where it is convenient for an *ex parte* application to be made orally in the course of the hearing of some other matter relating to the same contemplated proceedings. For example, if there is an *ex parte* application for an interim interlocutory injunction, such as a *Mareva* injunction before issue of the proceedings, it is clearly convenient for the commercial judge to hear the application under RSC Order 11 on the same hearing. On such occasions a composite affidavit can be used.

If, upon consideration of the documents tendered in support of an *ex parte* application under RSC Order 11, the commercial judge takes the view that the matter is not one that ought to be tried in the Commercial Court because it does not have a sufficiently commercial character, he has power to adjourn the Order 11 application to be heard by a Master.[16]

If the commercial judge refuses to give leave to serve the proceedings outside the jurisdiction an appeal will lie to the Court of Appeal, but only with leave of the commercial judge (for which an oral hearing would be needed) or, failing that, of the Court of Appeal.

It frequently happens that it is necessary to serve outside the jurisdiction proceedings which have to be commenced by originating motion, for example, in relation to English arbitration proceedings. An application to remove an arbitrator or umpire for misconduct[17] under section 23(1) of the Arbitration Act 1950 or to

---

13. RSC Order 11, rule 7.
14. RSC Order 72, rule 4(2). This procedure only applies to those actions where proceedings are to be issued out of the Central Office and not to Liverpool and Manchester Commercial actions where application under RSC Order 11, rule 4 should be made to the District Registrar.
15. RSC Order 72, rule 4(3).
16. RSC Order 72, rule 4(4).
17. RSC Order 73, rule 2(1)(b).

set aside or remit an award under sections 22 or 23(2) must be made by originating motion.[18] So also must applications for leave to appeal under section 1(2) of the Arbitration Act 1979[19] and for the determination of questions of law in the course of a reference under section 2(1) of that Act,[20] as well as appeals from arbitrators under section 1(2)[21] and applications for declarations that awards are not binding due to want of jurisdiction.[22] In all these cases it is necessary to obtain leave to serve notice of the motion outside the jurisdiction.[23] The procedure is the same as that for writs and originating summonses where the action is to be pursued in the Commercial Court. An important distinction is that in those cases which relate to arbitration proceedings and whether the matter is to be brought before the Court by motion or originating summons it is not necessary for the affidavit in support to depose to facts bringing the dispute within any of the categories listed in RSC Order 11, rule 1(1) provided that the affidavit shows that the arbitration to which the summons or motion relates is governed by English law or has been, is being, or is to be held, within the jurisdiction of the English Courts.[24]

Pleadings

Since its foundation, the Commercial Court has strongly set its face against unduly long and complex pleadings. From the outset it was recognised that most commercial disputes did not involve issues which were so complicated that they could only be identified by means of abstruse and intricately worded pleadings. At the time when the Court was founded it was felt that whereas it was essential to identify by some means all the issues in advance of the trial so that surprise was avoided[25] the use of the elaborate pleadings then frequently found in Queen's Bench Division actions was highly undesirable because such documents unnecessarily increased the cost of litigation to the parties and interfered with the speedy resolution of disputes. In *Hill* v. *Scott*,[26] where the issue was whether the defendant carrier was liable for damage to a consignment of wool belonging to the plaintiff, the commercial judge, on hearing the summons to transfer the action to the Commercial List after delivery of the statement of claim, ordered that the defendant's solicitors should write a letter to the plaintiff's solicitors indicating what defence was raised and that the action should be tried on that basis. When in the Court of Appeal counsel for the defendant attempted to argue a defence

---

18. See, generally, p. 127 below.
19. RSC Order 73, rule 2(1)(d).
20. RSC Order 73, rule 2(1)(e).
21. RSC Order 73, rule 2(2).
22. RSC Order 73, rule 2(3).
23. RSC Order 11, rule 9(3).
24. RSC Order 73, rule 7(1).
25. See the comments of Lord Esher, M.R., in *Hill* v. *Scott* (1895) 1 Com.Cas. 200, at pp. 203–4.
26. (1895) 1 Com.Cas. 200.

not raised in this letter Lord Esher, M.R., commented adversely on this departure from the judge's order and went on:

> "There has been established in that Court, . . . a procedure which is intended and calculated to avoid both expense and delay in the trial of commercial causes, by abridging all those useless and idle proceedings of which litigants can under the present rules avail themselves before an action comes on for trial . . . One of the great means whereby litigation might be cheapened and quickened was to do away with those preliminary opportunities for the wasting of time and money, to get rid of pleadings, with all the unnecessary delay that pleadings involve, delay which seems to be inveterate in solicitors' offices, and to make the parties state under the direction of the judge what was the real question at issue between them".

Trial without pleadings

In the early years of the Commercial Court a determination to avoid where possible unduly formal, complex and time-consuming interlocutory procedure led to the frequent making of orders that pleadings be dispensed with and that they should be replaced by informal exchanges between the parties, letters defining the issues or by a statement of issues developed by the commercial judge at the hearing of the summons to transfer to the Commercial List.[27]

It is now less common for orders to be made dispensing with pleadings. The main reason for this is that except in matters of great urgency it is now unusual for the commercial judge to see the action until after the pleadings are closed and sometimes until after completion of discovery. Where the action is commenced in the Commercial Court under the automatic procedure in RSC Order 72, rule 4, which is now normally the case, there is no need for a summons for transfer in the early interlocutory stages and it is usually not until the summons for directions and for a date for trial that the commercial judge sees the papers for the first time. Unless, therefore, the plaintiff applies to the Court for an order dispensing with pleadings at an early interlocutory stage the judge has no opportunity to intervene or encourage the use of a more efficient procedure until many months or even years after the issue of the writ.

Nevertheless, there may be cases where pleadings can be regarded as an unnecessary feature of an action. It will probably be found that where the facts are not substantially in dispute the more convenient course is to commence the proceedings by originating summons, a procedure for which pleadings are not

---

27. See, for example, *Tyser* v. *Shipowners' Syndicate (Reassured)* (1895) 1 Com.Cas. 224, a claim against reinsurers of an urgent nature when the writ was issued on 22nd November 1895, and on the application to transfer and for an early trial it was ordered that three issues should be tried and the action should be set down for trial on 29th November. Matthew, J., gave judgment on 5th December 1895.

usually ordered.[28] Where the matter proceeds by writ and points of construction are the main matters in issue both parties may find that it is convenient and economical to invite the commercial judge to make an order that pleadings be dispensed with. Order 18, rule 21 of the Rules of the Supreme Court makes provision for such an order and for an order giving directions as to how the issues are to be defined, because it is usually desirable that some formal record of the issues should be made. In cases of difficulty where the parties are unable to agree a statement of issues the judge is given power to settle the statement himself.[29] Where, however, the plaintiff's claim and also presumably the defendant's counterclaim are based on allegations of fraud or where the claim or counterclaim are for libel, slander or malicious prosecution pleadings may not be dispensed with.[30]

Various different means of recording the issues between the parties have been adopted in lieu of pleadings but it is desirable that maximum flexibility of procedure should be preserved so that the Court can be free to adopt in each case whatever contributes the more effectively to saving time and costs and to sufficient definition of the issues. The commercial judge may make a note of the issues as part of his order.[31] There may be a combination of mutual admissions of fact and mutually-agreed issues[32] or a combination of an agreed statement of facts and agreed issues.[33] A letter from the plaintiff's solicitors to the defendant's solicitors stating the heads of claim combined with admissions by the defendant and an agreed issue has been ordered to be the basis of an action.[34] Points of defence may sometimes conveniently be replaced by a letter from the defendant's solicitors outlining the points to be taken in defence.[35] Occasionally it may be possible, upon the defendant's admission of the material facts appearing in the indorsement on the writ, for the parties simply to invite the commercial judge to order the trial of the claim without further formal identification of issues, for example where there is a point of construction in issue.[36]

---

28. For an account of the procedure by originating summons see p. 34 above.

29. RSC Order 18, rule 21(2).

30. RSC Order 18, rule 21(4).

31. *Tyser* v. *Shipowners' Syndicate (Reassured)* (1895) 1 Com.Cas. 224. *Petersen* v. *Dunn* (1895) 1 Com.Cas. 8.

32. *Asfar & Co.* v. *Blundell* (1895) 1 Com.Cas. 71.

33. *Papayanni and Jeromia* v. *Grampian Steamship Co. Ltd.* (1896) 1 Com.Cas. 448; *Walker* v. *Vzielli* (1896) 1 Com.Cas. 452; *Central Argentine Railway* v. *Marwood* [1915] A.C. 981.

34. *R. Buchanan* v. *London and Provincial Marine Insurance Co.* (1895) 1 Com.Cas. 165.

35. *Hill* v. *Scott* (1895) 1 Com.Cas. 200.

36. *Union of India* v. *Compania Naviera Aeolus S.A.* [1960] 1 Lloyd's Rep. 112; [1961] 1 Lloyd's Rep. 132 (C.A.), and [1964] A.C. 868 (H.L.); *Jones Construction Co.* v. *Alliance Assurance Co. Ltd.* [1960] 1 Lloyd's Rep. 264.

If a more formal statement of admissions and agreed issues is required in lieu of pleadings it may be convenient for the parties to agree upon a special case for the opinion of the Court.[37] If that is done they must then obtain an order under Order 33, rule 3. The special case itself should normally, but not necessarily, be settled by counsel and if so it should be signed by counsel or otherwise by the parties' solicitors. It should set out first all the material facts which are agreed between the parties, then all the issues of fact which the Court is invited to determine and, finally, all issues of law or mixed law and fact. It is no longer necessary that a special case agreed by the parties should be confined to issues of law or construction: questions of fact may also be raised.

Commercial Court pleadings

In those actions where pleadings are required they must be in the form of Points of Claim, Points of Defence and Points of Reply.[38] The words "Points of" are intended to emphasize the objective of brevity and simplicity. Order 72, rule 7(1) requires that they "must be as brief as possible". Unfortunately, in practice, pleadings of considerable length are often found in actions in the Commercial Court. The Report of the Commercial Court Users' Conference, 1962,[39] regarded the delay and expense involved in the preparation and delivery of long and prolix pleadings as a major defect in the procedure of the Commercial Court:

> "We express our dissatisfaction with both the prolixity of modern pleadings in the Commercial Court and the time which is consumed in their delivery.
> "The original conception in the Commercial Court of short 'Points of Claim' and 'Points of Defence' seems now to have been forgotten and pleadings in the Commercial Court have become as lengthy as the more formal pleadings current in the Common Law Courts. Further, it has become the exception rather than the rule for either of the parties to deliver their pleadings within the times specified in the Order for Directions, and extensions of time are freely and frequently agreed. We find that much of the delay in bringing commercial cases to trial is due to the preparation and delivery of pleadings.
> "We appreciate that pleadings can perform a useful function in preventing either party being taken by surprise at the trial. We agree that in the comparatively rare commercial cases in which fraud or misrepresentation is alleged pleadings are essential. But we recommend that, subject to these safeguards, pleadings should be avoided in the Commercial Court wherever possible and that far more use should be made than at present of trial on agreed statements of fact".[40]

---

37. *Niarchos (London) Ltd.* v. *Shell Tankers Ltd.* [1961] 2 Lloyd's Rep. 496.

38. RSC Order 72, rule 7(1).

39. Cmnd. 1616.

40. ibid., para. 17. See also the memorandum submitted to the Conference on behalf of the Shipowners' Associations at p. 28 of the Report:

> "'Points of Claim' and 'Points of Defence' have become elaborate counterparts of Statements of Claim and Defence. In the anxiety of litigants (advised, as is recognised, by their lawyers) to miss no point however small lest it should be found to have a bearing on the case, pleadings have increased in volume and complexity, time over interlocutory proceedings is occupied beyond that which was ever in the contemplation of the founders of the Court and the issues, instead of being sharply defined, become obscure and complex".

In his Practice Direction of October 1962[41] Megaw, J., stated that:

> "Pleadings in commercial actions have tended to become much lengthier than formerly. When pleadings are required . . . their object is to define the real issues and avoid surprise. If this object is kept in mind—and the Court will have it in mind—it ought to be possible to shorten and simplify the pleadings in many commercial cases with a saving of time and costs".

In spite of these criticisms of the length and complexity of pleadings in the Commercial Court the modern practice of the Court is to work with pleadings which are often long and complicated. This is usually because pleaders are often not in a position to decide at the time when they produce the pleadings which points in their clients' favour can be abandoned. They may not be able to give up many perfectly pleadable points until after they have had before them all the material documents and that may often not be until after completion of discovery only a short time before the trial. The practice, therefore, tends to be to keep alive on the pleadings many points, often alternative ways of putting one party's case, which are ultimately abandoned following completion of discovery. The Commercial Court Committee has not recommended that the state of pleadings in the Court requires action and no further Practice Directions have been issued on the subject in recent years. Accordingly, apart from the general exhortation to brevity in Order 72, rule 7(1), there is in modern practice nothing in form to distinguish Points of Claim and Points of Defence from their equivalent Queen's Bench pleadings.

It is therefore no longer possible to recommend for use in commercial actions the extremely brief forms of pleadings which were in use at the end of the nineteenth century.[42] They are so short and tersely expressed usually because they only raise one or very few issues and it would be quite impossible to compress into so few words the average multi-issue shipping case now frequently before the Commercial Court. While brevity of pleading may often save time and costs in the interlocutory stages it is suggested that if the pleadings do not achieve an accurate definition of the issues by the time the matter has to be prepared for trial or comes on for trial a great deal of time and expense may be wasted and injustice may occur because new points are raised or old points not abandoned. Witnesses may be interviewed and documents copied which may ultimately be found quite irrelevant to the live issues. It is thus perhaps more to be emphasised that, whatever the length or complexity of the pleadings may be, solicitors and counsel should do their utmost *in good time before the trial* to ensure that *all* the issues that are going to be raised at the trial are raised in the pleadings and that no point

---

41. [1962] 1 W.L.R. 1216.
42. Examples of these short-form pleadings can be found in Matthew's *Practice of the Commercial Court* (1st edn., 1902).

which is not going to be taken at the trial is left undeleted in the pleadings. Any initial savings through brief and uninformative or not fully informative pleadings may be thrown away and far outweighed by the costs incurred and time lost in allowing the accurate definition of the real issues to be left until the last minute. In *Palamisto General Enterprises S.A.* v. *Ocean Marine Insurance Co. Ltd.*,[43] the leading case on particulars in scuttling actions, Buckley, L.J., gave the following useful account of the purpose of particularity in pleading:

> "The broad objectives of the rules requiring particularity in pleading are that actions should be tried as fairly and with as much economy of time and expense as the circumstances of each case permit. These objectives, which are in the interests of the parties and in the public interest, are sought to be attained by means which are directed to (a) ensuring that the issues of fact between the parties, which are relevant to the claims and defences raised, are defined with as much clarity as the circumstances permit; (b) ensuring that each party knows what case he has to meet—i.e. what is alleged against him—as well as how far, if at all, his own case is admitted; (c) avoiding any party being taken by surprise, with the consequence that he has not a fair opportunity at the trial of dealing with some part of the case made against him; (d) avoiding the need for any party to come prepared to call evidence on aspects of the case which turn out to be irrelevant, and (e) limiting discovery. Of these, (b) to (e) may be said to be merely aspects or consequences of (a)".

Amendment of pleadings

If in order to define the real issues it is necessary for a party to amend the pleadings after the summons for directions and the fixing of the trial date, the course which is usually most efficient in time and expense is to inform the opposing solicitors of the proposed amendments by sending to them a copy in draft and by inviting them to indicate whether they will consent to or oppose an application to amend. If the amendment is to be opposed a summons for leave to amend can be issued. If the application is not opposed the application for leave to amend and for the opposing party to make any consequential amendments can usually be made to the trial judge at the opening of the trial.

Particulars

Only those particulars need be given which are necessary to enable a party to be informed of the case he has to meet or are for some other reason necessary to secure the just, expeditious and economical disposal of any question at issue in the action.[44] It is very doubtful whether this in any way differs from the principles

---

43. [1972] 2 Q.B. 625, at p. 639.
44. RSC Order 72, rule 7(2).

which govern the pleading of non-commercial actions. Order 72, rule 7(2) expressly states that it is without prejudice to Order 18, rule 12(1).[45]

Although it is not strictly necessary to plead particulars of knowledge or of an allegation that somebody ought to have known a particular fact it is now usual for pleadings in commercial actions, if possible, to set out such particulars without waiting for the opposing party to make a formal request.

Particulars of scuttling

Until 1972 it was the practice of the Commercial Court that particulars of an allegation of scuttling, that is, that the loss of the vessel was caused by the wilful misconduct of the plaintiffs in procuring or conniving at the casting away of the vessel, raised by marine underwriters in defence to a claim in respect of the total loss of a vessel under a marine policy, need not be given and would not be ordered. In *Astrovlanis Compania Naviera S.A.* v. *Linard*[46] and *Palamisto General Enterprises S.A.* v. *Ocean Marine Insurance Co. Ltd.*[47] it was held by the Court of Appeal that such practice was inconsistent with the requirement under Order 18, rule 12(1) that particulars of fraud should be given and that therefore if the underwriters wished to advance at the trial an affirmative case that the vessel had been deliberately cast away with the privity of the plaintiff they must give particulars of how the loss of the vessel was deliberately procured and of any other matters relied on to support the allegation that the casting away of the vessel was wilfully procured or connived at by the plaintiffs.[48]

Particulars of damage

The calculation of damages is very often a complex matter in commercial actions and much time and expense can be saved in preparation for the trial if claims for damages are sufficiently particularized at an early stage. The plaintiff must in the ordinary way give particulars of all *special* damage making up his claim. This

---

45. RSC Order 18, rule 12:
    "(1) Subject to paragraph (2), every pleading must contain the necessary particulars of any claim, defence or other matter pleaded including without prejudice to the generality of the foregoing words—
    (a) particulars of any misrepresentation, fraud, breach of trust, wilful default or undue influence on which the party pleading relies; and
    (b) where a party pleading alleges any condition of the mind of any person, whether any disorder or disability of mind or any malice, fraudulent intention or other condition of mind except knowledge, particulars of the facts on which the party relies".
46. [1972] 2 Q.B. 611.
47. [1972] 2 Q.B. 625.
48. ibid., at p. 650.

means that all the damage which at the time of the pleading[49] has crystallized into a quantifiable monetary loss[50] must be pleaded and particularized so that the defendants can see exactly how the calculation of the total and any sub-totals has been made. If one or more alternative special damages cases are to be advanced at the trial each alternative ought to be pleaded and particularized.[51] In complex cases where the defendant proposes to advance at the trial an affirmative case as to the computation of special damages it may be desirable in the interests of saving time and expense and to avoid surprise if particulars of the defendant's case are given in the Points of Defence. *General* damages, that is to say loss which at the time of the trial cannot be the subject of exact monetary calculation either because it is prospective loss or because it is loss of a kind which cannot be directly quantified in monetary terms,[52] should be pleaded in sufficient detail to enable the defendant to know what method of calculation the plaintiff will invite the Court to adopt and, in particular, whether there are any unusual or special circumstances which it is said should be taken into account.[53] Defendants should be given sufficient information to enable them to calculate the total monetary extent of the plaintiff's claim and to see how the constituent parts of that claim have been calculated. Informative and accurate pleading of damages claims not only saves time and expense before and during the trial but also facilitates the settlement of actions by enabling the defendant to calculate exactly what his exposure to damages is likely to be if the plaintiff succeeds on liability. The defendant may then more easily be able to decide whether to make a payment into Court.[54]

Further and better particulars

Requests for further and better particulars of points of claim are normally served at the same time as the points of defence, and requests in respect of the points of defence are normally served at the same time as the points of reply, if any. Applications to the commercial judge for orders that further and better particulars be delivered should not in ordinary cases be made before the summons for directions. If the particulars requested are wholly or mainly of matters which it may be anticipated will be evidenced by or will be likely to emerge from the opposing party's documents, application for an order should not be made until after discovery unless the preparation of the case by the applicant is seriously

---

49. The pleading may have to be amended to bring it up to date at the time of the trial if loss is continuing.
50. *Ilkiw* v. *Samuels* [1963] 1 W.L.R. 991.
51. *Anglo-Cyprian Trade Agencies Ltd.* v. *Paphos Wine Industries Ltd.* [1951] 1 All E.R. 873.
52. *Ilkiw* v. *Samuels*, above.
53. *Perestrello e Companhia Lda.* v. *United Paint Co. Ltd.* [1969] 1 W.L.R. 570; *Domsalla* v. *Barr* [1969] 1 W.L.R. 630.
54. *Domsalla* v. *Barr*, above.

impeded or he is otherwise seriously prejudiced by lack of information as to his opponent's case. Because of the emphasis on brief and, so far as practicable, non-technical procedure in Commercial List cases the Court should be inclined to look more critically at an application for particulars in such a case than it might in an ordinary civil action.[55] Orders for further and better particulars may be refused where there has been inexcusable delay in making the application or where one consequence of granting the application would probably be that the date for trial would have to be vacated and the trial considerably delayed.[56]

Time for pleadings

The official time for service of pleadings in the Commercial Court does not differ from that in the High Court in general, namely:

Points of Claim:	either with the writ or before the expiration of 14 days after the defendant has given notice of intention to defend.[57]
Points of Defence:	either before the expiration of 14 days after the time limited for acknowledging service of the writ or after the points of claim are served, whichever is the later.[58]
Points of Reply:	before the expiration of 14 days after the service of the points of defence.[58a]

It is, however, common practice for extensions of time, often very considerable ones in complex cases, to be agreed between the parties without application to the Court. Where extension of time cannot be agreed there must be an application to the commercial judge for such extension.

---

55. *Palamisto General Enterprises S.A.* v. *Ocean Marine Insurance Co. Ltd.* [1972] 2 Q.B. 625, *per* Buckley, L.J., at p. 641.
56. *Astrovlanis Compania Naviera S.A.* v. *Linard* [1972] 2 Q.B. 611.
57. RSC Order 18, rule 1.
58. RSC Order 18, rule 2.
58a. RSC Order 18, rule 3(4).

CHAPTER 5

INTERLOCUTORY PROCEDURE IN THE COMMERCIAL COURT

Functions of the commercial judge

One of the major procedural differences between the Commercial Court and the remainder of the High Court of Justice, with the exception to some extent of the Admiralty Court, is that in the Commercial Court all interlocutory applications in London actions are always heard by the commercial judge. The Masters of the Queen's Bench Division play no part in the interlocutory work. Order 72, rule 2(3) provides:

> "The judge shall have control of the actions in the Commercial List and, subject to the provisions of this Order and to any directions of the judge, the powers of a judge in chambers (including those exercisable by a master or registrar) shall, in relation to any proceedings in such action (including any appeal from any judgment, order or decision of a master or registrar, given or made prior to transfer of the action to the Commercial List), be exercisable by the judge".

This provision reflects in substance the procedure originally introduced by the Notice as to Commercial Causes of 1895[1] whereby all applications in chambers were made to the judge. The underlying purpose of this procedure is to enable the judge to become acquainted with the action at an early stage and to exercise a measure of control over the interlocutory stages with some knowledge of what the case is about. This has the effect of facilitating the saving of time and expense in bringing the case on for trial and at the trial itself.[2] The prevailing approach of the commercial judges to interlocutory applications and to preparation of cases

---

1. See p. 7 above.
2. See, generally, the Introduction to Vol. I of *The Times Reports of Commercial Cases:*
   "The learned judge was guided in the course he adopted by the obvious objections to the existing methods of administering the law. It was clear that, if the legal advisers of the parties were willing to assist the Court, commercial disputes might be settled as promptly as by an arbitrator. But to attain this end it was necessary that the judge should be made acquainted at the earliest possible stage of the proceedings with the nature of the plaintiff's and the defendant's case. . . . The course of procedure followed in chambers has been to ascertain, upon the making of the order for the transfer of the case to the Commercial List, what directions were needed to secure a trial at the earliest convenient date. . . . As a result of this preliminary discussion before the judge many cases have been put in train for settlement".

for trial has always been to deal as flexibly with procedural requirements as may be necessary to encourage the fair, economical and expeditious bringing to trial of the action. Any procedure which causes avoidable delay or avoidable costs will be actively discouraged unless the commercial judge is convinced that it is essential to the fair trial of the action.

Until 31st December 1982 it was only in relation to "proceedings before final judgment" that the commercial judges replaced the Queen's Bench Division Masters in dealing with interlocutory applications. After final judgment the procedure for enforcement was the same as that for any other Queen's Bench Division action and recourse could not normally be had to the commercial judges but to the Masters. The procedure has now been changed[3] with effect from 1st January 1983 and all matters of enforcement are now within the jurisdiction of the commercial judges instead of the Queen's Bench Division Masters. However, by a practice direction issued by Lloyd, J., on 28th February 1983 it was ordered as follows:—

> "Unless on the application of any party to the action the judge otherwise orders, all proceedings for the enforcement of any judgment or order for the payment of money in actions in the Commercial List are hereby referred to the Masters of the Queen's Bench Division".

It remains to be seen by reference to what considerations the commercial judges will exercise their new jurisdiction.

Commercial actions outside London

Where a commercial action has been commenced in the Commercial Court by the automatic procedure of marking the writ or originating summons in accordance with RSC Order 72, rule 4(1), and the proceedings have been issued out of the District Registry of Liverpool or that of Manchester all interlocutory applications in the action are heard by the registrar of the relevant registry, with the sole exception of applications to remove an action from the Commercial List under Order 72, rule 6[4] which must be made to the commercial judge. The District Registrar may, if he sees fit, and shall if requested to do so by any party, adjourn any such interlocutory application to enable it to be heard by the commercial judge.[5]

When a commercial action has been commenced in the ordinary Queen's Bench Division but issued out of the District Registry of Liverpool or Manchester an application to transfer it to the Commercial List can be made to the commercial

---

3. 1982 S.I. No. 1786, para. 19.
4. RSC Order 72, rule 3.
5. RSC Order 72, rule 3.

judge but may instead be made to the District Registrar.[6] He has the power to transfer it forthwith or refer the matter to the commercial judge. He must adjourn the matter to the judge if requested by any party to do so.

Where proceedings in a commercial action are to be issued out of a District Registry other than that of Liverpool or Manchester, the writ or originating summons cannot be marked for automatic entry in the Commercial List. If, on the hearing of a summons in an action in the Queen's Bench Division issued out of a District Registry other than that of Liverpool or Manchester, any party requests the registrar to adjourn the summons so that it can be heard by the commercial judge, the registrar must adjourn the summons so that it can be heard by the commercial judge and it is then treated as a summons for transfer. On such an application, if there is an order that the action be transferred to the Commercial Court, the judge may also order the action to be transferred from the District Registry to the Royal Courts of Justice in London.[7]

The District Registrars of Liverpool and Manchester have a duty to liaise with the Commercial Court in London so as to keep it informed of the general progress of actions entered in their respective registries in the Commercial List and in particular as to dates for the trial of commercial actions in Liverpool and Manchester.[8] Although such trials are expressly provided for in Order 72 they are at present very rare. Arrangements can usually be made for such actions to be tried by one of the commercial judges if planned sufficiently well in advance to interlock with their commitments in London and on circuit.

Summons for transfer

When the Commercial Court was first established great importance was attached to the summons to transfer the action to the Commercial List. It was expected that the parties would be represented by counsel and that they would be in a position to inform the judge of all the major issues in the action so as to enable him at the outset to make positive suggestions for the speedy and economical trial of the matter, such as dispensing with pleadings, the limitation of oral evidence to those facts which could not be the subject of documentary proof, and the trial of preliminary issues. With the introduction in 1964 of the system of automatic entry in the Commercial List by marking the writ or originating summons in accordance with Order 72, rule 4, the summons for transfer of commercial actions to the Commercial List is only necessary where the plaintiff has not adopted the automatic entry procedure and he or one of the other parties subsequently wish

---

6. RSC Order 72, rule 5.
7. RSC Order 72, rule 5. This will usually be the convenient course.
8. RSC Order 72, rule 3(2).

to have the action heard in the Commercial Court. Awards in the form of a special case stated by arbitrators under section 21 of the Arbitration Act 1950 in arbitrations subject to that Act[9] must be formally transferred by summons to the Commercial List.

On the hearing of the summons for transfer the judge has a general discretion to decline to order the transfer to the Commercial List of any action which is not of a sufficiently commercial flavour.[10] Even if all parties consent to the transfer the judge will not make an order unless satisfied that it is appropriate that the action should be tried in the Commercial Court. If transfer is contested the parties should be represented by counsel who have been fully instructed as to the real issues likely to be raised at the trial.

Although the summons for transfer may be heard at any stage in the proceedings[11] the time at which it is most convenient to issue it will depend on the circumstances of each case. If the matter is urgent and a speedy trial is needed or where the trial of preliminary issues may be envisaged, it will usually be most helpful to all parties for the action to be transferred as soon as possible after the commencement of proceedings: similarly, where the action involves highly complex issues which may involve special orders as to pleading or discovery or arrangements for the trial. If the transfer of the action to the Commercial List is likely to be contested the summons should be issued as soon as possible after the commencement of proceedings. There may, however, be many cases which have no special features and where it will be just as convenient to apply for transfer after close of pleadings when the summons for directions is heard.

There may be cases proceeding in the Queen's Bench Division in which on the hearing of a summons before the Queen's Bench Master or judge in chambers or in the course of the trial it appears to the Court that the action may be suitable for trial in the Commercial Court and that one or more of the parties may wish the action to be transferred. In that event the Court may adjourn the hearing and the matter is then heard by the commercial judge and treated by him as a summons to transfer the action to the Commercial List.[12] Where the action is issued in the District Registry of Liverpool or Manchester the registrar has jurisdiction to transfer the action to the Commercial List forthwith,[13] although he may in his discretion and must, if requested to do so by one of the parties, adjourn

---

9. See p. 124 below.

10. For a discussion as to what constitutes a commercial action and when jurisdiction will be declined, see p. 23 above.

11. RSC Order 72, rule 5(1). Until 31st December 1982 transfer could be applied for only before trial. By 1982 S.I. No. 1786, para. 19 transfer may be applied for at any time in the proceedings—even after the start of the trial.

12. RSC Order 72, rule 5(3).

13. RSC Order 72, rule 5(4).

the summons or hearing to be heard by the commercial judge, whereupon it will be treated as a summons for transfer.[14]

Order 72 makes no provision for the transfer to the Commercial Court of actions pending in the Chancery Division. The Notice as to commercial causes of 1895 expressly provided for such transfer.[15] What must now be done is for a summons to be issued in the Chancery Division asking for the action to be transferred to the Queen's Bench Division.[16] Upon the order being made it would be necessary to issue a further summons for transfer under Order 72, rule 5(1).

Where following the hearing of an interlocutory application by a Queen's Bench Master one or more of the parties wishes to appeal against the Master's decision and also to have the action transferred to the Commercial List or where any other party wishes the action to be so transferred that party can issue a summons for transfer under Order 72, rule 5(1) and if the order for transfer is made the commercial judge may then proceed to hear the appeal from the Master's order.[17]

An appeal will lie to the Court of Appeal with leave of the commercial judge or of the Court of Appeal against an order that an action should be transferred to the Commercial Court or against an order refusing transfer.[18] The Court of Appeal will not normally interfere with the decision of the commercial judge.[19]

On the summons for transfer costs are normally costs in the cause.

Summons for removal from the Commercial List

The introduction of the procedure under Order 72, rule 4 for automatic entry of actions in the Commercial List by marking the writ or originating summons in the prescribed manner made it necessary for the defendants or third parties to be given the opportunity of challenging, if they saw fit, the pursuit of the action in the Commercial List. Accordingly, Order 72, rule 6 makes provision for applications for removal of such actions from the Commercial List. Application must be made to the commercial judge by summons within seven days after the applicant has given notice of intention to defend. The principles applicable upon such applications are discussed at page 23 above.

---

14. RSC Order 72, rule 5.
15. Paragraph 2, see p. 7.
16. RSC Order 4, rule 3.
17. This is the effect of RSC Order 72, rule 2(3) as amended which alters the procedure noted in the Supreme Court Practice, 1982, Vol. 1, p. 1197, para 72/5/1.
18. *Barrie* v. *Peruvian Corporation* (1896) 1 Com.Cas. 269; *Sea Insurance Co.* v. *Carr* [1901] 1 K.B. 7.
19. *Hudson's Bay Co.* v. *J.P. Byrne* (1920) 2 Ll.L.Rep. 192; but see *Sea Insurance Co.* v. *Carr* [1901] 1 K.B. 7.

Order 14 procedure

Applications for summary judgment under Order 14 in commercial actions which are commenced in the Commercial Court or which are transferred to it before the issue of the Order 14 summons are heard by the commercial judge sitting in chambers. Actions which are straightforward debt-collecting exercises, where it is obvious from the outset that there is no defence, should not be commenced in the Commercial Court: they can conveniently be heard under Order 14 by the Queen's Bench Division Masters and the Commercial Court will usually give no procedural advantage to either party. There may, however, be cases in which the claims arise out of unduly complex transactions of an essentially commercial character where, although it may appear on careful analysis that there is or may be no arguable defence, it would be advantageous and appropriate for the application for summary judgment to be heard by the commercial judge who would probably be familiar with the commercial background and with transactions and disputes of the kind under investigation. In such cases, Order 14 applications may properly be pursued in the Commercial Court. If the commercial judge takes the view that any particular application for judgment under Order 14 should not have been entered in the Commercial List he may of his own motion exercise his discretionary power to order the action to be removed from the Commercial List.[20] This power is being vigorously exercised.[21]

Where it is intended to proceed under Order 14 the Points of Claim must preferably be indorsed on the writ or served with it but may also be served after notice of intention to defend has been given. There can be no application for summary judgment under Order 14 until the defendant has given notice of intention to defend. Service of the summons and affidavit in support must be effected not less than 10 clear days before the return date. That date must be obtained from the Commercial Court Listing Officer at Room 198, Royal Courts of Justice, in the same way as for any other summons. Solicitors must mark the summons with an estimate of the time which is expected to be required for the hearing and if it subsequently appears that this estimate is likely to prove inaccurate, as often appears when the defendant's affidavit in reply is received, solicitors should notify the Commercial Court Listing Officer of the revised estimate. This is essential so as to assist in the allocation of sufficient time for summonses.[22]

---

20. RSC Order 72, rule 6(1).
21. See Commercial Court Committee Report 1981 and the Practice Direction of Parker J., of 15th March 1982, [1982] 1 Lloyd's Rep. 534 set out at p. 173 and see also p. 56 below.
22. *Per* Donaldson, J., Practice Statement [1967] 1 W.L.R. 1545.

Summons for directions

In those cases—now the vast majority of cases—where the action has been commenced in the Commercial List under the automatic entry procedure under Order 72, rule 4(1), and where consequently there is no need for a summons for transfer, the summons for directions should be issued at that time when the giving of directions as to interlocutory matters and as to the hearing of the action is likely to enable the parties to proceed to trial as speedily and as economically as possible. The Commercial Court has a very flexible approach to the giving of directions before trial and to this end Order 72, rule 8(1) expressly provides that "any party to an action in the Commercial List may take out a summons for directions in the action before the pleadings are closed". This is to facilitate the giving of directions in urgent cases or straightforward cases where it may be appropriate to dispense with pleadings altogether or to abbreviate them or to substitute inter-solicitor correspondence or the judge's note to define the issues so that an early trial can take place.[23] Indeed, an essential feature of the Commercial Court is its ability and the determination of the commercial judges to proceed to trial with immense rapidity if the urgency of the case requires it. Lord Justice Scrutton remarked in *Butcher Wetherly & Co.* v. *Norman*[24] that "I have known a writ being issued on a Monday and the case being heard on the Wednesday". The sense of urgency is particularly strong in those cases which involve disputes under or as to the continuation in force of existing contracts where great losses may be needlessly sustained if the parties cannot obtain an immediate and binding ruling on their legal rights.[25] In the case of *Gatoil Anstalt* v. *Omennial Ltd.* (*The Balder London*)[26] the issue under a time charter was whether the disponent owners were entitled to withdraw the vessel by reason of the charterers' failure to comply with the provisions as to the payment of hire. The dispute arose on 21st April 1980

---

23. For a full discussion of this practice in relation to dispensing with pleadings see pp. 39 to 41 above.

24. [1934] 1 K.B. 475, at p. 479. In *S.A. Commercial* v. *National S.S. Co.* [1935] 2 K.B. 313 the trial of the action took place two days after the issue of the writ.

25. Mr Justice Goff gave interesting examples in an article in the *Law Guardian Gazette*, 29th October 1980, p. 1053:

> "To give one or two examples, last year a dispute arose as a result of which a supertanker was about to be kept waiting off Freeport in the Bahamas. The matter was brought to the attention of the Court at 11 a.m. one morning; by 3.30 p.m. on the same day, judgment had been given in open Court, and the ship was able to commence discharge later that afternoon. In another case, earlier this year, a substantial dispute arose over discovery in a very large arbitration (being a claim for over £100 million). After appearing before the arbitrators on a Saturday and Sunday, the parties applied to the Court on Monday. The hearing was fixed for Thursday; after two days of argument, judgment was given between 6 p.m. and 7 p.m. on Friday".

26. [1980] 2 Lloyd's Rep. 489.

with a notice of withdrawal. The writ was issued on 28th April 1980. The points of claim were served on 2nd May, the points of defence and counterclaim on 8th May and the matter came on for trial on 14th May.

Ordinary commercial actions which have been commenced in the Commercial List do not involve the giving of any orders for directions before close of pleadings.[27] The parties are expected to get on with the exchange of pleadings, whether in strict accordance with the Rules or within such extended periods as may be agreed upon. It is intended that except where there is some special reason for an early summons for directions under the provisions of Order 72, rule 8(1) considered above, the summons for directions, unless the parties to the action agree to extend the time, will be issued in accordance with Order 25, rule 1. This requires that the summons for directions must be taken out within one month after close of pleadings. However, the effect of Order 25, rule 1(3) is that in practice the taking out of the summons for directions should be directly related to discovery and should not take place until 14 days after the time for exchange of lists of documents has expired. The time for exchange of lists of documents is prescribed by Order 24, rule 2 as being 14 days after the pleadings are deemed to be closed; but this period of time may be extended by order of the judge or by agreement between the parties and where such extension of time does take place the summons for directions must be taken out within 14 days after the extended period has expired,[28] but regardless of whether discovery by exchange of lists of documents has actually been completed or effected at all.

The summons for directions must be on Form P.F. No. 159, obtainable from the Inland Revenue Department, Royal Courts of Justice. At least 14 clear days must be allowed between issue of the summons and the return date. Service should be effected promptly after the issue of the summons. The return date must be obtained from the Listing Officer of the Commercial Court at Room 198, Royal Courts of Justice.[29] Solicitors must mark the summons with an estimate of the time required for the hearing and if subsequently that estimate appears likely to be inaccurate they must inform the Listing Officer of the corrected estimate.[30]

Summonses are normally heard on Fridays[31] when all the commercial judges then hearing commercial actions in London are normally available to try summonses. Where counsel are involved in more than one summons listed for a particular date, notification of that fact must be made to the Commercial Court

---

27. For those periods of time allowed by the Rules for the service of pleadings, see p. 46 above.
28. RSC Order 25, rule 1(3).
29. Telephone No. 01–405 7641, ext. 3826; Telex 296983 COMM.G.
30. *Per* Donaldson, J., Practice Statement [1967] W.L.R. 1545.
31. Practice Direction of Parker, J., [1981] 3 All E.R. 864. See p. 170 below.

Office by counsel's clerks not later than 9.30 a.m. on the day *prior to* the return date.

In practice it is frequently the case that discovery has not been completed at the time of the hearing of the summons for directions. Nonetheless, it is the duty of those advising the parties to give all such information and produce all such documents on the hearing as the Court may reasonably require for the purposes of enabling it properly to deal with the summons.[32] This is particularly important in multi-party proceedings involving complex factual and legal issues. If the salient points cannot be sufficiently explained to the judge by those representing the parties on the hearing of the summons for directions much time and costs may be wasted. By a Practice Direction issued by Parker, J., on 15th March 1982[33] it was directed that all documents relevant to the summons should be lodged in Room 198, Royal Courts of Justice, by noon two days before the date fixed for the hearing. Any affidavits previously filed should be bespoken and the exhibits to such affidavits should be lodged with the other documents. On the first occasion when there is an *inter partes* application in the action the documents lodged should always include the main pleadings and the parties should be prepared, if necessary, to justify the retention of the action in the Commercial List. Failure to comply with that direction, it was stated, would normally result in the application not being heard on the date fixed for the hearing at the expense of the party in default. It was also directed that a copy of the notice as to lodgment of documents should be attached to the copy of the application to be heard when that application is served on any other party to the proceedings. In complex actions it may therefore be advantageous to the parties to agree to postpone the summons for directions until both sides have had an opportunity of seeing the main body of documents forthcoming on discovery. In such cases discovery often leads to amendment of the pleadings and it may therefore be convenient to combine an application for leave to amend the pleadings with the summons for directions because the real issues will then be more readily identifiable. It is not uncommon for there to be applications for further discovery and it is therefore convenient for these to be dealt with at the same hearing.

In those cases where the action has not been commenced in the Commercial List by the automatic entry procedure, and a summons for transfer is subsequently taken out, the hearing is treated as a summons for directions.[34] It is then usual for the judge to give directions as to the service of pleadings, exchange of lists of documents, and inspection of documents. Unless the matter is urgent or is likely

---

32. RSC Order 25, rule 6(1).
33. [1982] 1 Lloyd's Rep. 534 and see for the precise text of the notice to be attached to all applications p. 173 below where the Practice Direction is set out.
34. RSC Order 72, rule 8(2).

to be sufficiently simple to be suitable for trial without pleadings or further directions a date for trial will not usually be fixed at such an early stage. If, however, there is a late application for transfer it may well be appropriate to fix a date for trial at the same hearing.

The commercial judges will in appropriate cases very readily use their powers under RSC Order 72, rule 6(1) to remove from the Commercial List actions which are not of a commercial character. To facilitate the proper monitoring of the disputes which come before the Court the main pleadings should always be lodged in Room 198, Royal Courts of Justice, by noon two days before the date fixed for the hearing of the first *inter partes* application in the action. In his Practice Direction of 15th March 1982[35] Parker, J., observed:

> "Many cases are launched in the Commercial List for no better reason than that one or other or both parties are banks, or shipping companies, or insurers, or commodity traders, or that the action is for breach of contract for sale of goods. If the issues in the cases are not commercial issues at all but, for example, a quality dispute in a sale of goods case, or a conversion or fraud, the resolution of which involves no commercial expertise, the case will normally be transferred to the Q.B. List".

Dates for trial

If the commercial judge is satisfied on the hearing of the summons for directions that sufficient information as to the major issues involved is available to enable those advising the parties to form a reasonably reliable estimate of the length of time required for the trial he will, if requested to do so, make an order fixing a date for trial. It is usually possible for those advising the parties to agree how long it will take for the action to be ready for trial, but in difficult cases where the parties are unable to agree, the judge will do his best to form a view as to how soon the action can be brought on for hearing without, on the one hand, giving rise to an unduly disorganised trial or injustice to any of the parties and without, on the other hand, allowing any of the parties an unnecessarily leisurely period of preparation during which there is a danger of the action going stale and the witnesses' memories failing. It will be usual for the Commercial Court Listing Officer to be in attendance on applications to fix dates so as to enable the judge and those representing the parties to be informed of what space is available in the Commercial Court diary. Otherwise dates can be arranged with the Commercial Court Listing Officer,[36] if necessary through counsels' clerks.

---

35. [1982] 1 Lloyd's Rep. 534 set out at p. 173 below.
36. Room 244A, Royal Courts of Justice, Strand, London WC2A 2LL, telephone number: 01–405 7461, ext. 3826; Telex 296983 COMM-G.

In matters of great urgency, where it is essential for the parties to have their rights determined as quickly as possible, for example, under a subsisting contract,[37] the Court will usually be able to find an early date close at hand. It will certainly always do its best to accommodate the parties, particularly if both parties are anxious to have the matter tried quickly and are clearly prepared to co-operate with each other and with the Court to facilitate an expedited hearing. Where only one of the parties, usually the plaintiff, asks for a speedy trial the judge usually investigates the matter with some care to ensure that the defendant is not being forced into a position where he cannot adequately organise his defence in time and that, if an order is made for a speedy trial, the parties will sufficiently prepare the case to ensure that the trial will be reasonably well organised, that documents will be sufficiently disclosed and prepared for trial, and that the issues will be sufficiently identified to enable the trial to go ahead.

Dates for trial are usually given on a "not before" basis. The hearing will not commence earlier than the date accorded to it but, subject to the availability of the commercial judges and to the overall state of the Commercial Court's diary, the start of the trial may be delayed for a few days. It is very unusual for very substantial delay to be experienced but it may occasionally happen if many of the previous fixtures being heard by the commercial judges substantially overrun their estimates[38] or there are exceptionally urgent matters which have to be given priority.

To enable the Commercial Court to provide an efficient service it is of great importance that it should be kept informed of any revision of estimates of length of those actions to which dates for trial have been given. If the parties are agreed that the estimate given at the time when the date was fixed is no longer accurate it is their solicitors' duty to inform the Listing Officer of the changed estimate. Equally, if the action has settled, the parties must inform the Listing Officer at the earliest possible opportunity. The estimate should be confirmed as accurate or changes should, if possible, be notified not later than six weeks before the date for trial.[39]

Unlike the remainder of the Queen's Bench Division, the Commercial Court sits during most of September and applications for dates for the trial of actions and matters arising in relation to arbitrations and for the hearing of summonses in September will be entertained in the same way as for fixtures during term time.[40] In order to obtain a date in September it is not necessary to establish that the matter is Long Vacation business under Order 64, rule 4.

---

37. See pp. 34 to 35 above.
38. In 1981 only 18 of the 446 cases given trial dates had to be stood out by the Court: Commercial Court Committee Report, 1981.
39. Practice Direction [1967] 1 W.L.R. 1545, Practice Direction [1974] 1 Lloyd's Rep. 239.
40. Practice Direction [1977] 1 All E.R. 912. Set out at p. 167 below.

Interrogatories

Although there is no specific prohibition on the granting in the Commercial Court of orders for interrogatories under RSC Order 26, it is most exceptional for such orders to be applied for or made. Since the foundation of the Commercial Court it has been the general philosophy to discourage such applications.[41] They often lead to avoidable extra costs and added delay. Requests for particulars of pleadings or further discovery of specific categories of documents will, in most cases, prove to be an effective means of obtaining the required information. Applications for interrogatories if made at all should not, therefore, be made until after close of pleadings and inspection of documents and then only if there is no other convenient and effective course. The party who wishes to apply for an order must be prepared on the application to satisfy the judge that he has made every effort to obtain the desired information by other means. It may, in certain cases, be appropriate in the interests of saving time and expense for the Court to order on an application for interrogatories that they should be answered informally by a letter from the other party's solicitors.[42] If it appears that an order for interrogatories may render it unnecessary for evidence to be taken on commission the application will usually be granted.

Order for the trial of preliminary issues

It has for long been the practice of the Commercial Court to encourage the trial of preliminary issues of law or construction provided that a decision one way will put an end to the litigation.[43] This will be particularly the approach where the trial of the preliminary issue can be disposed of very shortly by comparison with the overall length of a full trial of all issues. It is unnecessary to satisfy the judge that a decision *either* way on the preliminary issue will put an end to the whole litigation.[44]

The general power to order a trial of a preliminary issue or of some issues before others is derived from RSC Order 33, rule 4, which provides that ". . . different questions or issues may be ordered to be tried at different places or by different modes of trial and one or more questions or issues may be ordered to be tried before the others". Where the parties agree before the trial that the Court

---

41. See Introduction to *The Times Reports of Commercial Cases*, Vol. 1, p. vii, and Scrutton, *Charterparties and Bills of Lading* (11th edn., 1923), p. 447.

42. This was the order made by Donaldson, J., in *De Maurier Jewels Ltd.* v. *Bastion Insurance Co. Ltd. and Coronet Insurance Co.* (13th September 1967) (unreported).

43. See Scrutton, *Charterparties and Bills of Lading* (11th edn., 1923), p. 447.

44. *Everett* v. *Ribbands* [1952] 2 Q.B. 198, at p. 206 *per* Romer, L.J., approved in *Carl Zeiss Stiftung* v. *Herbert Smith & Co.* [1969] 1 Ch 93.

should try preliminary issues their agreement should be embodied in an order which should define the preliminary issues.[45]

In *Chippendale* v. *Holt*[46] the preliminary issue ordered as between marine hull underwriters and their reinsurers was as to the meaning of the words in the reinsurance policy "to pay as may be paid thereon". In *The Maori King*[47] there was a preliminary issue as to whether the exceptions clauses in the bill of lading precluded the implication of a term that at the time of the shipment the vessel and her refrigerating machinery were fit to carry frozen meat on the voyage. In *Queensland National Bank* v. *P. & O. Steam Navigation Co.*,[48] where the plaintiffs claimed under a bill of lading in respect of the loss of a box of sovereigns, it was ordered that there should be a trial of the preliminary issues whether there was an implied warranty by the shipowners under the bill of lading that the room in which the box was stowed was so constructed as to be reasonably fit to resist thieves and if so and such warranty were broken whether it was superseded by the bill of lading exceptions. In *Court Line* v. *Finelvet A.G.*,[49] where the 49 pages of pleadings raised extremely complex issues of fact and various issues of construction of a time charter relating to the grounding of the vessel *Jevington Court* in the River Plate, McNair, J., made an order in terms previously agreed between the parties that there should be a trial of six preliminary issues, largely of construction of the time charter, but partly of fact. The parties had previously been able to agree certain facts as to the grounding and subsequent detention of the vessel. Roskill, J., ultimately tried these issues within a week and the whole litigation was thereby concluded. In *The Yasin*[50] there was a preliminary issue as to whether cargo underwriters could by subrogation bring an action in the name of certain cargo receivers against the shipowners for breach of the bill of lading contract in a case where the shipowners themselves had, in accordance with an express term of the charter-party, taken out and paid premium on a policy for the benefit of receivers. In *Ellerman Lines Ltd.* v. *Lancaster Maritime Co.*[51] a preliminary issue was ordered as to whether time charterers' lien on the vessel for hire paid in advance but not earned gave the time charterers an equitable interest in the proceeds of insurance against the banks who were mortgagees of the vessel and had control over the insurance proceeds. In *Impex Transport Aktieselskabet* v.

---

45. *Atlantic Shipping & Trading Co. Ltd.* v. *Louis Dreyfus & Co.* [1922] A.C. 250, at p. 259 *per* Lord Sumner.
46. (1895) 1 Com.Cas. 197.
47. [1895] 2 Q.B. 550.
48. (1897) 2 Com.Cas. 229.
49. [1966] 1 Lloyd's Rep. 683.
50. [1979] 2 Lloyd's Rep. 45.
51. [1980] 2 Lloyd's Rep. 497.

A.G. Thames Holdings Ltd.[52] there was a preliminary issue as to whether a claim for demurrage to a consignment of fruit was time-barred under the C.M.R. Conditions. In *Schiffahrt und Kohlen* v. *Chelsea Maritime*[53] a preliminary issue was ordered as to whether the plaintiff cargo owners could sue the shipowners in tort in respect of damage to the plaintiffs' goods occurring before the plaintiffs acquired any proprietary interest in the goods. In *Lamport & Holt Lines Ltd.* v. *Coubro & Scrutton (M. and I.) Ltd.*[54] there was a claim by shipowners for negligently allowing a derrick to fall on to the deck of the plaintiff's vessel and preliminary issues were ordered as to which defendants contracted to re-stow and which defendants did re-stow the derrick, whether the relevant standard contract conditions were incorporated into the contract and, if so, whether the conditions excluded the defendant's liability in negligence.

It occasionally happens that title of the plaintiff to sue is a major issue which, if decided one way, will wholly dispose of the litigation; and in such cases it will often be convenient and appropriate for title to sue to be tried as a preliminary issue.

It is often the case that complicated questions of calculation of damages can be left to the agreement of the parties without being put before the trial judge and in such cases it is the practice for only the questions of liability to be referred to the Court. There may, however, be some cases where the issues relating to damages are so complex that it is necessary or more appropriate that they should be tried by the commercial judge. The issues as to causation may be inextricably related to the issues on liability and in such cases it may be particularly helpful to have damages tried by the judge who tried the issues as to liability.[55] He will already be closely acquainted with the facts and evidence and there will be consequent savings of time and expense if a detailed knowledge of such facts and evidence is directly relevant to the calculation of damages. Where the ascertainment or calculation of the damages does not involve detailed knowledge of the facts or evidence proved or given at the trial of liability but the parties cannot agree the amount of damages, the commercial judge will normally refer damages to the Official Referee. Although general average adjustments often come before the Commercial Court, it is not normal practice for the commercial judge to try questions of apportionment of sacrifice or expenses between general and particular average, valuation of contributing interests, allowances new for old, matters of

---

52. [1981] 2 Lloyd's Rep. 566.
53. [1981] 2 Lloyd's Rep. 635.
54. [1981] 2 Lloyd's Rep. 659.
55. This course was adopted by Goff, J., in *Westfalische Central-Genossenschaft* v. *Seabright Chemicals* (13th March 1979) (unreported).

adjusting practice or the computation of adjustments. The Court will normally insist that such matters should be agreed between the parties' average adjusters.

Special orders in complex actions

In those cases where many parties are involved in the same proceedings and where there are therefore many different firms of solicitors and many different counsel involved it may be appropriate, because of the complexity of the issues, for special interlocutory orders to be made so as to facilitate the smooth and efficient conduct of the trial.

If there are likely to be vast quantities of documents it may be appropriate for an order to be made that the main bundles of documents should be agreed by a specified date before the trial date.[56] In preparing the bundles of documents for the trial it is essential that solicitors and, if necessary, junior counsel, should exercise sensible selectivity so as to avoid burdening the bundles with useless material. The mere fact that a document has been disclosed on discovery does not mean that it must necessarily be included in the trial bundle. Documents which no party can reasonably envisage having to refer to at the trial should be excluded. In *Commonwealth Insurance Co.* v. *Groupe Sprinks S.A.*,[57] a reinsurance action involving many parties in which there were 452 pages of pleadings and many documents, Lloyd, J., in giving judgment, observed:

> "Finally, I should mention a practice which has grown up, particularly in these cases, of including every relevant document in the agreed bundles of correspondence. It is said to be cheaper than instructing counsel to select the correspondence that matters. In the present case . . . the agreed bundles comprise 2,876 pages. Within a few days of the start of the trial counsel helpfully created a working bundle from the mass of documents, comprising 773 pages. Less than 350 of those pages were in fact referred to during the proceedings and only about 100 pages have, in my estimation, proved to have any real significance".

Where there are many complex issues in a multi-party action, it may be appropriate for an order to be made for a pre-trial conference in chambers at which all parties would be entitled to raise before the commercial judge who was to try the case any matters relating to the preparation of the action for trial and to the conduct of the trial. Such matters would cover not only routine points relating to pleadings, particulars and discovery of documents, but also such matters as dates for exchange of experts' reports, additional expert evidence, arrangement

---

56. In *Philadelphia Manufacturers Mutual Insurance Co.* v. *Unigard Mutual Insurance Co.*, a multi-party reinsurance dispute, Donaldson, J., on 3rd July 1978 made an order that bundles of documents should be agreed by a date about three months before the trial date.

57. [1983] 1 Lloyd's Rep. 67, at p. 89.

of documents for the trial, the order of presentation of the different parties' cases at the trial, if necessary, the order in which specific issues should be tried, and whether particular matters of evidence should be proved by documents or orally by witnesses, and in what order.[58]

Where the issues in a multi-party action are closely inter-dependent it may be appropriate for an order to be made that epitomes of evidence of fact or even proofs of evidence of witnesses of fact be exchanged between all parties by a specific date before the date for trial. In *Philadelphia Manufacturers Mutual Insurance Co.* (3rd July 1978) unreported, Donaldson, J., made an order that epitomes of evidence of fact and/or proofs of witnesses of fact be deposited with the clerk to the Commercial Court on or before a certain date and that they should be released to the parties to the action on the following day. This order was subsequently approved by Parker, J., at the pre-trial conference.

It will often be helpful and convenient for an order to be made that at the commencement of the trial counsel for each of the parties should in turn give a brief opening, outlining the gist of their party's case, and this should be followed by the opening of the documentary evidence by the plaintiffs and by comments on such evidence by the other parties. Such an order was made before the trial by Donaldson, J., in *Philadelphia Manufacturers Mutual* v. *Unigard Mutual* and by Lloyd, J., at the commencement of the trial in *Commonwealth Insurance Co.* v. *Groupe Sprinks*.[59] Orders may also be made that summaries of issues affecting each party to the action should be prepared and agreed if possible and, if not agreed, should be delivered separately by a specified date.[60] It may in many cases—even those which do not rank as highly-complex multi-party actions—be appropriate for an order to be made that the expert evidence from all parties should be postponed until after the whole of the evidence of fact has been heard from all parties.

The taking of evidence abroad

With the relative simplicity of air travel and the consequent ease with which foreign witnesses can be moved around the world at relatively small cost and with

---

58. Such a pre-trial conference took place before Parker, J., on 2nd December 1978 in *Philadelphia Manufacturers Mutual Insurance Co.* v. *Unigard Mutual Insurance Co.* This immense reinsurance action involving over 70 parties, many groups of whom were separately represented, never came on for trial: it was settled some weeks before the hearing date.

59. [1983] 1 Lloyd's Rep. 67.

60. Such an order was made by Donaldson, J., in *Philadelphia Manufacturers Mutual Insurance Co.* v. *Unigard Mutual Insurance Co.* (3rd October 1978).

the advent of the provisions as to admissibility of written statements under section 2 of the Civil Evidence Act 1968 it is thought that there are now few applications for evidence to be taken abroad. The power to order the taking of evidence abroad by letters of request, either by oral examination by the parties or accompanied by written lists of interrogatories and cross-interrogatories, or by an examiner, usually a British Consul, is contained in RSC Order 39, rule 2. The most appropriate method of taking such evidence will depend in each case on the laws of the country in which the evidence is to be obtained and in particular whether Britain has a bilateral convention with that country or the country has ratified the Hague Convention on the Taking of Evidence Abroad in Civil or Commercial Matters, 1970. Lists of convention countries will be found in the notes to RSC Order 39, rule 2 in the Supreme Court Practice.

Applications for the taking of evidence abroad should not be made until some reasonable attempt has been made to obtain the evidence by other means, such as witnesses who are or can be brought within the jurisdiction, documents disclosed in the action or admissions by the other parties. The application should be made by summons in the action and where the application is opposed the usual practice is that the applicant indicates to the commercial judge what witnesses he proposes to call and what evidence the witness is expected to give. Where the facts to be proved by the witness are disputed, the judge may suggest that a statement of evidence on affidavit should be obtained from the proposed witness and should be made available to the other party or parties and that if discovery has not yet been completed all relevant documents should meanwhile be disclosed. If the parties consent, the affidavit can then be used in evidence at the trial. If this course is not acceptable to both parties the judge in a proper case then grants the application that evidence should be taken abroad and reserves the question of costs for the trial. If in the event the evidence obtained abroad does not substantially differ from that contained in the disclosed documents or from other available sources, the whole or part of the costs of taking evidence abroad may fall on the party who pursued the application.

Applications for ship's papers

This application arises in actions in the Commercial Court brought against insurers on marine insurance policies where the defendant insurers allege that the loss has been caused by the wilful misconduct of the assured. The effect of the order for ship's papers is that the assured is required to give discovery on oath and to produce for inspection all the ship's papers after service of the points of claim and before service of the points of defence. This procedure originated at the beginning of the nineteenth century before discovery was a generally available remedy in the Courts of Common Law and when the defendant insurers would otherwise have to apply to the Court of Exchequer to obtain disclosure of the plaintiff's documents.[61] It is now provided for by RSC Order 72, rule 10.[62]

Prior to the introduction of RSC Order 31, rule 12A in 1936 the insurers were entitled to the order almost as of right; but since then and now under Order 72, rule 10 the remedy is discretionary and the Court has to be satisfied that the circumstances of the case are such that it is necessary or expedient for the order to be made. Further, although there is referred to in Order 72, rule 10 that form of the order which is set out in Form No. 94 in Appendix A of the Supreme Court Practice,[63] it is made quite clear that the form of the order is in the discretion of the Court. "This form is so long, so full of repetitive detail, and so obscure that it must have been drafted by a conveyancer in the days when payment was so much a folio".[64] Indeed, in *Probatina Shipping Co. Ltd.* v. *Sun Insurance Office Ltd.*[65] all the members of the Court of Appeal recognised that this form of order was unsatisfactory and in need of revision. The trial judge—Kerr, J.—observed:[66]

> "The relative uselessness of the general wording of Form 94 is also illustrated by the fact that in many applications for ship's papers counsel for the insurers readily agree that if an order is made it may be more helpful, instead of making it in the terms of Form No. 94, for the parties to try to agree on a form of order containing classes of documents which are really relevant to the particular facts of the case".

Later in his judgment, Kerr, J., went on:[67]

> "The present rule gives a wide discretion and enables the Court in effect to consider and decide what documents or classes of documents should be disclosed in so far as the parties may be at issue about this. In my view this is the right

61. *Goldschmidt* v. *Marryat* (1809) 1 Camp, at p. 562.
62. RSC Order 72, rule 10:—
    (1) Where in an action in the Commercial List relating to a marine insurance policy an application for an order under Order 24, rule 3, is made by the insurer, then, without prejudice to its powers under that rule, the Court, if satisfied that the circumstances of the case are such that it is necessary or expedient to do so, may make an order, either in Form 94 in Appendix A or in such other form as it thinks fit, for the production of such documents as are therein specified or described.
    (2) An order under this rule may be made on such terms, if any, as to staying proceedings in the action or otherwise as the Court thinks fit.
    (3) In this rule "the Court" means the judge, the District Registrar of Liverpool or the District Registrar of Manchester, as the case may be.
63. The Order for ship's papers is reproduced at p. 69 below.
64. *Probatina Shipping Co. Ltd.* v. *Sun Insurance Office Ltd.* [1974] 1 Lloyd's Rep. 369, at p. 371, *per* Lord Denning, M.R.
65. *Supra.*
66. [1973] 2 Lloyd's Rep. 520, at p. 528 with which Buckley, L.J., expressly agreed at [1974] 1 Lloyd's Rep. 373.
67. [1973] 2 Lloyd's Rep. 530, with which Buckley, L.J., expressly agreed at [1974] 1 Lloyd's Rep. 373.

line on which to proceed. The defendants' solicitors should as soon as possible request the production of such further documents or classes of documents as they consider to be material. The plaintiffs' solicitors should then consider such request with equal expedition. In effect, the parties should therefore in the first instance try to agree what should be the contents of an order for the balance of ship's papers at this stage. If and to the extent that they cannot agree, the matter should come back to the Court for decision. All the documents disclosed, whether in the past or hereafter as the result of agreement or further order, should then be verified by the plaintiffs on affidavit. There should be no stay meanwhile, and the defendants should serve their points of defence within a time on which I will hear counsel".

In that case the Court of Appeal considered the principles on which the judge's discretion should be exercised. The substance of the approach should be that it is up to the assured who claims on marine underwriters to produce to them *at the outset* all papers relevant to his claim, together with all other papers that they may reasonably ask to see.[68] If he does not do so, but instead goes ahead with his action, it will be open to the defendant underwriters to apply for an order for ship's papers before defence. The order is not, however, to be given automatically. Roskill, L.J., considered[69] that:

"the crucial question—not necessarily the only question—which the commercial judge should ask himself is not . . . whether there is a *prima facie* case for pleading scuttling but whether, when the application for ship's papers is made, the plaintiffs have already voluntarily given sufficient disclosure of documents whether before or after the action brought. If they have, I see no reason why in such cases the points of defence should not be delivered with the best particulars then available. But if the plaintiffs have not, than I think a judge can and should order further discovery either in Form 94 or in such other form as he thinks fit, as for example by ordering discovery of specific classes of documents with or without a stay".

In the exercise of the Court's discretion the judge should also have regard to the relative advantage in obtaining further documents compared with the disadvantage of the consequent delay and expense. Buckley, L.J., expressed this consideration:[70]

"In my judgment it is the duty of a judge, who is asked to make an order for ship's papers, to weigh the advantages which may result in the search for truth against the disadvantages of delay and expense involved in discovery of this kind. That delay and expense may be very substantial. If the judge considers that the advantages outweigh the disadvantages, he will make an order for ship's papers; but otherwise, in my opinion, he should not, notwithstanding that the defendants indicate that they intend to plead scuttling. It goes without saying

---

68. *Per* Lord Denning at [1974] 1 Lloyd's Rep. 372.
69. ibid., at p. 377.
70. ibid., at p. 373.

that the judge should not make such an order if he has reason to suppose that it is being sought as a means of extorting a settlement".

The Court of Appeal also considered whether counsel for the insurers appearing on the application for ship's papers was obliged to disclose to the judge and, if so, in what detail, the grounds on which the insurers proposed to advance the plea of wilful misconduct. The Court took the view that this was a matter for the discretion of counsel in each case and that he was under no obligation to disclose the evidential basis for underwriters' suspicions.

> "It cannot . . . be right to require counsel to disclose his client's case at an interlocutory stage in the action and more particularly before pleadings are closed, but counsel may very possibly feel able to indicate the nature of the defendants' belief or suspicions without making any undesirable disclosure and he may think that to do so will assist him in his application for ship's papers. The court should not . . . readily suppose that an experienced and responsible counsel would associate himself with an allegation of something . . . without sufficient reason; but some indication of the basis of the allegation may well be necessary for deciding what kind of discovery of documents would fit the case".[71]

As appears from RSC Order 72, rule 10(2) whether an order for ship's papers should also incorporate an order staying the action is a matter for the judge's discretion. In *Probatina Shipping Co. Ltd.* v. *Sun Insurance Office Ltd.*[72] Kerr, J., declined to grant a stay and his decision was upheld by the Court of Appeal. Merely because an order is made for the production of ship's papers it does not automatically follow that a stay should also be ordered. It is important that there should not be undue delay of the proceedings[73] but there may be cases where the plaintiff has been so unco-operative and so unforthcoming that it would be proper to stay the proceedings until he does give the discovery that is asked.

The general approach of the trial judge and of the Court of Appeal in *Probatina Shipping* v. *Sun Insurance Office*[74] can therefore be summarised as being that the stringency of the order made upon an application for ship's papers will depend heavily upon the degree of co-operation in the provision of documents and information generally which has been afforded by the plaintiff prior to the application.

The order may be made against a party interested in the vessel who claims under a marine policy but yet who did not operate or have possession of or direct control over the vessel, such, for example, as a mortgagee of the vessel. In that

---

71. *Per* Buckley, L.J. at p. 373. Roskill, L.J., expressed similar views at p. 377.
72. *Supra.*
73. *Supra, per* Lord Denning, M.R., at p. 372.
74. *Supra.*

case the order imposes a duty to take all reasonable steps to procure discovery of the ship's papers by the owners or from whichever other party may have them.[75]

The fact that the plaintiff claims on a policy of reinsurance is not in itself a reason for refusing an order for ship's papers.[76]

The order is not confined to claims brought under policies on hull and machinery but may also be made where the claim is made under a cargo policy where the insurers propose to rely by way of defence on the allegation that the assured was a party to or aware of the loss of the cargo by wilful misconduct, such as where there is a conspiracy to scuttle the vessel with the cargo on board or to simulate a shipment.[77]

There may be cases where, although the proceedings do not in form embrace a claim under a marine policy, the substance of the claim will justify an order for ship's papers. Such a case would be a claim by insurers to recover money paid to an assured in respect of a fraudulent claim under a marine policy.[78]

The order is not available in cases where the carriage was exclusively land carriage.[79] Where the carriage includes but is not confined to overland transit the better view is that the order for ship's papers will be made in appropriate cases, even where the loss for which the claim is advanced occurred during land transit.[80]

The commercial judge's exercise of discretion in granting or withholding an order for ship's papers will not usually be reversed by the Court of Appeal.[81]

It is unnecessary for the application for ship's papers to be supported by an affidavit. But discovery made pursuant to an order will usually be required to be by affidavit. The affidavit must show the precise interest of the person swearing the affidavit or those whom he represents.[82]

If the affidavit provided pursuant to the order for ship's papers is unsatisfactory, the insurers may apply for a further and better affidavit.[83]

Setting down for trial

The order made on the summons for directions, at which the final directions for the trial are given, will include a provision that the action should be set down for

---

75. *West of England Bank* v. *Canton Insurance Co.* (1877) 2 Ex.D. 472, per Cleasby, B., at p. 474. See also *China S.S. Co.* v. *Commercial Ass. Co.* (1881) 8 Q.B.D. 142, *Graham Joint Stock Shipping Co.* v. *Motor Union Insurance Co.* [1922] 1 K.B. 563 and *Teneria Moderna Franco Espanola* v. *New Zealand Ins. Co.* [1924] 1 K.B. 79.
76. *China Traders' Co.* v. *Royal Exchange Assurance Corpn.* [1898] 2 Q.B. 187.
77. *British Isles Marine & General Insurance Co. Ltd.* v. *Bostandji* (1920) 5 Ll.L.Rep. 202 and *Teneria Moderna Franco Espanola* v. *New Zealand Insurance Co.* (*supra*).
78. *Boulton* v. *Houlder* [1904] 1 K.B. 784 and *British Isles Marine & General Insurance Co. Ltd.* v. *Bostandji* (*supra*).
79. *Schloss* v. *Stevens* (1905) 10 Com. Cas. 224.
80. *Harding* v. *Bussell* [1905] 2 K.B. 83 and *Leon* v. *Casey* [1932] 2 K.B. 576.
81. *Keevil* v. *Boag* [1940] 3 All E.R. 346.
82. *Avon* v. *Miall* (27th November 1975) unreported. Brandon, J.
83. *Abdela* v. *Mutual Property Investment Ltd.* [1921] W.N. 23.

trial within a certain number of weeks from the date of the order or before the trial date. This is in accordance with RSC Order 34, rule 2.[84] Except in cases of particular urgency it is usual to allow at least six weeks between setting down and the start of the trial, but in many cases a longer period will be appropriate.

Commercial actions are set down for trial in the Commercial List.[85] The procedure for setting down for trial in London[86] is that the plaintiff must deliver by post or otherwise, to the Head Clerk, Crown Office and Associates Department (Room 478), Central Office, Royal Courts of Justice, Strand, London WC2 (1) a request that the action may be set down for trial in the Commercial List at the Royal Courts of Justice and (2) two bundles each consisting of one copy of each of (a) the writ, (b) the pleadings (including any affidavits ordered to stand as pleadings), any request or order for particulars and the particulars given, and (c) all orders made on the summons for directions. Each bundle must be in chronological order, except that further and better particulars and voluntary particulars of pleadings are to be placed in the bundle immediately after the pleading to which they relate. The bundle which is to serve as the record (the other one being for the use of the trial judge) must be stamped denoting payment of the fee payable on setting down the action and have indorsed on it the names and addresses and telephone numbers of the solicitors for all parties or, in the case of a party who has no solicitor, of the party himself.

When a party has set down the action for trial he should notify the other parties and also the Commercial Court Listing Officer at the Commercial Court Office, Room 198, Royal Courts of Justice.[87] If the action is subsequently settled or

---

84. See the Lord Chief Justice's Practice Direction of 31st July 1981 [1981] 1 W.L.R. 1296, at para. 14 set out at p. 169 below. RSC Order 34, rule 2:—

Time for setting down action (O. 34, r. 2).

2.—(1) Every order made in an action which provides for trial before a judge shall, whether the trial is to be with or without a jury and wherever the trial is to take place, fix a period within which the plaintiff is to set down the action for trial.

(2) Where the plaintiff does not, within the period fixed under paragraph (1), set the action down for trial, the defendant may set the action down for trial or may apply to the Court to dismiss the action for want of prosecution and, on the hearing of any such application, the Court may order the action to be dismissed accordingly or may make such order as it thinks just.

(3) Every order made in an action in the Queen's Bench Division which provides for trial before a judge (otherwise than in the commercial list or the special paper or any corresponding list which may be specified for the purposes of this paragraph by directions under rule 4) shall contain an estimate of the length of the trial and, if the action is to be tried at the Royal Courts of Justice, shall, subject to any such directions, specify the list in which the action is to be put.

85. Lord Chief Justice's Practice Direction 31st July 1981. [1981] 1 W.L.R. 1296, para. 12: see p. 169 below.

86. See RSC Order 34, rule 3.

87. Lord Chief Justice's Practice Direction 31st July 1981, para. 14, *supra:* see p. 169 below.

withdrawn or if the estimate of the length of trial is revised it is the duty of all parties to notify the Listing Officer without delay.

Order for Ship's Papers in Marine Insurance Action
[RSC Order 72, rule 10]

[*Heading as in action*]

Upon hearing   [and upon reading the affidavit of   filed the   day of   19]:

It is ordered that the plaintiff and all other persons interested in this action, and in the insurance the subject of this action, do produce and show to the defendant, his solicitors or agents on oath [*or* by oath of their proper officer] all insurance slips, policies, letters of instruction or other orders for effecting such slips or policies, or relating to the insurance or the subject-matter of the insurance on the ship   , or the cargo on board thereof, or the freight thereby, and also all documents relating to the sailing or alleged loss of the said ship, cargo or freight, and all correspondence with any person relating in any manner to the effecting of the insurance on the said ship, cargo or freight, or any other insurance whatsoever effected on the said ship, cargo or freight, on the voyage insured by the policy sued on in this action, or any other policy whatsoever effected on the said ship, or the cargo on board thereof, or the freight thereby on the same voyage. Also all correspondence between the captain or agent of the ship and any other person with the owner or any person before the commencement of or during the voyage on which the alleged loss happened. Also all books and documents, whatever their nature and whether originals, duplicates or copies, which in any way relate or refer to any matter in question in this action and which are now in the custody, possession or power of the plaintiff or any other person on his behalf, his or their, or any of their brokers, solicitors or agents, with liberty for the defendant, his solicitors or agents to inspect and take copies of, or extracts from, any of those books or documents. And that in the like manner the plaintiff and every other person interested as aforesaid do account for all other books and documents relating or referring to any matter in question in this action which were once but are not now in his custody, possession and power.

And that [in the meantime all further proceedings be stayed and that] the costs of and occasioned by this application be costs in the action.

Dated the   day of   19 .

CHAPTER 6

"MAREVA" INJUNCTIONS

Purpose and basis of the jurisdiction

Since 1975 a major part of the work of the Commercial Court has been the hearing of applications for "*Mareva* Injunctions".[1] The purpose of this form of relief is to prevent the injustice of a defendant making himself "judgment-proof" by taking steps to ensure that he has no available or traceable assets within the jurisdiction on the day of judgment against which a judgment could be enforced.

Until 1981 the basis of the Court's jurisdiction to grant such injunctions was the Supreme Court of Judicature (Consolidation) Act 1925, section 45(1), which provided:

> "The High Court may grant a mandamus or an injunction or appoint a Receiver, by an interlocutory order in all cases in which it appears to the Court to be just or convenient to do so".[2]

This sub-section has now been replaced by section 37 of the Supreme Court Act 1981 which provides:

> "(1) The High Court may by order (whether interlocutory or final) grant an injunction or appoint a Receiver in all cases in which it appears to the Court to be just and convenient to do so.

---

1. In 1980 applications to the Commercial Court were at about the same rate as in 1979, namely 20 per month, as observed by Mustill, J., in *Third Chandris Shipping Corporation* v. *Unimarine S.A.* [1979] 1 Q.B. 645, at p. 650. The remedy was first given by the Court of Appeal in *Nippon Yusen Kaisha* v. *Karageorgis* [1975] 1 W.L.R. 1093; 2 Lloyd's Rep. 137 upon an *ex parte* application and was confirmed by the Court of Appeal, also upon an *ex parte* application but upon consideration of *Lister* v. *Stubbs* (1890) 45 Ch.D. 1, in *Mareva Compania S.A.* v. *International Bulk Carriers* [1975] 2 Lloyd's Rep. 509. The first *inter partes* hearing by the Court of Appeal was in August 1975 in *MBPXL Corporation* v. *Intercontinental Banking Corporation* (1975) CAT 411 in which an injunction was refused because it was not established that the defendants had assets within the jurisdiction of the English Courts. In March 1977 in *Rasu Maritima S.A.* v. *Persusahaan Pertambangan Minyak Dan Gas Bumi Negara (Pertamina)* [1978] Q.B. 644, after very full argument, the Court again confirmed that the Court did have jurisdiction to grant *Mareva* injunctions in appropriate cases. The only case involving a *Mareva* injunction yet to come before the House of Lords has been *The Siskina (Cargo Owners)* v. *Distos Compania Naviera* [1979] A.C. 210, but in that case the Court's jurisdiction to grant *Mareva* injunctions in appropriate cases was not challenged, and the House therefore was not required to consider whether the previous decisions of the Court of Appeal upholding the *Mareva* injunction jurisdiction were correct.

2. *Nippon Yusen Kaisha* v. *Karageorgis* [1975] 1 W.L.R. 1093; *Rasu Maritima S.A.* v. *Pertamina* [1978] Q.B. 644.

"(2) Any such order may be made either unconditionally or on such terms and conditions as the Court thinks just.

"(3) The power of the High Court under sub-section (1) to grant an interlocutory injunction restraining a party to any proceedings from removing from the jurisdiction of the High Court, or otherwise dealing with, assets located within that jurisdiction shall be exercisable in cases where that party is, as well as in cases where he is not, domiciled, resident or present within that jurisdiction".

Until 1980 the Courts regarded the risk of removal of the defendants' assets from the jurisdiction of the English Courts as being an essential feature of the *Mareva* jurisdiction.[3] Sir Robert Megarry, V.-C., was reflecting the prevailing view when in *Barclay-Johnson* v. *Yuill*[4] he said:

"If the assets are likely to remain in the jurisdiction, then the plaintiff, like all others with claims against the defendant, must run the risk, common to all, that the defendant may dissipate his assets, or consume them in discharging other liabilities, and so leave nothing with which to satisfy any judgment".

Although in form the injunction usually granted was in terms restraining the defendants from removing from the jurisdiction *or otherwise disposing of* any of their assets or particular assets, the purpose of the words in italics was treated as being to prevent the defendant from transferring assets into the hands of a recipient inside the jurisdiction with the ultimate purpose of having them removed from the jurisdiction.[5]

This limitation originated in the early *Mareva* cases from a misunderstanding of the effect of the much earlier decision of the Court of Appeal in *Lister* v. *Stubbs*.[6] In that case the plaintiffs claimed that the defendant, who was their agent, had taken bribes and held the money so received on trust for the plaintiffs. They argued that they were therefore entitled to an order that the money should be paid into Court and that there should be an interlocutory injunction restraining the defendant from dealing with land in which part of the bribes had been invested by the defendant. It does not appear from the report that it was argued that the plaintiffs were entitled to an interlocutory injunction even if they had no proprietary interest in the funds or the land. Nor does it appear that there was any evidence that there was a substantial risk that the defendant might be about to

---

3. See *Etablissement Esefka International Anstalt* v. *Central Bank of Nigeria* [1979] 1 Lloyd's Rep. 445, at pp. 448, 449; *Third Chandris Corporation* v. *Unimarine S.A.* [1979] 1 Q.B. 645, at pp. 652, 653, 669, 673; *Iraqi Ministry of Defence* v. *Arcepey Shipping S.A.* [1980] 1 Lloyd's Rep. 632, at p. 635; *Barclay-Johnson* v. *Yuill* [1980] 1 W.L.R. 1259, at p. 1264.

4. *Supra*, p. 1264.

5. See *Iraqi Ministry of Defence* v. *Arcepey Shipping Co. S.A.* [1980] 1 Lloyd's Rep. 632, *per* Goff, J., at p. 636.

6. (1890) 45 Ch.D. 1. See, in particular, *Mareva Compania S.A.* v. *International Bulk Carriers* [1975] 2 Lloyd's Rep. 509.

dissipate the property in issue or his assets in general for the purpose of avoiding execution of any judgment. The Court of Appeal was therefore concerned to emphasise that if a plaintiff had no proprietary interest in the assets in question he was not entitled by way of an interlocutory injunction or order for payment into Court to obtain security for his claim for damages or debt, however strong it might be, unless he obtained an order upon an application under Order 14. The Court was not called upon to consider whether an interlocutory injunction should be available in those cases where there was a substantial risk that the defendant would deliberately and imminently put his assets out of reach of the plaintiffs.

Apart from *Lister* v. *Stubbs*,[7] in view of the power of the Court to set aside voluntary conveyances in fraud of creditors originally under the Statute of Elizabeth, 1571, and subsequently under section 172 of the Law of Property Act 1925, in cases where there had been a disposal of assets *within the jurisdiction* into friendly hands in order that the transferor might avoid having to satisfy his creditors, it was clearly both illogical and quite contrary to the long-standing policy of the law not to extend the *Mareva* jurisdiction so as to protect potential creditors from the very injustice against which section 172 had been directed.

Predictably, it was Lord Denning, M.R., who first indicated that the *Mareva* jurisdiction should not be limited to cases where there was a risk of disposal *abroad* of the defendants' assets. In *Rahman (Prince Abdul) bin Turki al Sudairy* v. *Abu Taha*[8] the defendants were of Kuwaiti origin but had lived in London for many years trading under a firm name registered in Liechtenstein. They failed to give the addresses of places of residence in their affidavit. They had given a cheque to the plaintiff but it had been dishonoured. Lord Denning, M.R., in allowing the plaintiff's appeal against the judge's refusal to grant an injunction, stated[9]:

> "So I would hold that a *Mareva* injunction can be granted against a man even though he is based in this country if the circumstances are such that there is a danger of his absconding, or a danger of the assets being removed out of the jurisdiction or disposed of within the jurisdiction, or otherwise dealt with so that there is a danger that the plaintiff, if he gets judgment, will not be able to get it satisfied".

The effect of section 37(3) of the Supreme Court Act 1981—in as much as it confirms the power of the High Court to grant an interlocutory injunction restraining a party to any proceedings from removing from the jurisdiction of the High Court, *or otherwise dealing with*, assets located within that jurisdiction—is to recognise the basis of the *Mareva* jurisdiction as defined by Lord Denning,

---

7. *Supra*.
8. [1980] 1 W.L.R. 1268.
9. [1980] 1 W.L.R. 1268, at p. 1273.

M.R., in the passage cited above. This has been held by the Court of Appeal in *Z Ltd.* v. *A–Z.*[10] It is therefore no longer necessary to satisfy the Court that there is a risk that the defendant will remove his assets from the jurisdiction. It is enough to show that the defendant may well take steps designed to ensure that his assets are no longer available or traceable when judgment is given against him.[11]

Form of "Mareva" injunction

The form of a *Mareva* injunction is exemplified by that which was granted in *Third Chandris Shipping Corporation* v. *Unimarine*[12] set out in the judgment of Mustill, J., at page 648:

> "It is ordered and directed that the defendants by their officers, agents or servants or otherwise be restrained and an injunction is hereby granted restraining them from removing from the jurisdiction or otherwise disposing of[13] any of their assets, including and in particular any moneys forming an account in the name of the defendants standing at the Bank of Credit and Commerce S.A., 100 Leadenhall Street, London EC3, save in so far as the sum exceeds U.S. $91,087.25".

The sum specified in the order will normally be the amount of the debt or damages claimed in the action. The purpose of inserting a maximum amount is to enable the defendant to have the use of the amount by which his assets exceed the amount of the plaintiff's claim. When notice is given to a bank or other agent of the terms of the injunction with the maximum amount thus specified, there will be many cases where the bank or other agent is in the extremely awkward position of not knowing what total assets the defendant may have within the jurisdiction and whether, depending on that, the bank or other agent may release any of his assets which it may hold. In some exceptional cases the best course may be to omit from the order any maximum amount—leaving it to the defendant to apply to the Court for the order to be varied, thereby necessarily disclosing the

---

10. [1982] 1 Lloyd's Rep. 240, *per* Lord Denning, M.R., at p. 243; *per* Kerr, L.J., at p. 251.
11. ibid., *per* Kerr, L.J., at p. 251.
12. [1979] 1 Q.B. 645.
13. The words "or otherwise disposing of" were originally included in order to prevent the defendant from transferring assets into the hands of a recipient inside the jurisdiction with the ultimate purpose of removing them from the jurisdiction. In *Iraqi Ministry of Defence* v. *Arcepey Shipping Co. S.A.* [1980] 1 Lloyd's Rep. 632, Goff, J., said, at p. 636; "As was made plain by Mr Justice Mustill in the *Third Chandris* case, the point of the *Mareva* jurisdiction is to proceed by stealth, to pre-empt any action by the defendant to remove his assets from the jurisdiction. To achieve that result the injunction must be in a wide form because, for example, a transfer by the defendant to a collaborator in the jurisdiction would lead to the transfer abroad by that collaborator". It has now been held by the Court of Appeal in *Z Ltd.* v. *A–Z* [1982] 1 Lloyd's Rep. 240 that it is enough that there is a risk of disposal of assets *within* the jurisdiction and that ultimate export of assets is not essential. Consequently, these orders must now be treated as restraining all disposals of assets.

whereabouts of his assets.[14] But in most cases it is more desirable to insert in the order a maximum amount, and in such cases where possible there should also be inserted an order specifically restraining the defendant from disposing of any sums standing to his credit in a specified bank account up to that maximum or from disposing of any identified items deposited at an identified branch for safe custody.[14] It will be very much a matter for the discretion of the judge in each case having regard on the one hand to the objective of preventing dissipation of the defendant's assets and on the other to attempting to avoid imposing unworkable support obligations on third parties. The safest course for a bank or other agent in doubt as to how to apply the specified maximum amount to assets in its hands is not to release anything to the defendant without either the plaintiff's consent or an order from the Court. The general approach of the Commercial Court is that banks and other third parties in that position are encouraged to seek the directions of the Court. In some cases it may be appropriate for the defendant to be permitted to use a pre-determined part of his assets for normal living expenses.[14a] If so, the order should specify the amount and it may be appropriate that a special account should be opened to hold such amount, but it should not be the bank's function or duty to monitor the use to which the defendant puts such sums.[15] A form of order is set out at page 104 below.

Order for delivery up of tangible assets

While the normal form of *Mareva* injunction restrains the defendant from disposing of assets, there may be special circumstances which justify an order giving the plaintiffs through their solicitors physical control over tangible assets. The circumstances which would justify such an order were considered by the Court of Appeal in *C.B.S. United Kingdom Ltd.* v. *Lambert*.[16] In that case, in

---

14. See, generally, *Z Ltd.* v. *A–Z* [1982] 1 Lloyd's Rep. 240, at pp. 245 and 253–4. As to tangible assets, see sub-section "Effect on tangible assets in the hands of third parties" at p. 76 below.

14a. See, for example, *PCW (Underwriting Agencies) Ltd.* v. *Dixon, The Times*, 21st January and 4th February 1983, in which the Court of Appeal varied a *Mareva* injunction to the effect that, whereas the defendant's entire assets in the jurisdiction should be frozen, he would be entitled to withdraw up to £1000 per week in respect of reasonable living expenses, such drawings to be (i) first against funds indisputably his own money and not impressed with any equitable interest of the plaintiff or others (ii) second against funds which the defendant reasonably believed not to be impressed with such beneficial interest and (iii) third against funds which the defendant did not know to be impressed with such beneficial interest. This complex order, which was supported by ancillary orders for the replacement from the defendant's own assets of funds withdrawn and subsequently held to have been impressed with a beneficial interest and for an accountant's report on the defendant's assets, cannot, it is submitted, be treated as appropriate for the typical *Mareva* injunction securing a claim merely for unliquidated damages. Here the plaintiffs were claiming additionally to be entitled to an equitable interest in the funds themselves and to trace the defendant's assets.

15. *Z Ltd.* v. *A–Z, supra*, at p. 246.

16. [1982] 3 W.L.R. 746.

which the plaintiffs were proposing to bring an action against the defendants, one of whom was alleged to be a self-confessed record pirate, for breach of copyright, there was evidence that the defendants were systematically turning the profits of their operations into easily-disposable assets in order to evade the enforcement of claims. The Court of Appeal held that it was appropriate that the injunction granted should not only require the defendants by affidavit to identify their bank accounts and the make, model and registration numbers of their various expensive cars, as well as giving their whereabouts, but should also order them to deliver up into the custody of the plaintiffs' solicitors all such cars with ignition keys and any registration documents and documents of title.

The Court of Appeal laid down guidelines for the making of orders for the delivery up of chattels.[17] These can be summarized as follows:—

(1) There should be clear evidence that the defendant is likely, unless restrained by order, to dispose of or ortherwise deal with his chattels in order to deprive the plaintiff of the fruits of any judgment he may obtain. The Court should be slow to order the delivery up of any of the defendant's property unless there is some evidence that the property has been acquired by the defendant as a result of his alleged wrongdoing. In that case the inference was that if the defendants were forewarned or left in possession of the cars those vehicles would be sold and the proceeds of sale dissipated or hidden so that the plaintiffs would be deprived not only of damages but also of the proceeds of sale of the copyright-infringing articles.[18]

(2) No order should be made for delivery up of the defendant's clothes, bedding, furnishings, tools of trade, farm implements, livestock, machinery (including vehicles) or other goods, such as materials or stock in trade, which he was likely to use for normal business purposes. But if, for example, furnishings included objets d'art of great value bought for the purposes of frustrating judgment creditors, they could be included in an order.

(3) All such orders should specify as clearly as possible what chattels or classes of chattels are to be delivered up.

---

17. ibid., at p. 752, *per* Lawton, L.J., delivering the judgment of the Court.

18. Although the judgment does not expressly adumbrate the point, it is suggested that it is implicit in the judgment that the Court should take the view that the defendant was unlikely to be deterred from disposing of his assets by the sanction of proceedings for contempt should he ignore the injunction. Unless the Court reaches this conclusion it is difficult to justify an order for delivery up merely on the grounds set out in guideline (1).

(4) The order must not authorise the plaintiffs to enter on the defendant's premises or to seize the defendant's property save by permission of the defendant.

(5) No order should be made for delivery up to anyone other than the plaintiff's solicitor or a receiver appointed by the High Court and a receiver should be appointed to take possession of chattels unless the Court is satisfied that the plaintiff's solicitor has arranged, or can arrange, suitable safe custody for what is delivered to him.

(6) If and in so far as the chattels are in the possession, custody or control of third parties the Court should follow the guidelines set out by the Court of Appeal in *Z Ltd.* v. *A–Z.*[19] These guidelines are discussed at page 77 below.

Effect of injunction

The effect of an order in the usual form is to prevent the defendant from disposing of *any* assets for any purpose whatsoever if and to the extent that the consequence of such disposal would be to leave in the particular bank account or in the jurisdiction a sum of money less than that specified in the order. If the defendant has less than the specified sum within the jurisdiction but has other non-monetary assets within the jurisdiction, such an order, it is submitted, would also preclude him from disposing of any of such other assets, at least without first obtaining the leave of the Court.

Effect on tangible assets in the hands of third parties

In the recent case of *Z Ltd.* v. *A–Z*[20] in the Court of Appeal, Kerr, L.J., considered in some detail the ambit and effect of *Mareva* injunctions in relation to the difficulties experienced by banks in locating or valuing certain types of asset. He considered that the order should not apply to shares, title deeds or articles in a safe deposit, even if a bank was able to locate them through its central record system,

> "unless these are . . . specifically referred to in the order because they are in some way connected with the subject-matter of the action. The reason is that the bank may not, and generally will not, know their precise value, and that the bank should not be expected to try to assess this in some way, even at the plaintiff's expense, unless the terms of the order are specifically drafted so as to include them".

This view on a point not expressly considered by Lord Denning, M.R., or Eveleigh, L.J., does appear on the face of it to exclude from the ambit of *Mareva*

---

19. [1982] 1 Lloyd's Rep. 240.
20. *Supra*, at pp. 254–5.

injunctions assets which in some cases may be all or most of what the defendant has within the jurisdiction. Whereas it is clearly highly desirable that whenever possible the plaintiff should, on the *ex parte* application, be able to identify tangible assets and also the bank branch or agent in whose custody they are, it is respectfully suggested that it is highly undesirable that where this is impossible there should be any blanket exclusion of such assets merely because it is difficult or inconvenient for the bank or other bailee to value them. It is suggested that the proper course for a bank which holds such assets and which, having received notice of an injunction specifying a maximum amount, appreciates that it applies to those assets, ought to be to apply to the Court for directions. If the Court takes the view that, having regard to the information then before it as to the location of these assets, what other assets, if any, are within the jurisdiction and what their value is, it is appropriate that the tangible assets should be subject to the injunction, it may also take the view, in order that the *Mareva* jurisdiction should be effectively exercised in that particular case, that it is necessary for those tangible assets or some of them to be valued. In that event it is suggested that the right course ought to be for the Court to give directions for valuation at the plaintiff's expense. When it received such valuation the Court could then decide which, if any, of the tangible assets ought to continue to be subject to the injunction.

On the other hand if, due to lack of a central record system, the bank does not appreciate that assets held by it are caught by the injunction it should not be treated as in contempt of Court. However, the Court of Appeal in *C.B.S. United Kingdom Ltd.* v. *Lambert*[21] has now approved the more restrictive approach of Kerr, L.J., in *Z Ltd.* v. *A–Z.*

Effect on the proceeds of letters of credit and bills of exchange received by banks

In *Z Ltd.* v. *A–Z*[22] Lord Denning, M.R., expressed the view that a *Mareva* injunction might apply to such proceeds as and when received by or for the defendant. Kerr, L.J., held that whereas the proceeds of such documents might be frozen if they came to be paid into an account of the defendant to which the order applied, they should not otherwise be comprised within the terms of the order to which the banks were obliged to give effect. This latter view was based on the inconvenience to the banks in not having any central record system enabling them to locate the receipt of payment under such documents. The great disadvan-

---

21. [1982] 3 W.L.R. 746.
22. *Supra*, at pp. 244 and 255.

tage of this limitation of the scope of *Mareva* injunctions is that it enables the wary defendant to preserve from the reach of the order assets received by a bank on his behalf by instructing it beforehand not to credit the money to any of his accounts at the bank but simply to pay the money away to himself or a third party. It is respectfully suggested that a better course would be that if the bank is actually aware that payments received by it are within the scope of a *Mareva* injunction it ought not to dispose of the moneys without first obtaining the direction of the Court. If, due to lack of a central record system, the bank failed to realise that money received by it for the defendant was subject to an injunction and disposed of that money in accordance with the defendant's instructions, it should not be treated as in contempt of Court on that account.

Terms of orders to be served on banks and other third parties

In *Z Ltd.* v. *A–Z*[23] the Court of Appeal has held that such orders should in the first part of the order bind the defendant in relation to his assets generally to the extent to which this is reasonably necessary and should in the second part make it clear that in relation to assets in the generality of the order it should only apply to such assets as are identified or referred to specifically but not otherwise. In relation to banks, the terms of the order should in general only apply to accounts held by a bank referred to in the order and only to the extent specified in the order. The second part of the order may conveniently be drawn so as to restrain the defendant from drawing on any "time, notice or demand deposit" which may be held in his sole name by any bank referred to in the order up to the maximum sum stated in the order.

Execution by third party judgment creditors

It has not yet been decided whether there would be a breach of the order if the defendant's creditors other than the plaintiff obtained a judgment against the defendant which they then attempted to enforce by levying execution by writ of *fieri facias* on the defendant's property and if the defendant in consequence then disposed of his assets to these creditors. It is submitted that such a disposal would not be in breach of the injunction. This was implicitly accepted by Goff, J., in *Iraqi Ministry of Defence* v. *Arcepey Shipping Co. S.A.*[24] It must also follow in principle from the fact that whereas the delivery to the sheriff of a writ of *fieri facias* or other writ of execution against the goods creates a charge upon the goods,[25] the granting of a *Mareva* injunction relating to the goods does not create

---

23. *Supra*, at p. 256, *per* Kerr, L.J.
24. [1980] 1 Lloyd's Rep. 632, at pp. 636–7.
25. Sale of Goods Act 1893, section 26(1), Benjamin's *Sale of Goods*, 2nd edn., para. 568.

a lien, charge or other proprietory interest in the goods but operates merely *in personam* as between the plaintiff and the defendant.[26]

Garnishee proceedings by third party judgment creditors

If the assets, disposal of which has been restrained by a *Mareva* injunction, include debts due or accruing due to the defendant by a debtor such as a bank within the jurisdiction of the English Courts, it will be open to a third party who may have obtained judgment against the defendant to apply for a garnishee order against that debtor.[27] By obtaining a garnishee order *nisi* the judgment creditor causes a charge to be created over the debt due to the defendant from the time of service of the garnishee order on the garnishee.[28] The garnishor can, on the return date, apply for a garnishee order absolute. If the order is made absolute, it is submitted that, notwithstanding a pre-existing *Mareva* injunction expressly referring to the debt, the garnishee is obliged to make payment to the garnishor. The garnishor gains priority by virtue of his charge over the debt and the *Mareva* injunction creates no such charge or other proprietary interest in the debt.[29]

Where defendant is insolvent

Where a defendant against whom a *Mareva* injunction has been granted is insolvent or probably where the assets which he has *within* the jurisdiction of the English Courts are insufficient to discharge all outstanding liquidated claims against him within the jurisdiction as well as the garnishor's judgment debt, a garnishee order absolute would probably not be granted. The garnishee order is an equitable remedy and once a debtor is insolvent the Courts will not permit the remedy to be used in order to enable the judgment creditor to obtain priority over other creditors.[30] As Buckley, L.J., stated in *D. Wilson (Birmingham) Ltd.* v. *Metropolitan Property Developments Ltd.*[31] and repeated in *Rainbow* v. *Moorgate Properties Ltd.*[32]:

---

26. *Cretanor Maritime Co. Ltd.* v. *Irish Marine Management Ltd.* [1978] 1 W.L.R. 966; *Iraqi Ministry of Defence* v. *Arcepey Shipping Co. S.A.* [1980] 1 Lloyd's Rep. 632 and see, generally, p. 80 below.

27. RSC Order 49, rule 1.

28. RSC Order 49, rule 3(2).

29. See fn. 26 above. It would, however, be prudent for the debtor who has been placed in this predicament to apply to the Court which granted the *Mareva* injunction in order to obtain approval to its paying the garnishor, for in that event the terms of the injunction would probably have to be varied to take account of the fact that the defendant's assets were to be depleted to the extent of the garnishèd debt.

30. *Pritchard* v. *Westminster Bank Ltd.* [1969] 1 W.L.R. 547.

31. Bar Library Transcript No. 383A of 1974.

32. [1975] 1 W.L.R. 788, at p. 793.

> "The position is, I think, that a Court in considering whether or not to exercise its discretion to make absolute a garnishee order in circumstances such as this must bear in mind, not only the position of the judgment creditor, the judgment debtor and the garnishee, but the position of other creditors of the judgment debtor and must have regard to the fact that proceedings were launched, for ensuring the distribution of the available assets of the judgment debtor company among the creditors *pari passu*".

Thus, where the *Mareva* injunction has been granted to a plaintiff whose claim is for a debt or other liquidated amount, if the defendant is insolvent or possibly has insufficient assets within the jurisdiction to meet both the plaintiff's claim and the garnished debt, the Court is likely to exercise its discretion against making an order absolute and the limited protection provided by the *Mareva* injunction will therefore be preserved until the plaintiff or the other creditors apply for a winding-up order against the defendant or, in the case of an individual, commence bankruptcy proceedings. If it is in doubt whether the judgment debtor and defendant is insolvent the Court can decline to make an order absolute until an investigation has been conducted into the judgment debtor's solvency and, if necessary, an order can be made that the garnished debt should be paid into Court pending the outcome of that investigation.[33] Where, however, a *Mareva* injunction has been granted to a plaintiff whose claim is for *unliquidated damages* as distinct from a debt or other liquidated amount, it is submitted that the amount of such claim should be left out of account in ascertaining whether the defendant is insolvent when the Court is deciding whether to grant a garnishee order absolute. Thus, until the plaintiff can convert his claim for unliquidated damages into a judgment debt and so establish that the defendant is insolvent, the assets of the defendant covered by the *Mareva* injunction will continue to be vulnerable to attack by third party creditors who obtain garnishee orders.

"Mareva" injunctions do not attach assets

The effect of a *Mareva* injunction is not to freeze the defendant's assets in the sense of attaching them or creating a lien, charge or proprietary interest over them. The plaintiff merely has a personal right to enforce the injunction against the defendant and against third parties[34] who, with knowledge of the injunction, assist the defendant in disposing of assets contrary to its terms.

Cretanor Maritime Co. Ltd. v. Irish Marine Management Ltd.

Thus, in *Cretanor Maritime Co. Ltd.* v. *Irish Marine Management Ltd.*[35] it was argued that, having obtained a *Mareva* injunction, the plaintiff shipowners had

---

33. *George Lee & Sons (Builders) Ltd.* v. *Olink* [1972] 1 W.L.R. 214.
34. See p. 99 below.
35. [1978] 1 W.L.R. 966.

rights over moneys in the defendant charterers' bank account which took priority over the rights to those moneys of the holder of a debenture over the charterers' assets who had appointed a receiver some time after the *Mareva* injunction had been granted. The Court of Appeal rejected this argument. Buckley, L.J., observed[36] that although in *Rasu Maritima S.A.* v. *Pertamina*[37] Lord Denning, M.R., appeared to have treated the *Mareva* injunction procedure as a form of attachment, his real meaning was that, applying the principle which underlay the old practice of foreign attachment, English Courts should now employ the remedy of an interlocutory injunction to achieve a broadly similar result. Buckley, L.J., continued[38]:

> "Indeed, it is, I think, manifest that a *Mareva* injunction cannot operate as an attachment. 'Attachment' must, I apprehend, mean a seizure of assets under some writ or like command or order of a competent authority, normally with a view to their being either realised to meet an established claim or held as a pledge or security for the discharge of some claim either already established or yet to be established. An attachment must fasten on particular assets . . . A *Mareva* injunction, however, even if it relates only to a particularised asset (as in the unreported case referred to by Lord Denning, M.R., in his judgment in the *Rasu Maritima*[39] case in which Parker, J., granted an injunction restraining a foreign defendant from removing an aircraft from the jurisdiction) is relief *in personam*. It does not affect a seizure of any asset. It merely restrains the owner from dealing with the asset in certain ways. All that the injunction achieves is in truth to prohibit the owner from doing certain things in relation to the asset. It is consequently, in my judgment, not strictly accurate to refer to a *Mareva* injunction as a pre-trial attachment".

Later in his judgment Buckley, L.J., continued[40]:

> "It seems to me, however, for reasons which I have already given when discussing pre-trial attachment, that it is not the case that any rights in the nature of a lien arise when a *Mareva* injunction is made. Under such an injunction the plaintiff has no rights against the assets. He may later acquire such rights if he obtains judgment and can thereafter successfully levy execution upon them, but until that event his only rights are against the defendant personally".[41]

---

36. At p. 973.
37. [1978] Q.B. 644.
38. At [1978] 1 W.L.R. 974.
39. At [1978] Q.B. 662.
40. At p. 977.
41. Nevertheless, in the event of assets covered by a *Mareva* injunction being transferred to a third party who received them with knowledge of the injunction, it is submitted that the plaintiff would be entitled to an order against the transferee, on the basis that he was in contempt of Court, that he should return to the defendant such of the assets as remain in his hands or, in the case of money, that he should pay into Court an equivalent amount to that received by him.

Bona fide payments in the ordinary course of business

If the defendant against whom a *Mareva* injunction has been granted wishes to use assets covered by the injunction in order to make *bona fide* payments in the ordinary course of his business, is he entitled to do so? The usual form of a *Mareva* injunction is so wide that any disposition of assets covered by it for whatever purpose would be in breach of its terms and in contempt of Court unless the transferee could establish a proprietary right to the asset, for example as a debenture holder having appointed a receiver,[42] or as a judgment creditor having taken out a writ of *fieri facias* and served it on the sheriff,[43] or as a judgment creditor, having obtained a garnishee order absolute and having served it on a bank or other debtor from whom the garnished debt was due to the defendant against whom the *Mareva* injunction had been obtained.[44]

The principle in Iraqi Ministry of Defence v. Arcepey Shipping Co. S.A. (The Angel Bell)

In *Iraqi Ministry of Defence* v. *Arcepey Shipping Co. S.A.*[45] the defendant shipowners, a one-ship Panamanian company, were indebted to a third party, Gillespie Brothers & Co. Ltd., to whom it had been intended to mortgage the defendants' vessel and also to assign the benefit of certain marine policies on the vessel as security for the defendants' debt. The plaintiff cargo owners had a claim for unliquidated damages for loss of their cargo when the defendants' vessel sank, and that claim far exceeded the proceeds of the marine policies and the defendants' indebtedness to Gillespie. The underwriters paid the proceeds of the policies to London brokers Brandts. The plaintiffs obtained a *Mareva* injunction, restraining the defendants from disposing of any of their assets and therefore covering the insurance proceeds if Gillespie had no proprietary interest in them. Gillespie was given leave to intervene in the proceedings and an issue was ordered to be tried as between Gillespie and the plaintiffs as to whether Gillespie did have such an interest. It was held by Donaldson, J., that Gillespie were equitable mortgagees of the vessel and assignees of the policies entitled to sue on them.[46] But pending an appeal by the plaintiffs against that decision, Gillespie applied for an order varying the *Mareva* injunction so as to permit the brokers, Brandts, to pay Gillespie the amount of the debt due from the defendants to Gillespie out of the proceeds of the policies. In view of the pending appeal, Gillespie's application

---

42. *Cretanor Maritime Co. Ltd.* v. *Irish Marine Management Ltd.* [1978] 1 W.L.R. 966, discussed at p. 80 above.
43. Discussed at p. 78 above.
44. Discussed at p. 79 above.
45. [1980] 1 Lloyd's Rep. 632.
46. [1979] 2 Lloyd's Rep. 491.

was argued on the basis that they were merely unsecured creditors of the defendants. The defendants admitted that they were indebted to Gillespie and signified that they wished Brandts to pay over to Gillespie the amount which was due. The indebtedness to Gillespie amounted to £200,000 and the policy proceeds were only £240,000. Thus if payment were made the defendants' only remaining asset which would be available to meet the plaintiffs' claim would be the balance of £40,000. The plaintiffs argued that the purpose of a *Mareva* injunction was to freeze a foreign defendant's assets within the jurisdiction of the English Courts to ensure that there would be a fund available within the jurisdiction from which the plaintiff would be able to satisfy a judgment. Robert Goff, J., held that the injunction ought to be varied to enable the payment to be made. Having observed that a party claiming unliquidated damages against a company could not present a winding-up petition before obtaining judgment and that if the plaintiffs were right, since their claim was only for unliquidated damages, they would be enabled to achieve the status of a judgment creditor before they had obtained a judgment, he continued[47]:

> "For my part I do not believe that the *Mareva* jurisdiction was intended to rewrite the English law of insolvency in this way. Indeed, it is clear from the authorities that the purpose of the *Mareva* jurisdiction was not in any way to improve the position of claimants in an insolvency but simply to prevent the injustice of a foreign defendant[48] removing his assets from the jurisdiction[49] which otherwise might have been available to satisfy a judgment . . . I find it difficult to see why, if a plaintiff has not yet proceeded to judgment against a defendant but is simply a claimant for an unliquidated[50] sum, the defendant should not be free to use his assets to pay his debts. Of course, if the plaintiff should obtain a judgment against a defendant company and the defendant company should be wound up, its previous payments may thereafter be attached on the ground of fraudulent preference, but this is an entirely different matter which should be dealt with at the stage of the winding-up. It is not to be forgotten that the plaintiff's claim may fail, or the damages which he claims may prove to be inflated. Is he in the meanwhile, merely by establishing a *prima facie* case, to preclude the *bona fide* payment of the defendant's debts?

---

47. [1980] 1 Lloyd's Rep., at p. 636.

48. If there is a danger that assets will be removed from the jurisdiction in order to avoid satifying the plaintiff's claim a *Mareva* injunction may be granted even if the defendant is not a foreigner or foreign-based: *Barclay-Johnson* v. *Yuill* [1980] 1 W.L.R. 1259; *Rahman (Prince Abdul) bin Turki al Sudairy* v. *Abu-Taha* [1980] 1 W.L.R. 1268. (C.A.) overruling *Gebr. Van Weelde Scheepvaart Kantor B.V.* v. *Homeric Marine Services Ltd. (The Agrabele)* [1979] 2 Lloyd's Rep. 117.

49. *Mareva* injunctions are now granted where there is a risk of disposal of assets *within* as distinct from outside the jurisdiction: See pp. 72 to 73 above and *Z Ltd.* v. *A–Z* [1982] 1 Lloyd's Rep. 240.

50. It is submitted that there is no difference in principle between a claimant for a liquidated sum and claimant for an unliquidated sum. In both cases the claimant is unsecured. Therefore, unless and until there is a winding up of the defendant company it should be entitled with the sanction of the Court to dispose of its assets *bona fide* and in the ordinary course of its business.

When taxed with this point (counsel for the plaintiff) suggested that in such circumstances the appropriate course of a defendant's creditors was to proceed to judgment because the enforcement of judgments by execution would not constitute breaches of the *Mareva* injunction against the defendant. This I consider to be an unsatisfactory answer. It does not make commercial sense that a party claiming unliquidated damages should, without himself proceeding to judgment, prevent the defendant from using his assets to satisfy his debts as they fall due and be put in the position of having to allow his creditors to proceed to judgment with consequent loss of credit and of commercial standing".

The application for variation of the terms of "Mareva" injunctions

Although in *Iraqi Ministry of Defence* v. *Arcepey Shipping Co. S.A.* the application for variation of the injunction was made not by the defendants but by the interveners, Gillespie, to whom the defendants wished to make payment, the more common course will be for the defendants themselves to apply for leave to make payments. Such an application should normally be supported by an affidavit setting out facts on the basis of which the Court can conclude that the proposed payment is made in good faith and in the ordinary course of business and not for the purpose of preserving the fund from the risk of being available to satisfy such judgment as the plaintiff may ultimately obtain against the defendant. The Courts have yet to work out what standard of evidence they will require before being satisfied that a *Mareva* injunction should be varied to enable a payment to be made.

In *A. v. C. No. 2*[51], where the defendant applied for the injunction to be varied to permit payment out from assets in a particular fund of the legal costs of defending the proceedings before the Court but it was not clear from the defendant's affidavit that those were the only assets from which the payments could be made, Goff, J., refused to vary the injunction, the defendant having failed to discharge the burden of proof that payment out of the fund would not conflict with the policy underlying the *Mareva* injunction. If there were other assets from which such payments could be made it would be open to the plaintiffs to contend that it would be wrong for the Court to vary the terms of the injunction.

It is submitted that the defendant ought to put before the Court all those documents which establish that the payment is due to a third party, such as, for example, the defendants' order for goods or services and the third party's acceptance of order and final invoice showing that the price is due or his demands for payment. In many cases it may be unnecessary to apply to the Court if the defendant first sends his affidavit and evidence to the plaintiff with a request to concur in the proposed payment. The plaintiff may then be satisfied that the evidence properly establishes that the payment will be made *bona fide* in the

---

51. (Note) [1981] 2 W.L.R. 634.

ordinary course of business and the parties may therefore be able to agree to a consent order varying the terms of the original injunction. This course should be encouraged. Applications for variation may in appropriate cases be granted even where the defendant wishes to make a payment in respect of an unenforceable liability, provided that the payment is made in good faith and is not a disguised method of removing assets from the jurisdiction. Thus it has been held that the repayment of a debt alleged to be unenforceable under the Moneylenders Acts would justify an order varying a *Mareva* injunction to permit such payment[52] as would the payment to a bank of amounts due under a company's guarantee of its chairman's overdraft on his personal account where the payment was alleged to be an unlawful payment away of company money and where it was further alleged that the duty to pay under the guarantee had not yet arisen.[53]

Procedure for obtaining a "Mareva" injunction

The application is made *ex parte* in chambers. An appointment for a hearing before the Commercial Court at very short notice can be obtained by telephone from the Commercial Court Listing Officer whose number is (01)405-7641, Extension 3826; Telex 296983 COMM-G. It is usual for the party applying to be represented by junior counsel and appointments for hearings can often conveniently be made in conjunction with counsels' clerks. The applicant must normally put before the Court a writ which has already been issued, but due to the urgency with which most applications are made there will not usually be sufficient time to have prepared points of claim. The applicant must put before the Court an affidavit which (1) sets out the nature of the claim and the amount of the claim and fairly states the points made against it by the defendant, (2) states facts showing or from which it can be inferred that the defendant has assets within the jurisdiction of the English Courts, if possible identifying particular assets or particular balances in identified bank accounts or at particular bank branches, (3) sets out evidence from which it can be inferred that there is a real risk that unless an injunction is granted the defendant will, in order to avoid enforcement of a judgment, remove his assets from the jurisdiction, for example, the fact that the defendant is resident or carries on business abroad or has close foreign connections

---

52. *Iraqi Ministry of Defence* v. *Arcepey Shipping Co. S.A.* [1980] 1 Lloyd's Rep. 632, at p. 637.

53. *Bakarim* v. *Victoria P. Shipping Co. Ltd.* [1980] 2 Lloyd's Rep. 193, *per* Parker, J., *obiter* at p. 199: "If a defendant outside the jurisdiction desires to use money within the jurisdiction to make a payment to or for the benefit of someone else within the jurisdiction and there is no question of the payment being a disguised method of removing assets from the jurisdiction, he is *prima facie* entitled to do so and is not bound to justify it up to the hilt". As the law has subsequently developed, the appropriate proviso, it is submitted, is that there should be no question of the payment being a disguised method of disposing of assets inside or outside the jurisdiction to make himself judgment-proof.

which would facilitate the rapid disposal of assets abroad, or that the defendant may well dispose of his assets within the jurisdiction to avoid satisfaction of a judgment, (4) deposes to the belief that if no injunction is granted any judgment obtained by the plaintiff in this country will not be satisfied and (5) makes full and frank disclosure of all matters in his knowledge which are material for the judge to know. The applicant should normally put forward a draft order setting out all the terms of the injunction requested including all the undertakings by the plaintiff.[54] The plaintiff must give an undertaking in damages in case he fails in his claim or the injunction turns out to be unjustified. In a suitable case this undertaking should be supported by a bond or security; and the injunction should only be granted on its being given or undertaken to be given.[55]

The nature of the plaintiff's claim

The applicant must satisfy the Court that he has a good arguable case. This was said by Lord Denning, M.R., in the Court of Appeal in *Rasu Maritima S.A.* v. *Pertamina*[56] and in *Etablissement Esefka International Anstalt* v. *Central Bank of Nigeria*.[57] In the former case, Lord Denning, M.R., stated that the test of a good arguable case was the same as that applied for giving leave to serve a defendant outside the jurisdiction as laid down in *Vitkovice Horni a Hatui Tezirstvo* v. *Korner*.[58] He did not consider it appropriate that the jurisdiction should be limited to those cases where the plaintiff's case was so strong that judgment would be given in his favour under Order 14. In *Fary-Jones (Insurance) Ltd.* v. *I.F.M. Funding G.m.b.h. and Others*,[59] the Court of Appeal, in dismissing an appeal from the refusal of Slade, J., to grant a *Mareva* injunction, applied the test of a good arguable case. Sir David Cairns said of the judgments of Lord Denning, M.R., and Orr, L.J., in *Rasu Maritime S.A.* v. *Pertamina*[56]:

> ". . . the result of those two judgments is that in order to obtain a *Mareva* injunction the plaintiff has to go beyond showing that there is an arguable case and has to satisfy the Court that he has a case of a certain strength. Obviously it is impossible to lay down any precise rule as to what sort of strength of case will justify the granting of the injunction; but I apprehend that the learned judge who hears the matter . . . is not only entitled, but is bound, to address his mind to the question of the strength of the plaintiff's case, and that in doing so he is entitled to take into account such materials as are put before him, by way

---

54. *Z Ltd.* v. *A–Z* [1982] 1 Lloyd's Rep. 240, *per* Kerr, L.J., at p. 253. For a suggested form of order see precedent at p. 104 below.
55. *Per* Lord Denning, M.R., in *Third Chandris Shipping Corporation* v. *Unimarine* [1979] 1 Q.B. 645, at p. 669.
56. [1978] Q.B. 644, at p. 661.
57. [1979] 1 Lloyd's Rep. 445, at p. 448.
58. [1951] A.C. 869.
59. (Unreported) C.A., 10th April 1979.

of documentary evidence or otherwise, as will give an indication as to whether what the plaintiff has is merely an arguable case or is something which can be described as a 'good arguable case'".

Buckley, L.J.,[60] observed that whereas it was not the function of the Court on an interlocutory application to attempt to resolve conflicts of evidence or issues of fact which arose on the evidence before the Court which ought to be determined at the trial, the judge was nevertheless entitled to form a provisional view on the material then before him as to the ultimate outcome of the action. Since the strength of the plaintiff's case was one of the circumstances which were relevant to the question whether an injunction should be granted the judge must take into consideration his provisional view formed on the basis of the evidence before him. In *Ninemia Maritime Corporation* v. *Trave Schiffahrtsgesellschaft m.b.h. und Co. K.G.* [60a] Mustill, J., held that a good arguable case in this context means "a case which is more than barely capable of serious argument, and yet not necessarily one which the judge believes to have a better than 50 per cent chance of success".

Difficulty of establishing a good arguable case

Where there are substantial issues of fact which will arise at the trial it may in practice be extremely difficult for a plaintiff at the interlocutory stage to build up anything more than an arguable case as distinct from a good arguable case. Thus, in *Bakarim* v. *Victoria P. Shipping Co. Ltd.*[61] Parker, J., discharged a *Mareva* injunction on the grounds that the plaintiff had not adduced sufficient evidence to establish that as undisclosed principal he was charterer of the defendants' vessel and therefore was not entitled to leave to serve notice of the writ outside the jurisdiction. However, Parker, J., held *obiter* that in any event, on the evidence before him, the plaintiff had failed to establish a good arguable case. The plaintiff's evidence was that coffee owned by him was shipped on board the defendants' vessel and lost when the vessel caught fire and sank. The defendants relied on clause 13 of the Baltime form and adduced evidence to support their case that the loss occurred without want of due diligence on the part of the owners or their manager to make the vessel seaworthy. Parker, J., observed that, although the loss of the cargo established a *prima facie* case, because the burden of proof was thereby passed to the defendants, the question whether the plaintiff had a good arguable case depended upon an assessment of the defendants' evidence. The defendants had put in a body of evidence to establish that all proper steps were taken to see that the vessel was in every respect seaworthy and properly equipped,

---

60. ibid.
60a. (Unreported) 10th May 1983.
61. [1980] 2 Lloyd's Rep. 193.

that she was subject to thorough surveys and drydocking only some three weeks before the loss, that she had recently-issued certificates covering her fire-fighting equipment, that the master and crew were properly and carefully selected and that nobody had made any suggestion that the shipowners or anyone else were in any way to blame for the loss. Parker, J., went on[62]:

> "It is of course possible that, if the presently pending arbitration proceedings go to trial on the merits, something will emerge which will change the present picture. At the present time, however, and on the evidence before me, I am unable to say that the plaintiffs have a good arguable case on the merits . . . (counsel for the plaintiffs) sought to convince me that, where a charterer has lost his goods and the vessel has been sunk, he can do no more than rely on his *prima facie* case unless and until he has obtained from the owners full particulars and discovery both documentary and by interrogatories on the details of what happened and what precautions the defendants had taken, because all such knowledge is in the owner's possession. The cargo owner is therefore, so it was argued, entitled to have his injunction until then. I cannot accept this. The *Mareva* injunction is a useful and very powerful remedy, but its grant is a serious matter which may do the defendants great damage, and in *The Genie* [1979] 2 Lloyd's Rep. 184, Lord Denning, M.R., at page 189[63] stated that it must not be stretched too far. It would, in my judgment, be stretching it too far to allow it in cases where a shipowner had advanced cogent evidence of lack of personal fault and the cargo owner had neither put in countervailing evidence nor advanced some credible hypothesis as to what, involving personal fault, had happened or might reasonably be inferred to have happened".

Thus, although a *Mareva* injunction may be granted on the initial *ex parte* application on the basis of fairly slender evidence establishing no more than that the plaintiff has a *prima facie* case, it may prove difficult in practice for a plaintiff to hold the injunction on an *inter partes* hearing to discharge the injunction, at which the defendant is able at short notice to put before the Court evidence which supports a defence but which may be quite incomplete and which cannot really be tested because it comes before pleadings, discovery of documents and interrogatories. This is particularly the position where most of the facts going to liability must be exclusively within the knowledge of the defendant, as in many claims by charterers and cargo owners against shipowners. Nevertheless, the authorities referred to above support the view that if on the material before him the judge forms the provisional view that the applicant's claim is not strong, although it may well be arguable, he would be justified in discharging the injunction. It is submitted that it is difficult to justify the requirement of a good arguable case having regard to the principles laid down by the House of Lords for the granting of interlocutory

---

62. At p. 198.
63. *Sub nom. Third Chandris Shipping Corporation* v. *Unimarine S.A.* [1979] 1 Q.B. 645, at p. 668.

injunctions in *American Cyanamid Co.* v. *Ethicon Ltd.*[63a] The difficulty of reconciling these cases has recently been recognised in *Ninemia Maritime Corporation* v. *Trave Schiffahrtsgesellschaft m.b.h. und Co. K.G.* [63b]

The Court must have jurisdiction in relation to the underlying claim

The claim in support of which the applicant applies for a *Mareva* injunction must be one in relation to which the English Courts have jurisdiction or in respect of which the Court has power to permit service of its process outside the jurisdiction under RSC Order 11 and considers that it is a proper case for ordering service abroad. Thus, in *Siskina (Cargo Owners)* v. *Distos Compania Naviera S.A.*[64], the House of Lords reversed the decision of a majority of the Court of Appeal and held that, if the underlying claim did not fall within any of the sub-rules of RSC Order 11, rule 1, sub-rule (i) could not form a basis for the Court to exercise its jurisdiction and thereby to grant a *Mareva* injunction. The *Mareva* injunction is interlocutory and not final and is ancillary to a substantive pecuniary claim for debt or damages.[65] Therefore where the underlying claim was not one in relation to which the Court would have had jurisdiction, the application for an injunction could not, on the proper construction of sub-rule (i), clothe the Court with a jurisdiction which it did not otherwise have.[66]

Defendant's assets within the jurisdiction of the English Courts

It must be established that the defendant has assets within the jurisdiction. In *Third Chandris Corporation* v. *Unimarine S.A.*[67] Lord Denning, M.R., stated:

> "The plaintiff should give some grounds for believing that the defendant has assets here. . . . In most cases the plaintiff will not know the extent of the assets. He will only have indications of them. The existence of a bank account in England is enough, whether it is in overdraft or not".

At first instance Mustill, J.,[68] indicated that the plaintiff was not required to produce concrete proof of precisely what assets were at the time of the application within the jurisdiction. He went on:

> "To require such a standard of proof would be to put *Mareva* relief out of reach in most cases. Since the defendant is *ex hypothesi* a somewhat elusive character it will usually be impracticable to establish exactly what assets he has available. All that can reasonably be asked, where moneys are the subject

---

63a. [1975] A.C. 396.
63b. (Unreported) 10th May 1983, *per* Mustill, J.
64. [1979] A.C. 210.
65. *Per* Lord Diplock, at p. 253.
66. *Per* Lord Diplock, at p. 257.
67. [1979] 1 Q.B. 645, at p. 668.
68. ibid., at p. 651.

matter of the attachment, is that a *prima facie* case is made out inferring that such moneys exist and where they may be found. For this purpose the plaintiff need, in my view, do no more than point to the existence of a bank account".

In that case there was evidence before the Court from the defendants' Luxembourg bank which indicated that the defendants' account was in overdraft at about the time when the *Mareva* injunction was initially granted, but the evidence also suggested that moneys were frequently paid into that account and there was no evidence from which it would be inferred that there were no assets within the jurisdiction or that there was no collateral security supporting the overdraft.[69] It is probably not enough to establish that although the defendant does not presently have funds within the jurisdiction he may in future acquire assets within the jurisdiction,[70] although once an injunction has been granted in the usual form it will apply to assets which the defendant subsequently acquires or brings within the jurisdiction.[71] In general, any asset in respect of which an order for a *Mareva* injunction is sought should be identified with as much precision as is reasonably practicable and the Court may make it a term of the injunction that the plaintiff give an undertaking to pay the costs of anyone other than the defendant, such as a bank, who sustains expense in ascertaining whether assets covered by the order are within his possession or control.[72]

The nature of the assets

The *Mareva* jurisdiction extends to all assets whether tangible assets or mere choses in action, provided that the defendant is the legal or beneficial owner of them. Although funds are the most common subject-matter of the jurisdiction the Courts have been prepared to extend it to machinery lying at Liverpool Docks,[73] an aircraft temporarily within the jurisdiction,[74] time charterer's bunkers and cargo on a ship about to enter a British port[75], and a ship which had called at Liverpool

---

69. ibid., *per* Lawton and Cumming-Bruce, L.JJ., at p. 673.

70. *Cybel Inc. of Panama* v. *Timpuship* [1978] CAT 478. It is understood that there have been a number of recent instances of *Mareva* injunctions being granted outside the Commercial Court on *ex parte* applications restraining disposal of defendants' assets in Scotland and in other jurisdictions. It is submitted that there is no jurisdiction to make such orders and that they are fundamentally inconsistent with the whole basis of the *Mareva* jurisdiction. The decision of the Court of Appeal in *Intraco* v. *Notis Shipping Corporation* [1981] 2 Lloyd's Rep. 256 supports this view.

71. *Cretanor Maritime Co. Ltd.* v. *Irish Marine Management Ltd.* [1978] 1 W.L.R. 966, *per* Buckley, L.J., at p. 973.

72. *Searose Ltd.* v. *Seatrain (U.K.) Ltd.* [1981] 1 W.L.R. 894, *per* Goff, J., at p. 897 and *Z Ltd.* v. *A–Z* [1982] 1 Lloyd's Rep. 240, at p. 245 and see, generally, p. 101.

73. *Rasu Maritime S.A.* v. *Pertamina.* [1978] 1 Q.B. 644, where an injunction was discharged on other grounds.

74. *Allen* v. *Jambo Holdings Ltd.* [1980] 1 W.L.R. 1252.

75. *Clipper Maritime Co. Ltd. of Monrovia* v. *Mineralimport-export* [1981] 1 W.L.R. 1262 and see, generally, p. 102.

in order to discharge her cargo.[76] The *Mareva* injunction procedure may in appropriate cases enable a plaintiff to restrain the departure of more than one of the defendant's vessels from this country, although it would not be open to that plaintiff to secure himself in this way by arresting more than one vessel in an action *in rem*. Before granting a *Mareva* injunction covering tangible assets, the Courts will look with particular care at the possible damage which such an injunction may inflict upon the defendant's business.[77] There will probably be few cases where the extension of the *Mareva* jurisdiction to tangible assets, particularly ships, will have much practical effect save to create a temporary inconvenience to the defendant. This is because a defendant will normally be able to show that his purpose in removing a particular tangible asset from the jurisdiction is in order to satisfy his ordinary commercial commitments and not in order to enable him to evade satisfaction of the plaintiff's claim. If so, it would be open to him to apply to have the *Mareva* injunction varied or wholly discharged under the principle applied in *Iraqi Ministry of Defence* v. *Arcepey Shipping Co. S.A.*[78] It will also be open to third parties who may be adversely affected by the injunction, such as the charterers of a vessel which is the subject-matter of an injunction, to intervene in order to protect their interests.[79] It was held by the Court of Appeal in *Intraco* v. *Notis Shipping Corporation*[80] that the Court ought not to grant a *Mareva* injunction restraining the defendant from making a demand under a bank guarantee or letter of credit in respect of the purchase price of goods (a ship) of which he was the seller because to do so would be to interfere with the principle that in the absence of fraud such security documents should be treated as equivalent to cash. There was, however, no reason in principle why a *Mareva* injunction should not apply to the fruits of such documents once they had been paid.

Assets to which a third party is beneficially entitled

There have been a number of cases in which *Mareva* injunctions have been discharged or have been held not to apply to particular assets on the grounds that a third party has a beneficial interest in some or all of the assets in question. In

---

76. *The Rena K* [1979] 1 Q.B. 377. See also *The Stolt Filia* (1980) 15 LMLN.

77. *Rasu Maritima S.A.* v. *Pertamina* [1978] 1 Q.B. 644, *per* Lord Denning, M.R., at p. 662; *per* Orr, L.J., at p. 664. See also *The Rena K* [1979] 1 Q.B. 377, at p. 410. The circumstances in which tangible assets may be the subject of *Mareva* injunctions and in which it is appropriate to make an order not merely restraining disposal of the assets but requiring delivery up were discussed by the Court of Appeal in *C.B.S. United Kingdom Ltd.* v. *Lambert* [1982] 3 W.L.R. 746 and which is considered more fully at pp. 74 to 75 above.

78. [1980] 1 Lloyd's Rep. 632. See p. 82 below.

79. *The Rena K* [1979] 1 Q.B. 377, at p. 410.

80. [1981] 2 Lloyd's Rep. 256. See also *Z Ltd.* v. *A-Z* [1982] 1 Lloyd's Rep. 240, at pp. 244, 255 and 256. This case is more fully discussed at p. 76 above.

Cretanor Maritime Co. Ltd. v. *Irish Marine Management Ltd.*[81] the injunction was discharged upon the application of a receiver who had been appointed after the granting of the injunction by the holder of a foreign debenture over the charterers' assets, the debenture holder having become equitable assignee of the bank deposit covered by the injunction. Similarly, in *Iraqi Ministry of Defence* v. *Arcepey Shipping Co. S.A.*[82] the interveners claimed to be equitable mortgagees of the vessel *Angel Bell* and assignees of hull and machinery policies as security for loans made to the shipowners. The vessel had sunk with the plaintiffs' cargo on board and the insurance moneys were held by London brokers. A *Mareva* injunction having been granted to the plaintiffs, Donaldson, J., ordered an issue to be tried as to whether the interveners were secured on the proceeds of the policies.[83] It was held that the interveners were secured creditors and were therefore entitled to payment notwithstanding the injunction. The same point arose in *Pharoahs Plywood Co. Ltd.* v. *Allied Wood Products (Pte) Ltd.*[84] In that case the defendants had sold timber through the plaintiffs acting as their agents to various buyers including M. The defendants had a claim against M for a substantial sum and they commenced an arbitration against M in order to recover this money. The defendants were indebted to the plaintiffs for £50,000 and in June 1976 the defendants' solicitors promised to pay the plaintiffs out of the proceeds of the arbitration. However, in order to purchase the timber the defendants had borrowed money from a bank and had, in April 1976, assigned the proceeds of the arbitration to the bank as security for the amount due, but had not given notice of the assignment to M. In April 1979 an award was made in the arbitration pursuant to which M paid $294,000 to the defendants' solicitors. The plaintiffs then issued a writ claiming £50,000 and applied for a *Mareva* injunction restraining disposal of an equivalent amount from the damages fund. The Court of Appeal held that an injunction should not be granted because the plaintiffs were merely unsecured creditors and not assignees of the fund, whereas the bank had a valid equitable assignment of the whole fund.

---

81. [1978] 1 W.L.R. 966. As observed by Buckley, L.J., at p. 978, the debenture-holder and not the receiver was the appropriate applicant for discharge of the injunction. See also *Oceanica Castelna Armadora S.A.* v. *Mineralimport-export* (1983) 87 LMLN.

82. [1979] 2 Lloyd's Rep. 491.

83. As suggested by Donaldson, J., at p. 493 and as emerges from the judgment of Goff, J., in *Iraqi Ministry of Defence* v. *Arcepey Shipping Co. S.A.* [1980] 1 Lloyd's Rep. 632 the interveners or the defendants could have successfully applied for the injunction to be varied to permit payment to them of moneys due in the ordinary course of business without being obliged to establish that they were beneficially entitled to such moneys as secured creditors.

84. (1980) 7 LMLN.

Risk of removal of assets from the jurisdiction

The risk of the defendant removing his assets from the jurisdiction and so stultifying any judgment given by the Courts was originally conceived as being the underlying reason for the *Mareva* jurisdiction.[85] Although in most cases where the *Mareva* jurisdiction is invoked it is likely that the method by which it is feared the defendant will attempt to make himself "judgment-proof" is by removing assets from the jurisdiction, the Court of Appeal has now held[86] that a *Mareva* injunction can be given even if there is a risk merely that the defendant will attempt to dispose of assets *within* the jurisdiction in order to avoid satisfying a judgment. This aspect of the *Mareva* jurisdiction has been more fully explained at page 72 above. Evidence that the defendant is resident abroad or does not carry on business within the jurisdiction are matters from which in some cases it can properly be inferred that there is a greater risk that the defendant may transfer his assets from the jurisdiction for the purpose of avoiding satisfaction of any judgment against him.[87] This inference may also be drawn where it is shown that although the defendant resides within the jurisdiction he is a foreign national having close ties with places outside the jurisdiction and is thus likely to leave at short notice and remove his assets to such places[88] or where, although the defendant is not a foreign national or foreign corporation, it has characteristics from which it can be inferred that there is a real risk that it will remove its assets from the jurisdiction of the English Courts. Thus, in *Barclay-Johnson* v. *Yuill* an injunction was granted against an English defendant who had left the country and was living on a yacht in the Mediterranean, there being no information as to when, if ever, he might return, and where there was evidence that on a previous occasion the defendant had gone to the United States when he had been in financial difficulties. If there is no real danger of the defendant dissipating his assets to make himself "judgment-proof" a *Mareva* injunction should not be granted merely so that a plaintiff can have security for his claim or where the real purpose is to exert pressure on the defendant to settle the action.[89]

---

85. *Etablissement Esefka International Anstalt* v. *Central Bank of Nigeria* [1979] 1 Lloyd's Rep. 445, at pp. 448, 449; *Third Chandris Corporation* v. *Unimarine S.A.* [1979] 1 Q.B. 645, at pp. 652, 653, 669, 673; *Iraqi Ministry of Defence* v. *Arcepey Shipping Co. S.A.* [1980] 1 Lloyd's Rep. 632, at p. 635; *Barclay-Johnson* v. *Yuill* [1980] 1 W.L.R. 1259, at p. 1264; *Rahman (Prince Abdul) bin Turki al Sudairy* v. *Abu-Taha* [1980] 1 W.L.R. 1268.
86. *Z Ltd.* v. *A-Z* [1982] 1 Lloyd's Rep. 240.
87. *Third Chandris Corporation* v. *Unimarine* [1979] Q.B. 645. *Barclay-Johnson* v. *Yuill* [1980] 1 W.L.R. 1259, at p. 1265.
88. *Chartered Bank* v. *Daklouche* [1980] 1 W.L.R. 107, at p. 112.
89. *Z Ltd.* v. *A-Z* [1982] 1 Lloyd's Rep. 240, *per* Kerr, L.J., at p. 251.

Circumstances relevant to the risk of removal of assets

There must be evidence before the Court from which it can be found that

(1) the defendant has some characteristic which suggests that he *can* readily export his assets if he chooses to do so;

(2) the defendant may in all the circumstances of the case take advantage of his opportunities to export his assets;

(3) if the defendant were to export his assets the enforcement of an English judgment against him would be substantially more difficult than if he were restrained from removing assets from England.

Thus in *Montecchi* v. *Shimco (U.K.) Ltd.*[90] a claim was made by the Italian plaintiffs on bills of exchange of which the defendants were the drawers and the defendants counterclaimed for breach of the contract in respect of which the bills had been issued. The defendants applied for a *Mareva* injunction to restrain the plaintiffs from removing the proceeds of a judgment under Order 14 for the amount of the dishonoured bill. The Court of Appeal rejected the application on the grounds that[91]:

(1) on the evidence before the Court the Italian plaintiffs were "persons of perfectly sound financial standing in Italy";

(2) if the defendants recovered judgment on their counterclaim such judgment would be enforceable in Italy under the procedure provided by the Foreign Judgments (Reciprocal Enforcement) Act 1933;

(3) there was some evidence that a defendant could deliberately delay enforcement proceedings in Italy but the evidence was not strong enough to show that if there were judgment on the counterclaim against the plaintiffs they would be liable to avoid satisfying it or would be unable to do so.

In *Third Chandris Corporation* v. *Unimarine S.A.*[92] the Court of Appeal made it clear that the mere fact that the defendant is abroad is not *by itself* a sufficient ground for concluding that there is a real risk of removal of assets in order to avoid satisfying a judgment. Lord Denning observed[93]:

"The mere fact that the defendant is abroad is not by itself sufficient. No one would wish any reputable foreign company to be plagued with a *Mareva* injunction simply because it has agreed to London arbitration. But there are some foreign companies whose structure invites comment. We often see in this

---

90. [1979] 1 W.L.R. 1180.
91. At p. 1184, *per* Bridge, L.J.
92. [1979] Q.B. 645, *per* Lord Denning, M.R., at p. 669; *per* Lawton, L.J., at p. 671; *per* Cumming Bruce, L.J., at p. 673.
93. At p. 669.

> Court a corporation which is registered in a country where the company law is
> so loose that nothing is known about it—where it does no work and has no
> officers and no assets. Nothing can be found out about the membership, or its
> control, or its assets, or the charges on them. Judgment cannot be enforced
> against it. There is no reciprocal enforcement of judgments. It is nothing more
> than a name grasped from the air, as elusive as the Cheshire Cat. In such cases
> the very fact of incorporation there gives some ground for believing there is a
> risk that, if judgment or an award is obtained, it may go unsatisfied".

Lawton, L.J., stated[94] that the affidavit in support of the application should set out
what inquiries have been made about the defendant's business and what information
has been revealed, including that relating to its size, origins, business domicile, the
location of its known assets and the circumstances in which the dispute has arisen.
Thus, in that case, the Court regarded as material to the assessment of the extent of
the risk of removal of assets the facts that the defendant company was registered in
Panama, that no director or officer of the company deposed to its financial standing,
that no balance sheet or statement of accounts were put before the Court, that there
was no evidence of the existence or location of any specific assets and that recently
it had delayed in meeting an arbitration award against it. In *Etablissement Esefka
International Anstalt* v. *Central Bank of Nigeria*[95] the defendant bank satisfied the
Court that it had ample resources to meet any judgment and the Court of Appeal
concluded on that evidence that there was no danger of the bank not satisfying a
judgment against it. The approach of the Courts was summarized by Mustill, J., in
the recent case of *Ninemia Maritime Corporation* v. *Trave Schiffahrtsgesellschaft
m.b.h. und Co. K.G.* [95a] as follows:—

> "It is not enough for the plaintiff to assert a risk that the assets will be
> dissipated. He must demonstrate this by solid evidence. This evidence may take
> a number of different forms. It may consist of direct evidence that the defendant
> has previously acted in a way which shows that its probity is not to be relied
> upon. Or the plaintiff may show what type of company the defendant is (where
> it is incorporated, what are its corporate structure and assets, and so on) so as
> to raise an inference that the company is not to be relied upon. Or, again, the
> plaintiff may be able to found his case on the fact that inquiries about the
> characteristics of the defendant have led to a blank wall. Precisely what form
> the evidence may take will depend upon the particular circumstances of the
> case. But the evidence must always be there. Mere proof that the company is
> incorporated abroad, accompanied by the allegation that there are no reachable
> assets in the United Kingdom apart from those which it is sought to enjoin, will
> not be enough".

---

94. At p. 672.
95. [1979] 1 Lloyd's Rep. 445.
95a. (Unreported) 10th May 1983.

Full and frank disclosure of material facts

The plaintiff must, when applying for a *Mareva* injunction, make full and frank disclosure to the judge of all matters within his knowledge which are material for the judge to know.[96] He ought to state the nature of the case and his cause of action and in fairness to the defendant he should disclose, so far as he is able, any defence which the defendant has indicated in correspondence or elsewhere. It is only if such information is put fairly before the court that a *Mareva* injunction can properly be granted.[96a] Thus, in *The Assios*,[97] the buyers of a ship, in respect of which completion under the sale contract was due to take place at one London bank in the late afternoon by payment by the buyers of the balance of the purchase price and provision of a letter releasing to the sellers from a joint account at another London bank the amount of the deposit, wished to secure themselves against a claim against the sellers under the sale contract for bottom damage to the vessel after her inspection. Therefore, earlier on the same afternoon, the buyers applied for and obtained a *Mareva* injunction restraining the sellers from removing any of their assets, and in particular the deposit, from the jurisdiction. Just prior to completion the buyers' solicitors informed the bank where the deposit was on joint account that an injunction had been granted but the buyers then proceeded to complete, receiving documents of title to the vessel without informing the sellers that an injunction had been granted. Mocatta, J., then discharged the injunction on the sellers' application on the grounds that the buyers had failed to disclose to them their plan for obtaining security and that if it had been disclosed on the *ex parte* application he might never have granted the injunction. The Court of Appeal upheld this approach.[98] In *Z Ltd.* v. *A–Z*[99] this type of trapping exercise was condemned as an abuse of the *Mareva* jurisdiction.

---

96. *Third Chandris Corporation* v. *Unimarine S.A.* [1979] Q.B. 645.

96a. *Bank Mellat* v. *Mohammad Ebrahim Nikpour* [1982] Com.L.R. 158, *per* Lord Denning, M.R., at p. 159.

97. *Negocios del Mar S.A.* v. *Doric Shipping Corporation S.A.* [1979] 1 Lloyd's Rep. 331.

98. In this case Mocatta, J., also raised the question whether the Court should grant a *Mareva* injunction at a time when there had been no completed breach of contract, in that case before delivery of the vessel in a damaged condition. The Court of Appeal did not consider this point but it is submitted that normally no injunction should be granted unless at the time of the application there is a completed cause of action for damages, although there may be exceptional cases where the defendant's conduct is such that at the time when the application is made a breach of contract or duty by the defendant is inevitable and possibly that there is a real risk that before the breach takes place the defendant will remove his assets from the jurisdiction in order to avoid execution. In *Ninemia Maritime Corporation* v. *Trave Schiffahrtsgesellschaft m.b.h. und Co. K.G.* (10th May 1983; unreported) Mustill, J., declined to grant a *Mareva* injunction in the absence of a completed cause of action at the time of the *ex parte* application, but granted an injunction on a further application on the following day after the cause of action had been completed.

99. [1982] 1 Lloyd's Rep. 240, at p. 251.

"Mareva" injunctions to secure claims under arbitration

It was held by Brandon, J., in *The Rena K*[100] that the Court had power under section 12(6)(*f*) and (*h*) of the Arbitration Act 1950 to grant a *Mareva* injunction for the purpose of protecting a claim arising under an arbitration and to do so in the case of an arbitration not yet commenced, subject to a term providing for the arbitration to be commenced within a specified time, together with other terms as it thought fit. In *Third Chandris Corporation* v. *Unimarine S.A.*,[101] in which the applicants were claimants in arbitrations, this decision was not challenged and the Court of Appeal did not suggest that it was wrong. A form of order appropriate in relation to an arbitration is set out at page 107 below.

Orders ancillary to "Mareva" injunctions

In order to enable the Courts to operate the *Mareva* jurisdiction more effectively and with greater precision it may, in particular cases, be necessary to ascertain further specific information about the value and whereabouts of the defendant's assets. Such information will often be wholly within the knowledge of the defendant or his bankers or agents. In such cases the Court may make orders for immediate discovery of documents by the defendant or for the answering of interrogatories or for the inspection and copying of entries in bank documents under section 7 of the Bankers' Books Evidence Act 1879 if such orders are likely to lead to disclosure of the required information. The Court's power to make such orders was fully considered by Goff, J., in *A and B* v. *C.D.E.F.G.H.*[102] In that case it was ordered that the first five defendants should disclose to the plaintiffs forthwith the sums at present standing in accounts in the names of any of the first five defendants or another party at the sixth defendant bank. Goff, J., observed[103] that the exercise of the *Mareva* jurisdiction might lead to problems:

> "The defendant may have more than one asset within the jurisdiction—for example he may have a number of bank accounts. The plaintiff does not know how much, if anything, is in any of them; nor does each of the defendant's bankers know what is in the other accounts. Without information about the state of each account it is difficult, if not impossible, to operate the *Mareva* jurisdiction properly; for example, if each banker prevents any drawing from his account to the limit of the sum claimed, the defendant will be treated oppressively, and the plaintiff may be held liable on his undertaking in damages. Again there may be a single claim against a number of defendants; in that event the same difficulties may arise. Furthermore, the very generality of the order creates difficulty for the defendant's bankers, who may, for example, be

---

100. [1979] Q.B. 377.
101. [1979] Q.B. 645.
102. [1980] 2 Lloyd's Rep. 200.
103. ibid., at pp. 202–3.

> unaware of the existence of other assets of the defendant within the jurisdiction;
> indeed, if a more specific order is possible, it may give much needed protection
> for the defendant's bankers, who are after all simply the innocent holders of
> one form of the defendant's assets".

If the Court were not able to make such ancillary orders a plaintiff, being ignorant
of the value of a particular asset, might in the examples given be deterred from
giving his undertaking in damages and thus be unable to obtain an injunction.
This decision was accepted by the Court of Appeal in *Bankers Trust Co.* v.
Shapira[104] and the Court of Appeal approved the use of such orders in *C.B.S.
United Kingdom Ltd.* v. *Lambert.*[105]

Ancillary orders against banks and other innocent parties

In cases where the plaintiff seeks an order *tracing* funds to which he claims to
be entitled and where there are good grounds for believing that such funds have
been paid into an account at a particular bank the Court may make an order
directing the bank to give full disclosure of all documents relevant to the operation
of any account into which the funds may have been paid. Such order can cover
correspondence with the other defendants concerning their account at the bank,
cheques drawn on any account at the bank in the defendants' names, debit
vouchers, transfer applications and orders and internal memoranda of the bank
relating to any material account. The Court of Appeal made an order of this kind
in *Bankers Trust Co.* v. *Shapira*[106] but made it clear that the jurisdiction to make
such ancillary orders should be carefully exercised. If plaintiffs apply for such
orders against banks they must give an undertaking in damages to the bank and
must pay all the bank's expenses incurred in making discovery.[107] The documents
and information disclosed by the bank must only be used for the purpose of
following and tracing the money.[108] Although in *A and B* v. *C.D.E.F.G.H.*[109]
Goff, J., did not limit the availability of an order for discovery against a bank or
other innocent parties to actions where the plaintiff was seeking to trace funds
which might have been transferred by other defendants to the bank or other
innocent party, it appears from the decision in *Bankers Trust Co.* v. *Shapira*[110]
that the Courts are likely to be reluctant to make similar orders, at least against
banks, in cases where the plaintiff has a mere claim for damages against the

---

104. [1980] 1 W.L.R. 1274.
105. [1982] 3 W.L.R. 746, at p. 751; and see also *PCW (Underwriting Agencies) Ltd.* v. *Dixon, The
Times,* 21st January and 4th February 1983, considered at fn. 14a above.
106. [1980] 1 W.L.R. 1274.
107. ibid., at p. 1282, *per* Lord Denning, M.R.
108. ibid., at p. 1282, *per* Lord Denning, M.R.; at p. 1283 *per* Waller, L.J.
109. [1980] 2 Lloyd's Rep. 200.
110. [1980] 1 W.L.R. 1274.

defendants and does not seek to trace funds. However, there may be exceptional cases where, as contemplated by Goff, J., in *A and B* v. *C.D.E.F.G.H.*,[111] it may be difficult or impossible to operate the *Mareva* jurisdiction effectively without information as to the value and whereabouts of the defendants' assets and where such information cannot be obtained from those defendants themselves. In such cases, even if no tracing order is sought, it may be appropriate for discovery to be ordered against banks and other innocent parties. The precise extent of the jurisdiction to grant such ancillary orders remains to be explored.

Ancillary orders not to be used for policing injunctions

The purpose of all such ancillary orders for discovery and interrogatories is to enable the Court to exercise the *Mareva* jurisdiction effectively: they must not be used in order to ascertain whether *Mareva* injunctions already granted have been broken. So held the Court of Appeal in *A. J. Bekhor & Co. Ltd.* v. *Bilton.*[112] In that case the evidence was such as to give rise to suspicions that the defendant might have disposed of assets in breach of a previous injunction. Parker, J., made an order that the defendant should by affidavit give very detailed information as to the value and whereabouts of his assets at different dates and an explanation of what he had done with his assets and how and when he had disposed of them. The Court of Appeal allowed an appeal against this order stating that the correct method of policing the *Mareva* injunctions in that case was to apply for leave to cross-examine the defendant on his affidavit or for the Court to make such an order of its own motion under RSC Order 38, rule 2, or for the plaintiffs to apply for the Court to revoke leave to dispose of part of the defendant's assets which the defendant had obtained on a previous occasion.

Effect of "Mareva" injunctions on banks, agents and other innocent parties

As soon as a bank or other agent is given notice of a *Mareva* injunction it must freeze the defendant's bank account or other assets. It must not allow any drawings to be made on such account or assets, either by cheques drawn before the injunction, nor by those drawn after it. The reason is because, if it allowed any such drawings, it would be obstructing the course of justice—as prescribed by the Court which granted the injunction—and it would be guilty of a contempt of Court.[113]

---

111. [1980] 2 Lloyd's Rep. 200, at pp. 202–3.
112. [1981] 1 Lloyd's Rep. 491.
113. For a general consideration of the position of banks and other innocent third parties see the judgments of the Court of Appeal in *Z Ltd.* v. *A–Z* [1982] 1 Lloyd's Rep. 240. The above text is based on the judgment of Lord Denning, M.R., at p. 244. In the same case Kerr, L.J., in agreeing with Lord Denning, relied on the additional reason that once the bank has notice of the injunction its authority to give effect to the instructions of the defendant is thereby revoked in the same way as in garnishee proceedings: see *Rekstin* v. *Severo, Sibirsto and the Bank for Russian Trade* [1933] 1 K.B. 47.

The above principle applies to tangible assets whether in the hands of banks or other agents.[114] A *Mareva* injunction does not, however, prevent payment by the bank to third parties under banker's irrevocable security documents such as a letter of credit, performance bond or guarantee.[115] Nor does it prevent payment under a credit card issued to the defendant and used by him unless used fraudulently or wrongly.[116] Once a *Mareva* injunction has been granted against a defendant, his bank may consider it prudent to withdraw cheque and credit card facilities if within its power to do so.[117]

Notice to banks, agents and other innocent parties

The plaintiff who has obtained a *Mareva* injunction should give notice of it to the bank or other agent of the defendant identifying with as much precision as possible the assets to which it is to attach. He should, if possible, identify the bank account by specifying the branch, number and heading of the account.[118] Where the plaintiff cannot identify the bank account or other asset with sufficient precision he may have to request the bank or other innocent third party to conduct a search so as to ascertain whether the bank or third party does hold assets of the defendant.[118] In some rare cases it may be appropriate that the injunction should specify a joint account but normally a *Mareva* injunction should not be taken as applying to a joint account.[119]

Once the bank or other agent has been given notice of the injunction it is bound by it, notwithstanding that notice may not yet have been given to the defendant himself.[120] Having obtained the injunction on an *ex parte* application, the plaintiff should give notice to the defendant, the bank and any other third party at once, either by telephone or telex, and he must follow that up by a written confirmation to be delivered by hand or other equally speedy means.[121]

If the bank to whom notice is given ascertains that the account of the defendant is in a currency different from that expressed in the order, the bank should convert the credit balance in the account into sterling (if that be the currency of the order)

---

114. *Z Ltd.* v. *A–Z, supra,* at p. 244. But such assets must be specified in the order: see the discussion of this qualification at p. 76 above.

115. *Intraco Ltd.* v. *Notis Shipping Corporation* [1981] 2 Lloyd's Rep. 256; *Power Curber International Ltd.* v. *National Bank of Kuwait* [1981] 2 Lloyd's Rep. 294; *Z Ltd.* v. *A–Z* [1982] 1 Lloyd's Rep. 240.

116. *Z Ltd.* v. *A–Z* [1982] 1 Lloyd's Rep. 240, at p. 244.

117. ibid., *per* Kerr, L.J., at p. 255.

118. ibid., at pp. 245 and 253. The bank's or agent's expenses in giving effect to the injunction or searching for the defendant's assets must be paid by the plaintiff: see p. 101 below.

119. ibid., at pp. 246 and 255.

120. ibid., at pp. 243 and 251-2.

121. ibid., at p. 246.

at the then buying rate to the extent necessary to meet the sum stated in the order.[122]

Expenses of innocent parties in complying with "Mareva" injunctions

Innocent parties who are not defendants to the proceedings, particularly banks, may be put to very considerable expense in complying with *Mareva* injunctions. For example, their systems of accounting, at the present time frequently computerised, may not enable them readily or instantly to isolate and monitor the operation of particular accounts belonging to or operated by the defendant. In *Rahman bin Turki al Sudairy* v. *Abu-Taha*[123] the Court of Appeal stated that where a bank which had been notified of the injunction was put to any expense in regard to it that expense must be paid by the plaintiff.

Undertaking in respect of banks' expenses

In *Searose Ltd.* v. *Seatrain (U.K.) Ltd.*[124] Goff, J., granted an injunction on condition that the plaintiffs undertook to pay the reasonable costs incurred by any person (other than the defendants) to whom notice of the terms of the injunction was given in ascertaining whether or not any asset to which the order applied was within his possession or control. He explained the need to protect innocent holders of assets such as banks who might be put to expense[125]:

> "It is well known to the judges who sit in the Commercial Court that, as *Mareva* injunctions have come to be granted more frequently, the banks in this country have received numerous notices of injunctions which have been granted. Sometimes the injunction identifies the bank account in question; sometimes it identifies the branch of a bank at which the defendant is said to have a bank account; sometimes it identifies the bank and no more; sometimes it does not even identify the bank. Now where the particular account is identified, I do not think the bank can reasonably complain. Every citizen of this country who receives notice of an injunction granted by the Court will risk proceedings for contempt of Court if he acts inconsistently with the injunction; and a bank, like any other citizen, must avoid any such action. But where the particular account is not identified, the situation is somewhat different. I do not think it is right that the bank should incur expense in ascertaining whether the alleged account exists, without being re-imbursed by the plaintiff for any reasonable costs so incurred . . . Even where the particular branch of the bank is identified, some expense is likely to be incurred in ascertaining whether the defendant has an account at the branch. But where the branch is not identified the bank will be put in a very difficult position".

---

122. ibid., at p. 256.
123. [1980] 1 W.L.R. 1268.
124. [1981] 1 W.L.R. 894.
125. [1981] 1 W.L.R., at pp. 895–6.

Goff, J., explained that the effect of the undertaking in the terms ordered would be that a bank to whom notice of the injunction was given could, before taking steps to ascertain whether the defendants had an account at any particular branch, obtain an undertaking from the plaintiffs' solicitors to pay their reasonable costs incurred in so doing. He observed that although the costs would be borne by the plaintiffs in the first place they might be able to seek indemnification from the defendants if they were ultimately successful when the question of costs arose. Although that case involved a bank, Goff, J., indicated that in principle a plaintiff should give an undertaking to pay the expenses of anyone who was put to similar expenses but was not party to the action. This approach was expressly approved by the Court of Appeal in *Z Ltd.* v. *A–Z*[126]

Undertakings in respect of the expenses of other innocent parties

That innocent parties may be put to substantial expense or loss other than the cost of identification of the assets in question was recognized by the decision in *Clipper Maritime Co. Ltd. of Monrovia* v. *Mineralimport-export.*[127] In that case an injunction was obtained by shipowners restraining the time-charterers of their vessel, which was approaching Barry, in Wales, from *inter alia* removing the defendants' cargo or bunkers from the jurisdiction so as to reduce the value of the defendants' assets within the jurisdiction below the sum claimed by the shipowners. Having regard to the fact that the port authority at Barry might not be able to move the vessel off the berth consistently with the injunction until after it lost income from use of the berth, that the port authority might in any event incur administrative expenses as a consequence of the injunction and that the port authority might have to move the vessel in the ordinary course of the good administration of the port, Goff, J., ordered the plaintiff shipowners to give an undertaking to pay the actual income lost and the administrative costs incurred by the port authority as a consequence of granting the injunction. The injunction in that case was also qualified by a proviso imposed by the Court that the port authority should have a discretion for operational reasons to move or order the movement of the vessel within the area of the jurisdiction of the High Court. Goff, J., indicated that the Court would in future impose similar terms on *ex parte* applications where the injunction ordered might affect ships in port. Having observed that the order was made as a result of representations made to the Court by solicitors for the British Ports Association, he went on:

---

126. [1982] 1 Lloyd's Rep. 240, at pp. 245 and 252. If the injunction would substantially interfere with the business rights of a third party the offer of a plaintiff's indemnity will not be enough and the injunction will not be granted: see *Galaxia Maritime S.A.* v. *Mineralimport-export* [1982] 1 W.L.R. 539.
127. [1981] 1 W.L.R. 1262.

"The Commercial Court is very anxious to provide a service to the commercial community which is sensitive to its needs: and in particular it is anxious that the *Mareva* jurisdiction, in the administration of which the Commercial Court plays so substantial a part, should be implemented in a manner which takes account of the interests of innocent third parties. Since initially *Mareva* injunctions are almost invariably granted on *ex parte* applications, orders may be made which affect third parties who are unrepresented at the hearing of the initial application. It is, therefore, of great assistance if the Court can be kept informed of any adverse effect which these injunctions are having upon third parties, as in the case of the clearing banks and port authorities, so that steps can be taken where possible to protect their interests. If any other bodies wish to make representations on this point, it would be most appropriate for them to address their representations to the secretary of the Commercial Court Committee at the Royal Courts of Justice, in which event they will immediately be drawn to the attention of the judge in charge of the Commercial List".[128]

This case was expressly approved by the Court of Appeal in *Z Ltd.* v. *A–Z.*[129]

"Mareva" injunction followed by judgment in default

Where the plaintiff obtains a *Mareva* injunction and serves his writ but the defendant then fails to give notice of intention to defend, it is not open to the plaintiff, without leave, to sign judgment in default of notice of intention to defend. This is because the plaintiff's claim in the writ includes a claim for an injunction in addition to the claim for damages or a liquidated sum and accordingly the plaintiff is unable to comply with RSC Order 13, rule 6.[130] In such cases the appropriate course is for the plaintiff to apply to the Court for leave to enter judgment in default of notice of intention to defend and for the *Mareva* injunction to be continued in force after the judgment in aid of execution. It is within the inherent jurisdiction of the Court to make such an order,[131] because otherwise it would be open to a defendant to defeat the whole purpose of *Mareva* injunctions by declining to give notice of intention to defend.

---

128. [1981] 1 W.L.R. 1264–5.
129. [1982] 1 Lloyd's Rep. 240, at pp. 245 and 252.
130. RSC Order 13, rule 6(1) provides:
   "Where a writ is indorsed with a claim of a description not mentioned in Rules 1 to 4 then, if any defendant fails to give notice of intention to defend, the plaintiff may, after the prescribed time, and if that defendant has not acknowledged service, upon filing an affidavit proving service of the writ on him and, where the statement of claim was not indorsed on or served with the writ, upon serving a statement of claim on him, proceed with the action as if that defendant had given notice of intention to defend".
131. *Stewart Chartering Ltd.* v. *C. & O. Managements S.A.* [1980] 1 W.L.R. **460 (Practice Note)**.

5

MAREVA INJUNCTION: PRECEDENTS

ORDER
(1) High Court Proceedings:

IN THE HIGH COURT OF JUSTICE
QUEEN'S BENCH DIVISION
COMMERCIAL COURT

BETWEEN:

WHITE SUGAR COMPANY LIMITED

Plaintiffs

— and —

BROWN SUGAR COMPANY LIMITED

Defendants

The Hon. Mr Justice
UPON HEARING counsel for the Plaintiff
ex parte

AND UPON READING the [draft] affidavit of JOHN SILENUS SMITH, sworn herein on the 9th day of July, 1982 [if not yet sworn see undertaking (4) below]

AND UPON the Plaintiff by its counsel undertaking:
(1) To abide by any Order this Court may make as to damages, in case this Court shall be hereafter of opinion that the Defendant should have sustained any by reason of this Order which the Plaintiff ought to pay.
(2) To indemnify any person (other than the Defendants, its servants or agents) to whom notice of this Order is given, against any costs, expenses, fees or liabilities reasonably incurred by it in seeking to comply with this Order.[1]

---

1. *Z Ltd.* v. *A–Z* [1982] 2 W.L.R. 288, 297, 307–8. For examples of more detailed undertakings of this type see *Searose Ltd.* v. *Seatrain Ltd.* [1981] 1 W.L.R. 894, 895 (bank accounts) and *Clipper Maritime* v. *Mineralimport-export* [1981] 1 W.L.R. 1262, 1264 (bunkers on board a vessel). If the injunction would substantially interfere with the business rights of a third party, the offer of an indemnity will not be enough and no injunction will be granted, see *Galaxia Maritime S.A.* v. *Mineralimport-export* [1982] 1 W.L.R. 539.

(3) To issue and serve upon the Defendants as soon as practicably possible the writ in this action,[2] this Order together with the affidavits specified above [and the Summons for the continuation of this Order].[3]

[(4). To cause the affidavit specified above to be sworn as soon as practicably possible.]

(5) To notify the Defendants of the terms of this Order as soon as practicably possible, by telex or cable if they are abroad.

(6) To notify and inform any third parties affected by this Order of their right to apply to this Court for this Order to be varied or discharged in so far as this Order affects the said third parties.

IT IS ORDERED[4] THAT

(1) The Defendant, whether by itself its servants or agents or otherwise howsoever, be restrained until further order from removing any of its assets out of the jurisdiction, or disposing of or charging or otherwise dealing with any of its assets within the jurisdiction so as to deplete the same below £450,000.[5]

(2) In particular and without prejudice to the generality of the foregoing the Defendant, whether by itself, its servants or agents, be restrained until further order:

(a) From drawing from, charging or otherwise dealing with any accounts (whether time notice or demand deposits) standing in its name at Ruritanian International Bank Ltd., Lombard Street Branch, 102b Lombard Street, London, SW1, except to the extent that any of those accounts exceed £450,000[5];

(b) From removing from the jurisdiction, disposing of, charging or otherwise dealing with a Rolls-Royce motor car, number plate SUGA 1, so as to deplete the value of the Defendant's assets within the jurisdiction below £450,000.[5]

(3) Without prejudice to the generality of the foregoing, any bank to whom notice of this Order is given, in relation to any assets held or controlled by it for or on

---

2. RSC Order 29, rule 1(3).

3. A summons for continuation will only be necessary where the order specifies an expiry date of the injunction before trial. In many cases it may be doubtful whether a time limit should be imposed, especially if the defendant is overseas, see Z Ltd. v. A–Z (supra) 299, 309.

4. Although guidelines as to the form of the order are set out in Z Ltd. v. A–Z (and this example follows them as closely as possible), these guidelines do not fetter the form of order for which a plaintiff may ask in a particular case or the discretion of judges on the hearing of an application for an order (see Z Ltd. v. A–Z (supra) 308, per Kerr, L.J.). See also Practice Direction (Judge in Chambers: Procedure) [1983] 1 W.L.R. 433, 434–5.

5. As to the desirability of fixing a "maximum" amount, the position is not entirely clear, see Z Ltd. v. A–Z (supra) 298 (Lord Denning, M.R.); 310–11 (Kerr, L.J.).

behalf of the Defendant, whether solely or jointly with others, shall have liberty lawfully to deal with the same, except insofar as those assets are specified in paragraph (2) herein.[6]

(4) Provided nothing in this Order shall prevent Ruritanian International Bank Ltd. from exercising any right of set-off it may have in respect of any facilities it may have afforded the Defendant before the date of this Order.[6a]

(5) Liberty to apply.

(6) Costs reserved.

Dated the   day of   19   .

---

(2) Arbitration Proceedings

In the case of an *ex parte Mareva* injunction ordered pursuant to the Court's power under Arbitration Act 1950 ss.12(6)(f) and (h)[7] the heading of the Order would be as follows:

---

6. A paragraph of this type should be added where it has been possible for the plaintiff to identify and evaluate some of the defendant's assets with sufficient precision to be sure that they will meet the likely amount of the claim. In such circumstances third parties (especially banks) should be free to deal at the defendant's request with other assets of the defendants which are under their control without having to inquire as to the value of those assets (see *Z Ltd.* v. *A–Z (supra)* 311–13, *per* Kerr, L.J.). In practice, however, it is often impossible for the plaintiff to identify and evaluate the defendant's assets in this way and this paragraph is often not included.

6a. Where bank accounts are subject to a *Mareva* Order, a paragraph of this type should be included to avoid the relevant bank having to apply to the Court for the variation of the Order to allow the bank to exercise any right of set-off it may have against the defendant's funds (see *Oceanica Castelana Armadora S.A.* v. *Mineralimport-export, Financial Times,* 2nd February 1983, Lloyd, J.)

7. See *The Rena K* [1979] Q.B. 377, 408.

IN THE HIGH COURT OF JUSTICE
QUEEN'S BENCH DIVISION
COMMERCIAL COURT

THE HONOURABLE MR JUSTICE

IN THE MATTER OF THE ARBITRATION ACTS 1950–1979
AND
IN THE MATTER OF AN ARBITRATION

BETWEEN:

WHITE SUGAR COMPANY LIMITED

Plaintiffs
(Claimants)

– and –

BROWN SUGAR COMPANY LIMITED

Defendants
(Respondents)

Further:

(1) Instead of undertaking to issue and serve the writ, the undertaking will be to commence the arbitration within a period specified by the Court.[8]

(2) The limit of the injunction will usually be, for example, "until 14 days after the publication of the award or further order". If, however, an earlier *inter partes* hearing is regarded as desirable and an originating summons issued, then the injunction will be expressed to run until the return date of the summons.

(3) If there is to be no summons, the order for costs should be "costs in the arbitration", if there is to be one, "costs reserved".

---

8. ibid., p. 409.

AFFIDAVIT

(1) High Court proceedings

IN THE HIGH COURT OF JUSTICE   1982 W.No.
QUEEN'S BENCH DIVISION
COMMERCIAL COURT

BETWEEN:

WHITE SUGAR COMPANY LIMITED

Plaintiffs

– and –

BROWN SUGAR COMPANY LIMITED

Defendants

AFFIDAVIT

I, JOHN SILENUS SMITH of 12a New Victoria Street, London, SW48, MAKE OATH and SAY as follows:[9]
1. I am an employee of Bigg, Head & Co., solicitors of the above address and I have the conduct of this matter on the Plaintiff's behalf. Insofar as the facts and matters to which I herein depose are within my own knowledge they are true; insofar as they are derived from statements I have heard or documents I have read, they are true to the best of my knowledge and belief.
2. There is now produced and shown to me marked JSS1 a bundle containing true copies of the documents to which I refer below.
3. The Plaintiff is a company incorporated and registered in England which has engaged in the sugar trade for over 50 years. The Defendant is a company incorporated and registered in England, but, according to the letter heading of its writing paper, it is a subsidiary of Strange Traders of Ruritania [JSS1, p. 1]. Both companies engage in the import and export of commodities.

The Dispute
4. By a contract evidenced by or contained in telexes dated 23rd April 1982 (JSS1 pp. 2–4), the Plaintiff agreed to sell, and the Defendant agreed to buy 4,000,000

---

9. For the guidelines as to the contents of the affidavit see *Third Chandris Shipping Corpn.* v. *Unimarine* [1979] Q.B. 645, 668–9.

kilos net of EEC No. 2 quality granulated white sugar in 80,000 jute bags c.i.f. Genoa, Italy, at price of £10 per bag.

5. The contract provides for payment by "cash against documents".

6. Pursuant to the contract, the Plaintiff shipped the sugar on board the M.V. WORLD SUCROSE, the master signing bills of lading in respect thereof on 18th June 1982 (JSS1, pp. 5–7). On July 24th 1982 the Plaintiff presented the bills of lading, the certificate of insurance and invoices (JSS1, pp. 8–9) to the Ruritanian International Bank ("the Bank") at its branch at 102b Lombard Street, London, SW1 for tender to the Defendants. The Defendants have failed to take up the documents, instruct the Bank to make payment or arrange for payment in any other way.

7. In these circumstances, I would humbly submit that the Plaintiffs have a claim against the Defendant for the following sums:

Contract Price of 4,000,000 kilos net of EEC No. 2 quality granulated white sugar in 80,000 jute bags @ £10 per bag	£800,000
Less market value of goods on June 24th, 1982: 80,000 bags @ £5 per bag	£400,000
	£400,000

Plus interest and costs.

8. From correspondence with the Defendant (JSS1, pp. 8–10) it appears that it may wish to raise the Defence that the sugar was not packed in jute bags, but in paper bags and was not in accordance with the contract description (and less able to withstand the stresses of the voyage). However, a certificate of inspection issued by Messrs. Blind, Eye & Co., cargo surveyors (JSS1, p. 11) states that on inspection of the cargo on its arrival in Genoa the cargo was packed in jute bags, and this agrees with the description in the bills of lading.

9. I am not aware that the Defendant has any other defence to this claim.

Grounds for Believing the Defendant has Assets within the Jurisdiction

10. I have been advised by Mr Terrance Chrystal, the managing director of the Plaintiff, that Mr Bruno Grain came to the offices of the Plaintiff in April, 1982 before the contract was concluded in a Rolls-Royce motor car, with the distinctive number plate of SUGA 1. Mr Grain told Mr Chrystal that it was a company car.

11. I am further advised by Mr Chrystal that he understood from Mr Grain that the Defendant had an account at the Ruritanian International Bank, to where the documents were to be sent. The Bank itself will neither confirm nor deny the existence of an account (JSS1, p. 12).

Grounds for Believing in the Risk of Removal of Assets

12. The Plaintiffs have engaged the services of Messrs. I. Spy & Sons, private investigators, who report (JSS1, pp. 13–15) that the address given by the Defendant on its letter heading as its registered office is merely a postal address. There are no offices there. Inquiries at the Companies Registry have revealed that the Defendant was formed in November 1980 with a share capital of £100 and is essentially an "off the peg" company. It has never filed any accounts. (JSS1, p. 16–18). Inquiries directed to Strange Trading of Ruritania have produced only one letter denying all responsibility (JSS1, p. 19). From that letter it appears that Mr Grain is a director of that company as well as of the Defendants.

13. In these circumstances, I verily believe that unless restrained by this Honourable Court there is a risk that the assets of the Defendant will be removed abroad or otherwise disposed of before the Plaintiff has obtained judgment and is in a position to levy execution.

SWORN BEFORE ME
ON THE   DAY OF
AT

SUMMONS

(1) High Court Proceedings

If a Summons is to be issued,[10] it will be in the general form of a summons in the action.[11]

[Title as in the Affidavit]

Let the BROWN SUGAR COMPANY LIMITED of 69, Treacle Street, London, SE1, attend before the Judge in the Commercial Court, Royal Courts of Justice, Strand, London, WC2A 2LL on Monday the 26th day of July, 1982 at 10.30 in the forenoon, on the hearing of an application on the part of the Plaintiff for an order that the order of the Honourable Mr Justice   dated the 9th day of July, 1982 be continued until further order and that the costs of the application before the Honourable Mr Justice   on the 9th day of July, 1982 and of this application be costs in cause.

Dated the 13th day of July, 1982.
This Summons was taken out by   etc.

---

(2) Arbitration Proceedings

If an originating summons is to be issued it must be in RSC Appendix A, Form No. 10, (unless there is an action pending, when the application is by an ordinary summons[12] in the action).[13]

---

10. As to which, see fn. 3 *supra*.
11. The form is at RSC, para. 206.
12. i.e. in the form of RSC, para. 206. The heading is as set out for the Originating Summons.
13. RSC Order 73, rule 3(3).

IN THE HIGH COURT OF JUSTICE   *1982 W. No.*
QUEEN'S BENCH DIVISION
COMMERCIAL COURT

IN THE MATTER OF THE ARBITRATION ACTS 1950–1979
AND
IN THE MATTER OF AN ARBITRATION

BETWEEN:

WHITE SUGAR COMPANY LIMITED

Plaintiffs
(Claimants)

– and –

BROWN SUGAR COMPANY LIMITED

Defendants
(Respondents)

Let the BROWN SUGAR COMPANY LIMITED of 69, Treacle Street, London, SE1, attend before the Judge in the Commercial Court, Royal Courts of Justice, Strand, London, WC2A 4LL on Monday the 26th day of July, 1982 at 10.30 in the forenoon, on the hearing of an application on the part of the Plaintiff for an order that the order of the Honourable Mr Justice   dated the 9th day of July, 1982 be continued until 14 days after the publication of the award or until further order and that the costs of this application before the Honourable Mr Justice   on the 9th day of July, 1982 and of this application, be costs in the arbitration.

And let the Defendant within 14 days . . . etc.[14]

---

14. Complete with the formal parts of Form No. 10, RSC, Appendix A.

CHAPTER 7

TRIALS IN THE COMMERCIAL COURT

Flexible approach to procedure

The trial of actions in the Commercial Court is conducted under the same procedural rules as those which apply to all actions in the Queen's Bench Division. However, the general approach of the Court is to maintain a highly flexible attitude to procedure with the object of achieving a speedy and efficient disposal of the issues before the Court. This approach manifests itself in a number of ways which are discussed in this Chapter. It must be remembered, however, that although the practice of the Court leans strongly in favour of the parties' not requiring strict proof of facts which can be gleaned from documents and particularly from routine records such as logs and survey reports and in favour of the parties' not taking pleading points without good reason in the course of the trial, the smooth working of this approach depends in many cases on the co-operation of the parties to the action and on the approach to the trial of those advising them. If, for example, solicitors and counsel go into a trial with the firm resolve never to concede the proof of any fact which only emerges as double-hearsay and is therefore inadmissible evidence in the documents, much time and cost may be taken up which more often than not will be quite contrary to the interests of either party to the action.

Departure from pleaded case

The Court's tendency to discourage excessive demands for particulars of pleadings and its discouragement of interrogatories has already been discussed at page 58 above. This approach is reflected in the practice of adopting a very flexible attitude to departure from a pleaded case in the course of a trial. It often happens that in the course of the trial primary facts emerge which were not anticipated when the trial started or when the expert witnesses wrote their reports. The whole basis of one party's expert evidence may be destroyed by unexpected primary evidence. New experts' reports may be required and in consequence either party may have to reconstruct his case while the trial is in progress. The new case may bear little or no resemblance to the case as pleaded. In that event the Commercial Court will tend to permit the new case to be advanced provided that it is satisfied that this can be done without prejudice to the other party and it may be that in appropriate cases this can be dealt with by special orders as to costs. There is usually a fairly strong disposition against long adjournments of the trial and the party who advances a new and unpleaded case is strongly encouraged to release to the other side at the earliest possible opportunity the substance of the new case without formality. Although an order will usually be made for the new case to be incorporated into the pleadings in due course, the predominant object will be to give the other side sufficient information so as to enable those advising it to consider their position as early as possible and to see whether there really is any need to ask for an adjournment.

Pleading points discouraged

The overall approach of those conducting trials in the Commercial Court will be to avoid taking pleading points at the trial unless they are satisfied that there will otherwise be unavoidable prejudice to the party they represent. There will be very few cases where the usual order that the party introducing a new case should bear the costs of and occasioned by the amendment of the pleadings will not amply protect the opposite party from the consequences of a late amendment. Much will depend upon the point in the trial at which the new case is first advanced and the extent to which it may involve either party's adducing further primary evidence. Thus, whereas there may be many actions in which a defendant will be permitted to advance a new case if this is fully developed before the plaintiff has closed his case, even if this may involve the plaintiff's adducing further primary evidence, the Court will be very much less inclined to permit the defendant to advance a new case after the plaintiff's case has been closed and will do so only in exceptional circumstances if in consequence the plaintiff will be obliged to adduce further primary evidence.

Expert evidence

Expert witnesses are called in a very substantial proportion of the witness actions which come before the Commercial Court. On the summons for directions it is very frequently the practice for the parties to agree that each should have leave to call experts and that there should be an exchange of experts' reports before the trial. It is usually the practice to make an order under RSC Order 38, rule 38 in terms that experts' reports or summaries of expert evidence shall be *exchanged* at some specified period before the trial rather than that each party should disclose his expert's reports. If that is the order and one party tenders an expert's report but the other does not have one to exchange, it is then not incumbent on the first party to hand over his report before trial unless the other party no longer wishes to call expert evidence.

Postponement of expert evidence

It is the practice of the Court to encourage the parties where convenient to agree to call their respective expert witnesses after both sides have called all their witnesses of fact.[1] This practice has much to recommend it. There are many cases where, until all the primary evidence has been put before the Court, the plaintiffs' expert witnesses can only give their evidence on a hypothetical basis because many of the facts directly relevant to their opinion can only be obtained from the defendants' witnesses. Typical of such cases are claims by cargo owners or charterers against shipowners for cargo loss or damage or claims for breach of a charter-party by reason of the unseaworthiness of the vessel. There may be other cases where the plaintiffs' expert witnesses have assumed some fact relevant to their reports which on cross-examination of the defendants' witnesses of fact turns out to be untrue or inaccurate. If the plaintiffs' experts have already given evidence it may then become necessary to recall them. New reports and calculations may have to be made. Much of the expert evidence already given may be invalidated. If all expert evidence is postponed until after all evidence of fact, much time and costs will thus be saved in such cases.

Disclosure of further expert evidence in the course of the trial

It often happens that an exchange of experts' reports is delayed and takes place only a few days before the start of the trial. Each expert may then revise his report or produce a riposte to the other side's expert. While there is no obligation to exchange such supplementary reports, with the object of saving trial time and costs, the Court leans very heavily in favour of encouraging the narrowing and definition of issues between opposing experts before they are called to give evidence. It will therefore be a matter for the judgment of counsel in each case to decide whether to disclose to the other side the whole or any part of his expert's supplementary report in the course of the trial. He will have to weigh the advantage of being able to confront and surprise the opposing expert in cross-examination with matters which that expert may have overlooked or neglected or miscalculated in his report with the prospective disadvantages of delay and cost if that expert, when called, revises his initial view and produces a new and unexpected approach to the case for which an exchange of supplementary reports might have prepared the first party's advisers. The Court will strongly discourage the surprise confrontation of expert witnesses in the course of cross-examination with complex sets of calculations without the experts having adequate opportunity

---

1. See also p. 62 above for the giving of directions to this effect before trial in complex multi-party actions. In more straightforward cases it would not usually be necessary for an order to this effect to be made before the trial.

to consider them. An adjournment may have to be ordered in such a case and in cases where such calculations could easily have been disclosed prior to cross-examination the Court may take the view that the need for such an adjournment should be reflected in a special order as to costs.

Definitions of issues between experts

Particularly in those cases where the calling of all expert evidence has been postponed until after the calling of all witnesses of fact, it is often a useful and economical practice for the expert witnesses to meet before giving their evidence in order to draw up a joint statement defining the common ground between them and the remaining areas of disagreement. This exercise will always be encouraged in the Commercial Court for it often leads to considerable savings of trial time and costs.

Impact of the Civil Evidence Act 1968

Before the changes in the law of evidence in civil actions introduced by the Civil Evidence Act 1968 it was the practice of the Commercial Court to encourage the parties to agree to permit facts to be proved by statements in documents or by affidavits or the signed statements of witnesses who could not conveniently be called to give evidence.[2] If, however, the parties could not agree on the adoption of such informal methods of proof the Court had only a limited and discretionary power to permit such a method to be used. At the least, witnesses' evidence had to be on affidavit and this in itself often gave rise to considerable cost and delay in obtaining evidence even of the less-important facts which a party had to prove. The Report of the Commercial Court Users' Conference 1962 recommended that the Court should have power to admit in evidence unsworn statements of witnesses and statements in documents even if the opposite party objected and that the Evidence Act 1938 should be amended to enable this reform to be introduced. The changes in the law of evidence introduced by Part I of the Civil Evidence Act 1968 were in some respects even wider than those proposed by the 1962 Conference, particularly in as much as the unsworn statements, even of interested persons, are now admissible as evidence of the facts contained in them if "that person is dead, or beyond the seas, or unfit by reason of his bodily or mental condition to attend as a witness or cannot with reasonable diligence be identified or found or cannot with reasonable diligence be expected (having regard to the time which has elapsed since he was connected or concerned . . . and to all the

---

2. See Mathew's *Practice of the Commercial Court,* 2nd edn., pp. 58–61 and 66-68.

circumstances) to have any recollection of matters relevant to the accuracy or otherwise of the statement".[3]

Unsworn statements of overseas witnesses

In commercial actions the practice of putting in the unsworn statements of overseas witnesses is now very widespread.[4] When deciding whether to call an overseas witness or to rely on an unsworn statement by him it is essential to have in mind the provisions of section 6(3) of the Civil Evidence Act 1968 as to the weight to be attached to such statements:

> "In estimating the weight, if any, to be attached to a statement admissible in evidence by virtue of sections 2, 3, 4, or 5 of this Act regard shall be had to all the circumstances from which any inference can reasonably be drawn as to the accuracy or otherwise of the statement and, in particular—
> (a) in the case of a statement falling within section 2(1) or 3(1) or (2) of this Act, to the question whether or not the statement was made contemporaneously with the occurrence or existence of the facts stated, and to the question whether or not the maker of the statement had any incentive to conceal or misrepresent the facts".

In deciding whether to incur the expense of locating and bringing from abroad a foreign witness whose unsworn statement could be put in under the Civil Evidence Act it is also always as well to remember that evidence given by a witness who has been exposed to and stood up to cross-examination will carry much greater weight where the facts are strongly contested than the evidence of the same witness neatly set out in a written statement in impeccable English which has been obtained by a solicitor as a result of a close and detailed interview, particularly when obtained a long time after the events. In particular, it is rarely advisable to rely merely on the statement of a witness who has an interest either direct or indirect in the outcome of the action or in his evidence being accepted by the Court.

Notice to admit facts

Where facts which have been put in issue on the pleadings can be proved only by the evidence of an overseas witness it is often advisable to obtain and place

---

3. Civil Evidence Act 1968, sections 1, 2 and 8. As to the weight to be attached to the unsworn evidence of interested person see section 6(3).

4. Notice must be given under RSC Order 38, rule 21 within 21 days of setting the action down for trial. The notice must contain those particulars required by RSC Order 38, rule 22. If the plaintiffs' solicitors fail to set down the action for trial until relatively close to the date for the trial either party may be enabled to serve such a notice at a very late stage before the start of the trial. This may have the consequence of severely embarrassing the other party. If, however, there is such delay in serving the notice under RSC Order 38, rule 21, it will often be too late for the party serving such a notice to test its effect by an accompanying notice to admit facts under RSC Order 27, rule 2, as to which see p. 118 below.

before the other parties to the action a signed statement from the witness, together with a notice to admit facts under RSC Order 27, rule 2[5] covering that witness's evidence. It is, however, important to serve the notice to admit facts not later than 21 days after the action has been set down for trial. If the party upon whom the notice to admit facts has been served refuses or neglects to admit the facts within seven days after service on him of the notice to admit or within such further period as may be allowed by the Court, the costs of proving the facts are to be paid by that party, unless the Court otherwise orders.[6]

Use of routine commercial documents as evidence

It is not always necessary or possible to obtain signed statements from overseas witnesses. Sometimes their evidence is to be found in survey reports, masters' notices of protest, log books, telex messages, internal reports or letters. These documents may often be the subject of notices given under the Civil Evidence Act 1968.[7] Such notices must be served not later than 21 days after the action has been set down for trial and they must contain the particulars set out in RSC Order 38, rule 22 or 23. It is the practice of the Court to encourage the admission of facts set out in routine commercial documents of the type referred to above but, where the contest between the parties depends to a large extent on the accuracy of statements in such documents, it is usually unwise to rely on the documents as evidence of the facts and it is advisable to call the witness to give evidence.

General average adjustments

The Commercial Court also encourages the admission of facts and calculations set out in general average adjustments. These often contain a more or less detailed account of the facts relating to the voyage, and may also set out survey reports and not infrequently the opinions of experts. In most cases involving claims for general average contribution the underlying dispute will involve investigation of the seaworthiness of the vessel and also an inquiry as to whether the shipowners exercised due diligence under the Hague Rules, Article III, rules 1 and 2. In such

---

5. RSC Order 27, rule 2:

"(1) A party to a cause or matter may not later than 21 days after the cause or matter is set down for trial serve on any other party a notice requiring him to admit, for the purpose of that cause or matter only, such facts or such part of his case as may be specified in the notice.

"(2) An admission made in compliance with a notice under this rule shall not be used against the party by whom it was made in any cause or matter other than the cause or matter for the purpose of which it was made or in favour of any person other than the person by whom the notice was given, and the Court may at any time allow a party to amend or withdraw an admission so made by him on such terms as may be just".

6. RSC Order 62, rule 3(5).
7. Under RSC Order 38, rule 21 or 23.

cases surveyors and ship's witnesses may well have to be called although their reports or statements may be set out in the adjustment. It will be a matter for counsel's judgment in each case whether the material set out in the adjustment will carry sufficient weight as evidence if the witness is not to be tendered for cross-examination at the trial. It must be remembered, however, that the citation of a witness's statement in an adjustment or the reference to the contents of a routine commercial document does not render admissible as evidence the facts set out in the statement or document. It is therefore necessary to serve notices under the Civil Evidence Act 1968 if such facts are to be relied on at the trial and are not admitted by the opposing party.

Agreement as to principles of general average adjustment encouraged

It is the practice of the Court to encourage agreement as to the principles and calculation of apportionment of general average expenditure. It is most exceptional for the Court to go behind the items brought into account in an average adjustment and to re-open the calculation of individual items. Should there be a dispute as to the method of applying the York-Antwerp Rules or the Rules of Practice the parties are strongly encouraged to make efforts to arrive at an agreed position. Most disputes concerning claims for general average contribution are therefore as to whether there has been a general average act and, if so, whether it was occasioned by the actionable default of the shipowners.[8]

Proof of facts referred to in average adjustments

The use of a notice to admit facts served under RSC Order 27, rule 2[9] may in many cases help in deciding whether to call the writer of survey reports, masters' notices of protest, log books, telex messages, internal reports, general correspondence and other material set out in general average adjustments. If the facts essential to prove the case are not admitted and there is a real risk that they may be effectively challenged by oral evidence, it is generally unwise to rely on documentary evidence put in under the Civil Evidence Act.

Preparation of documents for trial

In many commercial actions large numbers of documents have to be put before the Court. The efficient and speedy conduct of the trial can often be severely impeded if the solicitors for the parties do not prepare the documents in a logical and convenient order. All bundles should be made up in chronological order and

---

8. See, generally, York-Antwerp Rules, rule D, and *Goulandris* v. *Goldman* [1958] 1 Q.B. 74.
9. See p. 118, fn. 5 above.

should be properly paged. Each separate bundle should be identified by a convenient number or letter.

Where at all possible the solicitors for all parties should agree several weeks before any trial involving a substantial number of documents which documents are to be put before the Court and how they should be bundled and paged. Where there has been no such agreement it is not incumbent upon solicitors representing a plaintiff to include in the bundles made up by them for use at the trial any documents which the plaintiffs do not rely upon. Failure to agree bundles of documents before trial will almost inevitably lead to considerable duplication of material, an unwieldy filing system for the trial and in consequence delay and increased costs.

Weeding out unnecessary documents

The practice of including in the bundles of documents prepared for the trial every single document which has been disclosed on discovery, regardless of whether it will be referred to at the trial, is now prevalent and is quite wrong.[10] It over-burdens the Court with unnecessary paper, makes it more difficult to locate and refer in the course of the trial to those documents which are to be referred to and therefore wastes time and adds unnecessarily to the costs. It is up to the solicitors representing the parties to the action to obtain in good time before the trial date an advice on evidence from counsel which should include advice on which of the disclosed documents will or will not be needed at the trial.

Clarity of copy documents

Bundles of photocopies of telex messages or other documents which are so faint that they are wholly or partly illegible will not be sympathetically received: in preparing bundles for trial it is the responsibility of solicitors to check them for faint copies and to prepare typescript copies if necessary. Where there are printed documents such as charter-parties, bills of lading, airway bills or invoices including small print, it is important that these should be available in legible form. The advent of more sophisticated photocopying equipment should now enable solicitors to prepare magnified copies of such documents for use at the trial.

---

10. See, in particular, the remarks on this practice made by Lloyd, J., in *Commonwealth Insurance Co.* v. *Groupe Sprinks S.A.* [1983] 1 Lloyd's Rep. 67, at p. 89. Cited at p. 61 above.

CHAPTER 8

THE COMMERCIAL COURT AND ARBITRATION
PROCEEDINGS

Introduction

For many years much of the business of the Commercial Court has been concerned with matters arising in relation to commercial arbitrations held in London and elsewhere in England and Wales. Most of the arbitrations have been either maritime arbitrations arising under the arbitration clauses in charter-parties, bills of lading or contracts for the sale or building of ships or they have been commodity contract arbitrations arising under the arbitration clauses in standard form commodity sale contracts. The maritime arbitrations[1] with which the Court has been concerned have usually involved hearings either before two arbitrators and an umpire appointed by them or before a sole arbitrator. It is not unusual for the umpire or sole arbitrator to be a Queen's Counsel. It is also fairly common for the parties to a maritime arbitration clause to agree to refer a particular dispute to a sole legally-qualified arbitrator in place of the two arbitrators who must also appoint an umpire in accordance with the clause. The maritime arbitrators are almost invariably members of the London Maritime Arbitrators' Association.[2] In contrast, arbitrations held in accordance with the arbitration rules of the various commodity trading associations have in the case of many such associations been through a two-tier arbitration procedure before the award comes before the Court.[3] The two-tier procedure usually initially involves an arbitration by two arbitrators and an umpire if the two cannot agree. This is then followed by an appeal board hearing at which the whole case is re-argued before a board consisting of from four to 10 members of the association, depending on its arbitration rules.

---

1. In the 1979 volumes of *Lloyd's Law Reports* there are reported 42 judgments in the Commercial Court, of which 13 were concerned with maritime arbitrations.

2. Those who wish to appoint a maritime arbitrator and for this purpose require the names of those experienced in this field can obtain the necessary information from: The Hon. Secretary, The London Maritime Arbitrators' Association, c/o The Baltic Exchange, 24 St. Mary Axe, London, EC3A 8DE.

3. In the 1979 volumes of *Lloyd's Law Reports* there are reported a total of 42 judgments in the Commercial Court, of which 11 were concerned with commodity arbitrations. Of these, eight were in relation to awards in the form of special cases stated by the Appeal Board of the Grain and Feed Trade Association (GAFTA). Judgments were also given in relation to arbitrations before other commodity trading associations, in particular, the Refined Sugar Association (1) and the Federation of Oil Seeds and Fats Association (FOSFA) (2).

121

It has not traditionally been the practice of the Commercial Court to hear matters relating to arbitrations which do not have a "commercial" subject-matter, such as building and civil engineering arbitrations, although there are a few instances of the Court having considered this type of case.[4] It remains to be seen whether one consequence of the new RSC Order 73, rule 6 will be that the Commercial Court widens its practice to cover the hearing of appeals and preliminary points of law in arbitrations relating to disputes of a kind which have not previously been entertained by the Court, such as disputes under R.I.B.A. contracts and civil engineering contracts. That rule provides that those matters which by RSC Order 73, rules 2 and 3 are to be heard by a judge, including, in particular, all applications under section 1 of the Arbitration Act 1979 for leave to appeal on a question of law arising out of an award, and all applications for orders that the arbitrators should give reasons for an award and the hearing of preliminary points of law under section 2 of the Arbitration Act 1979, are to be heard by a commercial judge unless such judge otherwise orders.

It is suggested that it would be inappropriate for the Commercial Court to determine disputes arising out of arbitrations unless the subject matter of those disputes were such that had they been litigated they would have had the flavour of a "commercial action" as indicated by RSC Order 72, rule 1.[5] There is, however, nothing in RSC Order 73, rule 6 which expressly requires the commercial judges to refrain from hearing matters relating to "non-commercial" arbitrations. It can nevertheless probably be anticipated that whenever a matter arising out of one such non-commercial arbitration comes before the commercial judges they will direct that the matter be heard by a High Court judge not sitting in the Commercial Court. There may, however, be cases which raise important points of construction or practice in connection with the Arbitration Act 1979 or the application of RSC Order 73 where, although the underlying dispute is not of a commercial flavour, it is appropriate that the application should be heard in the Commercial Court.

Proceedings relating to arbitrations under the Arbitration Act 1950 and not subject to the Arbitration Act 1979

The procedure set out under this heading relates only to those arbitrations which do not fall within the Arbitration Act 1979, that is to say all those arbitrations commenced before 1st August 1979.[6]

---

4. An example is *Lind* v. *Constable Hart* [1979] 2 Lloyd's Rep. 248.
5. RSC Order 72, rule 1(2):
    ". . . 'commercial action' includes any cause arising out of the ordinary transactions of merchants and traders and, without prejudice to the generality of the foregoing words, any cause relating to the construction of a mercantile document, the export or import of merchandise, affreightment, insurance, banking, mercantile agency and mercantile usage".
6. Arbitration Act 1979 (Commencement) Order 1979 (S.I. 1979, No. 750). It is by the terms of the Order open to the parties to arbitrations commenced *before* that date to agree in writing that the 1979

That provision of the Arbitration Act 1950 which led more than any other to the enactment of the 1979 Act was section 21.[7] This provided for awards to be stated by the arbitrators or umpire in the form of a special case for the decision of the Court and for any question of law arising in the course of the reference to be similarly so stated; the latter being commonly known as the consultative case procedure. In view of the fact that section 21 of the 1950 Act has now been repealed by the 1979 Act the number of arbitrations now likely to give rise to a special case or a consultative case is rapidly diminishing and it is therefore only necessary in this book to give a brief outline of the applicable practice and procedure.

Act shall apply to their arbitration as from 1st August 1979 or the date of their agreement, whichever be the later. For the time when an arbitration is commenced see section 29(2) of the Arbitration Act 1950, section 34(3) of the Limitation Act 1980 and fn. 44 on p. 131 below.

7.   "21 (1) An arbitrator or an umpire may, and shall if so directed by the High Court, state—
        (a) any question of law arising in the course of the reference; or
        (b) an award or any part of an award,
in the form of a special case for the decision of the High Court.
    "(2) A special case with respect to an interim award or with respect to a question of law arising in the course of a reference may be stated, or may be directed by the High Court to be stated, notwithstanding that proceedings under the reference are still pending".
    The disadvantages of the special case procedure are discussed in the Report on Arbitration of the Commercial Court Committee 1978 (Cmnd 7284). In summary, these disadvantages are as follows. In order to justify the stating of an award in the form of a special case and in order to obtain from the Court an order directing arbitrators to state such a case it is enough to show that there is a real and substantial point of law appropriate for decision by a Court, the resolution of which is necessary for the proper determination of the case: see *Halfdan Grieg & Co. A/S* v. *Sterling Coal & Navigation Corpn.* [1973] Q.B. 843. In effect unless the point is unarguable, provided the application is not obviously made in bad faith, the Court will order a special case. The procedure therefore provides respondents who have little prospect of having the arbitrator's decision reversed with a readily-available means of delaying satisfaction of the claim against them. Secondly, parties to an arbitration have to formulate their questions of law for a special case before they know what findings of fact or decision on the law the arbitrators will make, a requirement which often gives rise to misdirected or entirely irrelevant questions. For a discussion of the difficulties that may arise and of the Courts' preference of a flexible approach to the form of the questions asked, see *Fawzi A. Ismail* v. *Polish Ocean Line* [1976] Q.B. 893. The arbitrator may have to make a decision on whether to accede to the request for a special case before he knows what findings of fact he will make and if he refuses to accede to the request for a special case a party may have to apply to the Court under section 21 of the Arbitration Act 1950 prior to the publication of an award and before it is known what findings of fact are going to be made. Thirdly, it is not open to the parties to a contract providing for English arbitration validly to contract out of the special case procedure: see *Czarnikov* v. *Roth Schmidt & Co* [1922] 2 K.B. 478. Fourthly, the drafting of an award in the form of a special case in cases where the facts are complicated, combined with the necessity of excluding from it conclusions of law which might render the award vulnerable to being set aside for error of law on its face, may prove an extremely difficult, time-consuming and therefore expensive undertaking on which lay arbitrators frequently require legal advice. Fifthly, the above defects were tending to deter parties to supranational contracts from referring their disputes to arbitration in London.

Special case procedure

Where in an arbitration commenced before 1st August 1979[8] an arbitrator or umpire does not accede to the request of one or other of the parties to the arbitration to state a question of law arising in the course of the reference or an award in the form of a special case for the decision of the High Court under section 21 of the Arbitration Act 1950, application to the Court to direct an arbitrator or umpire to state a question of law or an award in the form of a special case is made by originating summons. Service should be effected on the opposite party to the arbitration and also on the arbitrators or umpire.[9] In a commercial arbitration, that is to say, one involving a dispute relating to any of the matters referred to under RSC Order 72, rule 1(2),[10] or to a dispute of a similar kind, the originating summons can be issued in the Commercial Court by marking it with the words "Commercial Court" in the upper left-hand corner in accordance with RSC Order 72, rule 4(1). Where the originating summons has not been issued in the Commercial Court and the defendant or the plaintiff on further consideration wishes to bring the special case before the Commercial Court he can issue a summons to transfer the proceedings to the Commercial Court under RSC Order 72, rule 5(1).

In order to obtain an order directing arbitrators to state an award in the form of a special case it must be shown that there is a real and substantial point of law, clear-cut and capable of being accurately stated which is open to serious argument and appropriate for decision by a Court as distinct from one which depends on the special expertise of the arbitrators, the resolution of which is necessary for the proper determination of the case. That the judge to whom application is made to direct a special case to be stated forms the impression at first sight that the issue of law is likely to be resolved in the same way as was decided by the arbitrators

---

8. This procedure had been abolished by sections 1(1) and 8(3) of the Arbitration Act 1979 and by the Arbitration Act 1979 (Commencement) Order 1979 (S.I. 1979, No. 750) for all arbitrations commenced on or after 1st August 1979. It is by the terms of the Order open to the parties to an arbitration commenced *before* that date to agree in writing that the 1979 Act shall apply to their arbitration as from 1st August 1979 or the date of their agreement, whichever is the later. For the time when an arbitration commences see section 29(2) of the Arbitration Act 1950, section 34(3) of the Limitation Act 1980 and fn. 44 on p. 131 below.

9. Arbitrators thus served not infrequently put before the Court an affidavit explaining their decision not to accede to the request for a special case, although it is not incumbent on them to do so. The appropriate response for an arbitrator served with proceedings to set aside an award for misconduct is discussed by Donaldson, J., in *Port Sudan Cotton Company* v. *Gowinda Swamy Chettiar* [1977] 1 Lloyd's Rep. 170, at p. 178.

10. "In this Order 'commercial action' includes any cause arising out of the ordinary transactions of merchants and traders and, without prejudice to the generality of the foregoing words, any cause relating to the construction of a mercantile document, the export or import of merchandise, affreightment, insurance, banking, mercantile agency and mercantile usage".

in the award is not a reason for refusing to direct a special case unless, perhaps, the point of law is unarguable or the application is obviously made in bad faith.[11]

An award in the form of a special case should be filed at the Crown Office and Associates Department, Room 478, Royal Courts of Justice, where the proceedings are set down for hearing in the Arbitration Case List established in accordance with the Lord Chief Justice's Directions for London of 31st July 1981.[12] Having been set down in the Arbitration Case List, the papers are then transmitted by the Crown Office to the Commecial Court Listing Officer. The date for the hearing can then be fixed by him in consultation with the parties' solicitors and counsels' clerks.

It has been held that RSC Order 73, rule 2(2) in the form which it took *prior to* 1st August 1979 from which date it was amended by the Rules of the Supreme Court (Amendment No. 3) Order 1979 still operates in relation to arbitrations commenced before 1st August 1979 so as to provide a procedure for the hearing of special cases.[13] Although the old form of RSC Order 73, rule 6 provided for the transfer to the Commercial List by summons of special cases and motions to remit under section 22 of the Arbitration Act 1950, it is no longer operated. As a matter of procedural convenience such special cases and motions to remit are now set down in the Arbitration Case List and are heard by the commercial judges as if they were covered by the new RSC Order 73, rule 2 and therefore also by the Lord Chief Justice's Directions for London of 31st July 1981.[14]

Setting aside or remitting an award for error of law or fact on the face of the award

Where in an arbitration commenced before 1st August 1979[15] an award has been published which on its face is bad in law in the sense that it is expressed on

---

11. *Halfdan Grieg & Co. A/S* v. *Sterling Coal & Navigation Corpn. (The Lysland)* [1973] Q.B. 843. This practice as to the exercise of discretion under section 21 of the 1950 Act is to be contrasted with the view of the House of Lords in *Pioneer Shipping Ltd.* v. *B.T.P. Tioxide Ltd.* [1981] 2 Lloyd's Rep. 239 as to what ought to be the practice as to granting leave to appeal an arbitration award under section 1 of the Arbitration Act 1979.

12. Directions for London [1981] 1 W.L.R. 1296, set out at p. 168 below. This Practice Direction makes no provision for the setting down of special cases or consultative cases under the Arbitration Act 1950 but it has been found convenient to treat them as if they were covered by the Practice Direction with regard to the Arbitration Case List and 1950 Act special cases and consultative cases are now treated administratively in a similar way to motions and other applications under RSC Order 73, rule 2.

13. So held by Parker, J. in *Compania Maritima Zorroza S.A.* v. *Maritime Bulk Carriers Corporation* [1980] 2 Lloyd's Rep. 186, at p. 189. The old Order 73, rule 2(2) provided:

"A special case stated for the decision of the High Court under section 21 of the Arbitration Act 1950 shall be heard and determined by a single judge".

14. *Supra*, set out at p. 168 below.

15. This procedure has been abolished by section 1(1) of the Arbitration Act 1979 and by the

its face to be based on some wrong proposition of law the Court will set it aside.[16] This procedure, which exists at common law, is by way of originating motion to a single judge in Court, although not expressly provided for by the Arbitration Act 1950.[17]

The application to the Court must be made and the notice of originating motion must be served within six weeks after the award has been made and published to the parties.[18] The notice of motion must be served at least two clear days before the day named for the hearing.[19]

The notice of originating motion must state the grounds of the application to set aside or remit the award.[20] When the application is founded on evidence by affidavit a copy of the affidavit to be used must be served with the notice of motion. For the purpose of setting aside or remitting an award for error of law it will normally be necessary only to put the award itself and any documents attached

---

Arbitration Act (Commencement) Order 1979 (S.I. 1979, No. 750) for all arbitrations commenced on or after 1st August 1979. This procedure has now been replaced by the Judicial Review procedure under section 1 of the Arbitration Act 1979. It is by the terms of the above Order open to the parties to an arbitration commenced *before* 1st August 1979 to agree in writing that the 1979 Act shall apply to their arbitration. For the time when an arbitration is commenced see section 29(2) of the Arbitration Act 1950, section 34(3) of the Limitation Act 1980 and fn. 44 on p. 131, below.

16. *British Westinghouse Electric Co.* v. *Underground Electric Railways* [1912] A.C. 673; *F. R. Absalom Ltd.* v. *Great Western (London) Garden Village Society Ltd.* [1933] A.C. 592. The defects of this procedure which led to its being abolished are: (1) that if the Court decides that there is an error of law on its face the award may be set aside in full so that the arbitration has to start again; (2) whether an error appears on the face of the award is a matter of chance usually unrelated to the substance of the matters in issue; (3) the dangers of having the award set aside deter arbitrators from giving reasons as part of their awards and this may make the awards more difficult to enforce in foreign jurisdictions.

17. RSC Order 73, rule 2(1).

18. If RSC Order 73, rule 5(1) applies to arbitrations commenced before 1st August 1979 and which are not subject to the Arbitration Act 1979 (see fn. 15 above and fn. 44 on p. 131) the relevant period is 21 days. However, it has been held by Parker, J., in *Compania Maritima Zorroza S.A.* v. *Maritime Bulk Carriers Corporation (The Marques de Bolarque)* [1980] 2 Lloyd's Rep. 186 that the form of Order 73 which was in force before 1st August 1979 applies to arbitrations commenced before that date and not subject to the 1979 Act. This decision has produced the surprising and bizarre result that two versions of Order 73 are simultaneously in force; that introduced as from 1st August 1979 applying only to arbitrations subject to the 1979 Act, and that form generally in force before 1st August 1979 and no longer printed in the current edition of the Supreme Court Practice. That form is as follows:

"5.—(1) An application to the Court—

  (a) to remit an award under section 22 of the Arbitration Act 1950, or

  (b) to set aside an award under section 23(2) of that Act or otherwise,

may be made at any time within 6 weeks after the award has been made and published to the parties.

  (2) In the case of every such application, the notice of motion must state in general terms the grounds of the application; and, where the motion is founded on evidence by affidavit, a copy of every affidavit intended to be used must be served with that notice".

There is power to extend time under RSC Order 3, rule 5 even if it has already expired.

19. RSC Order 8, rule 2(2).

20. RSC Order 73, rule 5(5).

to and forming part of it before the Court without further evidence and this should be exhibited to an affidavit. When the motion is set down for hearing two copies of the notice of motion must be left at the Crown Office Department, together with either the original award and one copy or with a copy verified by affidavit and an extra copy. The original and one copy of any affidavit to be used at the hearing must be lodged with an extra copy. It sometimes happens that where an award has been stated in the form of a special case the unsuccessful party wishes to apply to set it aside for error of law on its face. In such cases the special case should be set down for trial and the motion to set aside should be heard at the same time as the special case.

Proceedings in relation to all arbitrations

The procedure set out under this heading relates to all arbitrations, but there are certain variations in procedure according to whether the arbitration is subject to the Arbitration Act 1979, that is to say, according to whether it was commenced before or on or after 1st August 1979.

The following applications must be made by originating motion. If subject to the 1979 Act they must be heard by the commercial judge unless he otherwise directs.[21]

(a) *Applications to remit an award under section 22 of the Arbitration Act 1950.*[22] This procedure is most commonly used where arbitrators have failed to make sufficient findings of fact to enable the Court to determine the question of law before it. This was occasionally a necessary procedure where a special case had been requested. It is anticipated that it may still be useful, in relation to reasoned awards in which the arbitrator or umpire have not made sufficient findings of fact. In relation to such awards, however, the Court is now given express powers under section 1(5) of the Arbitration Act 1979 to remit to the arbitrators or umpire an

---

21. RSC Order 73, rules 2(1) and 6. Prior to the 1979 Act such applications were not confined to the Commercial Court. They could be made to any Division of High Court. Henceforth, the Commercial Court will have control over the development of the practice as to those matters reserved for the decision of a judge alone in all arbitrations except those which because they are of a non-commercial nature are upon the direction of the commercial judge heard by the other High Court judges. If the arbitration is not subject to the 1979 Act it appears to follow from *Compania Maritima Zorroza S.A.* v. *Maritime Bulk Carriers Corporation* [1980] 2 Lloyd's Rep. 186 that RSC Order 73, rule 6 does not apply.

22.   "(1) In all cases of reference to arbitration the High Court or a judge thereof may from time to time remit the matters referred, or any of them, to the reconsideration of the arbitrator or umpire.

       "(2) Where an award is remitted, the arbitrator or umpire shall, unless the order otherwise directs, make his award within three months after the date of the order".

For the principles applicable and for illustrations of the exercise of the power to remit awards otherwise than in cases of misconduct see: *Halsbury Laws of England,* 4th edn., Vol. 2, para. 617 and *Universal Cargo Carriers* v. *Citati* [1957] 1 W.L.R. 979 (C.A.).

award which does not or does not sufficiently set out the reasons for the award and to order the arbitrators or umpire to state the reasons for the award in sufficient detail to enable the Court to consider any question of law arising out of the award if an appeal should be brought against the award. There is thus probably something of an overlap of powers in relation to arbitrations subject to the 1979 Act. The power to remit may also be used in cases where there has been misconduct by the arbitrators or umpire but where in all the circumstances it would not be appropriate to set aside the award and in those cases where new evidence has come to light after the arbitration hearing.[23]

The application to remit must be made by notice of originating motion. A precedent is set out at page 159 below. In arbitrations to which the 1979 Act applies the motion must be heard by a commercial judge unless he otherwise orders and must be served within 21 days after the award has been made and published to the parties.[24] The Court has power to extend this period of time even if it has already expired.[25] Applications for an extension of time should normally be combined in a single notice of originating motion with the application to remit. The notice of originating motion must be served at least two clear days before the day named for the hearing in the notice.[26]

The motion must be set down in the first instance in the Arbitration Case List and is then referred to the judge in charge of the Commercial List for his consideration as to its suitability for retention in that List. If he decides that it ought to be heard by a commercial judge any party can then apply for a date for trial of the motion.[27]

---

23. See *Whitehall Shipping Co. Ltd.* v. *Compass Schiffahrtskontor (The Stainless Patriot)* [1979] 1 Lloyd's Rep. 589, in which Donaldson, J., held that a party seeking leave to remit must at least establish: (1) that he did not have the evidence at the time of the arbitration; (2) that he could not then have obtained the evidence by exercising due diligence; (3) that if he had obtained the evidence at the time it would probably have had a substantial effect on the arbitrator's award; (4) that he did not have the opportunity of inviting the arbitrators to delay the award while he considered whether it was possible to obtain evidence of the type which he applies to be allowed to adduce. See also *Bjorn-Jensen & Co.* v. *Lysaght (Australia) Ltd. (The Gamma)* [1979] 1 Lloyd's Rep. 494 and *Andre & Cie S.A.* v. *Tradax Export S.A.* [1983] 1 Lloyd's Rep. 254, C.A. in which Kerr, L.J., usefully sets out many of the relevant authorities and citations at pp. 267–8.

24. RSC Order 73, rules 5(1) and 6. In arbitrations to which the 1979 Act does not apply it seems that the form of RSC Order 73, rule 5 in force for all arbitrations before 1st August 1979 still has effect: the period of time within which applications must be made is six weeks after the award has been published and the motion need not be heard by a commercial judge: see *Compania Maritima Zorroza S.A.* v. *Maritime Bulk Carriers Corporation* [1980] 2 Lloyd's Rep. 186.

25. RSC Order 3, rule 5.

26. RSC Order 8, rule 2(2).

27. Directions for London given by the Lord Chief Justice on 31st July 1981, [1981] 1 W.L.R. 1296, para. 14; see p. 168 below.

(b) *Applications to remove an arbitrator or umpire for misconduct under section 23(1) of the Arbitration Act 1950*[28] *and applications under section 23(2) to set aside an award for misconduct or because the arbitration or the award has been improperly procured.*[29] The application to the Court to set aside an award for misconduct must be made by notice of originating motion and in the case of arbitrations to which the 1979 Act applies the motion must be heard by a commercial judge unless he otherwise orders and the notice of originating motion must be served within 21 days after the award has been made and published to the parties.[30] The Court has power to extend this period of time even if it has already expired.[31]

An application under section 23(1) of the Arbitration Act 1950 to remove an arbitrator or umpire for misconduct must be made by notice of originating motion, which in the case of arbitrations to which the 1979 Act applies must be heard by the commercial judge.[32] Such applications are not subject to a 21-day time limit.

The notice of originating motion must in the case both of an application to remove an arbitrator or umpire for misconduct under section 23(1) and of an application to set aside the award under section 23(2) be served at least two clear days before the day named for the hearing in the notice.[33]

The motion must be set down in the first instance in the Arbitration Case List and it is then referred to the judge in charge of the Commercial List for his consideration as to its suitability for retention in that List. If he decides that it ought to be tried by a commercial judge any party can apply for a date for trial of the motion.[34]

---

28. RSC Order 73, rules 2(1)(b) and (6). Section 23(1) provides "where an arbitrator or umpire has misconducted himself or the proceedings, the High Court may remove him". For the principles applicable and for illustrations of the exercise of the power of removal of arbitrators for misconduct, see the recent decisions of the Court of Appeal in *Modern Engineering (Bristol) Ltd.* v. *Miskin & Son Ltd.* [1981] 1 Lloyd's Rep. 135, and of Pain, J., in *Pratt* v. *Swanmore Builders Ltd.* [1980] 2 Lloyd's Rep. 504. See also the decision of the Court of Appeal in *Fisher* v. *P.G. Wellfair Ltd.*, The Times, 8th May 1981.

29. RSC Order 73, rule 2(1)(c). Section 23(2) provides "Where an arbitrator or umpire has misconducted himself or the proceedings, or an arbitration or award has been improperly procured, the High Court may set the award aside". For the principles applicable and for illustrations of the exercise of the power to set aside awards for misconduct, see *Halsbury Laws of England*, 4th edn., Vol. 2, para. 622.

30. RSC Order 73, rules 5(1) and 6. In arbitrations to which the 1979 Act does not apply it seems that application must be made to a judge, but not necessarily a commercial judge, within six weeks of publication of the award in accordance with the form of RSC Order 73, rule 5 in force for all arbitrations before 1st August 1979: see *Compania Maritima Zorroza S.A.* v. *Maritime Bulk Carriers Corporation* [1980] 2 Lloyd's Rep. 186.

31. RSC Order 3, rule 5.

32. RSC Order 73, rules 2(1)(b) and 6.

33. RSC Order 8, rule 2(2).

34. Directions for London, 31st July 1981, [1981] 1 W.L.R. 1296, para. 14, set out at p. 168 below.

Proceedings in relation to arbitrations subject to the Arbitration Act 1979

The Arbitration Act 1979, as was to be expected, is having a greater impact on the work of the Commercial Court than any other legislation in the recent past. It was in the Commercial Court that the defects of the special case procedure[35] and the power to set aside awards for error of law on their face[36] had become obvious, particularly since 1970, and it was therefore appropriate that the recommendations in the Report of the Commercial Court Committee,[37] published as a Command Paper in July 1978, should form the basis of the new Act which came into force on 1st August 1979. The two main resulting changes in the work of the Commercial Court are the gradual disappearance of awards in the form of a special case stated under section 21 of the Arbitration Act 1950[38] which can now only emerge from arbitrations which were commenced before 1st August 1979[39] and the large number of applications for leave to appeal against arbitration awards made under section 1(2) of the Arbitration Act 1979. The introduction of the new RSC Order 73, rule 6 has the effect that, unless a commercial judge otherwise directs, applications for leave to appeal under section 1(2),[40] applications for orders that arbitrators shall give reasons for their awards under section 1(5),[41] the determination of preliminary questions of law under section 2(1),[42] and applications for the extension of the powers of arbitrators under section 5[43] of the 1979 Act, are reserved exclusively to the Commercial Court.

Applications for leave to appeal against awards

Section 1 of the Arbitration Act 1979 sets out a comprehensive system for the judicial review of arbitration awards which replaces the special case procedure and the setting aside or remission of awards for error of law or fact on their face. The Report of the Commercial Court Committee considered it a matter of overriding importance that uniformly consistent principles of law should be applied in commercial arbitrations and in the Commercial Court. Unless the legal principles applied in arbitration awards were subject to some supervisory control by the Courts consistency of principle would or might be lost and with it the element of certainty of principle which has for so many years made English Law the preferred system for the great majority of international commercial contracts.

---

35. See fn. 7 on p. 123.
36. See fn. 16 on p. 126.
37. Report on Arbitration of the Commercial Court Committee 1978 (Cmnd 7284).
38. See p. 124 above for the appropriate procedure.
39. Arbitration Act (Commencement) Order 1979 (S.I. 1979, No. 750).
40. See p. 132 below.
41. See p. 143 below.
42. See p. 145 below.
43. See p. 147 below.

Hence, the 1979 Act has introduced a system of judicial review which maintains for the Commercial Court an element of supervisory control over arbitration awards by means of the appeal procedure and the associated introduction of the requirement for reasoned awards, but which attempts to avoid the disadvantages of the special case procedure by permitting appeals only with leave of the Court and by permitting exclusion agreements under section 3 of the Act whereby the right of appeal can in certain circumstances be excluded by agreement of the parties to the arbitration.

The new system applies to arbitrations commenced on or after 1st August 1979,[44] save that it is open to the parties to an arbitration commenced *before* that date to agree in writing that the 1979 Act shall apply to their arbitration as from 1st August 1979 or from the date of their agreement, whichever is the later.

Section 1 provides as follows:—

"(2) Subject to subsection (3) below, an appeal shall lie to the High Court on any question of law arising out of an award made on an arbitration agreement; and on the determination of such an appeal the High Court may by order—

(a) confirm, vary or set aside the award; or

(b) remit the award to the reconsideration of the arbitrator or umpire together with the Court's opinion on the question of law which was the subject of the appeal;

and where the award is remitted under paragraph (b) above the arbitrator or umpire shall, unless the order otherwise directs, make his award within three months after the date of the order.

"(3) An appeal under this section may be brought by any of the parties to the reference—

(a) with the consent of all the other parties to the reference; or

---

44. Arbitration Act (Commencement) Order 1979 (S.I. 1979, No. 750). For the time when an arbitration is commenced see section 29(2) of the Arbitration Act 1950:

". . . an arbitration shall be deemed to be commenced when one party to the arbitration serves on the other party or parties a notice requiring him or them to appoint or concur in appointing an arbitrator or, where the arbitration agreement provides that the reference shall be to a person named or designated in the agreement, requiring him or them to submit the dispute to the person so named or designated".

See also section 34(3) of the Limitation Act 1980 to similar effect and *The Agios Lazaros* [1976] 2 Lloyd's Rep. 47, in which Lord Denning, M.R., stated at p. 51 that in a case where the reference is to two arbitrators, one to be appointed by each party

". . . the arbitration is deemed to commence when the one party, expressly or by implication requires the other to appoint his arbitrator. If he simply says: 'I require the difference to be submitted to arbitration in accordance with our agreement' that is sufficient to commence the arbitration: because it is by implication a request by the other to appoint his arbitrator".

For there to be a commencement of arbitration within the Arbitration Act (Commencement) Order 1979 there must be a live dispute at the time when the arbitrator is appointed: see *Peter Cremer G.m.b.H. & Co.* v. *Sugat Food Industries Ltd.* [1981] 2 Lloyd's Rep. 640.

(b) subject to section 3 below,[45] with the leave of the court.

"(4) The High Court shall not grant leave under subsection (3)(b) above unless it considers that, having regard to all the circumstances, the determination of the question of law concerned could substantially affect the rights of one or more of the parties to the arbitration agreement; and the Court may make any leave which it gives conditional upon the applicant complying with such conditions as it considers appropriate".

An application for leave to appeal must be made by originating motion to a judge in the Commercial Court. This is the practice notwithstanding that the arbitration from which the application arises is not of a commercial character.[46] The appeal itself is also to be made by originating motion to a judge in the Commercial Court and heard by a commercial judge unless he otherwise orders[47] and notice of the appeal may be included in the notice of application for leave to appeal where leave is required, that is to say, in those cases where all the parties to the reference do not consent. Notice of application for leave to appeal and notice of the appeal itself should be combined in a single notice of originating motion in order to save time and costs. A precedent is set out at page 155 below. In the earlier cases of applications for leave to appeal it was usually the practice that where possible the application for leave and the appeal itself would be heard at the same time,[48] but this practice has not continued and is now discouraged and it is believed that in practically all cases the argument of appeals now takes place at a separate hearing.[49] In *Tor Line A.B.* v. *Alltrans Group of Canada Ltd.*[50] Bingham, J. considered whether, as a general practice, the Court, having granted leave to appeal, should go on at the same hearing to determine the appeal itself. He said this:

"The hearing of the application is not intended to be of a length and depth necessary to lead the judge to a final conclusion but only to enable him to form a provisional view whether the arbitrator was wrong or whether a strong *prima facie* case has been made out that he was wrong, as the case may be. For this

---

45. Section 3 provides that if the parties to the reference have entered into an exclusion agreement which excludes the right of appeal in relation to that award the High Court shall not grant leave to appeal.

46. RSC Order 73, rule 2(1)(d). It was held by the Court of Appeal in *F.G. Whitley & Sons Co. Ltd.* v. *Clwyd C.C.* (*The Times*, 6th August 1982) that the appropriate time for the commercial judge to decide whether to retain the appeal in the Commercial Court under RSC Order 73, rule 6 is *after* leave to appeal has been granted and the Commercial Court has changed the previous practice accordingly.

47. RSC Order 73, rule 2(2) and 6. For a discussion as to the circumstances in which a commercial judge might order that the appeal should be heard outside the Commercial Court by a High Court judge see p. 122 above.

48. *International Sea Tankers Inc.* v. *Hemisphere Shipping Co. Ltd., The Wenjiang* [1981] 2 Lloyd's Rep. 308, at p. 313, *per* Goff, J.

49. ibid., in the Court of Appeal [1982] 1 Lloyd's Rep. 128, *per* Lord Denning, M.R., at p. 130.

50. [1982] 1 Lloyd's Rep. 617, at pp. 626–7.

purpose full argument and citation of authority are not called for. It makes no sense of the authoritative guidelines if full-dress hearings take place at the stage of seeking leave, and the business of the Court would become seriously overloaded if this became a regular practice. . . . There may be exceptional cases where the point of law is so short and clear and self-contained that a final decision can be taken on the application for leave and any further hearing would be futile, but such cases must be rare. The Court will in general strongly discourage attempts to convert applications for leave into full appeal hearings".

In that case Bingham, J., held that in view of there having been full argument and citation of authority on the application for leave it was not right that the parties should be put to the expense of a further hearing.

Notwithstanding the practice that has now developed it is the view of many in the legal profession that the separation of the hearing of the substantive appeal from the application for leave to appeal is an undesirable waste of time and costs and that the two hearings should in the interests of efficient litigation be combined into one, the judge going on to hear the substantive appeal immediately after giving leave. Against this view, if the two hearings were to be combined into one, the organization of the Court's time would become somewhat more difficult because the time likely to be taken by combined hearings would become extremely difficult to predict since it would depend upon whether leave to appeal were given. In addition, the combined hearing would make it more difficult to give effect to the intention behind the appeals procedure under the 1979 Act in as much as the decision on whether leave to appeal is to be given should not depend on such detailed legal argument as might be required for consideration of the appeal itself.

Notice of the appeal must be served and the appeal entered within 21 days after the award has been made and published to the parties, save that where reasons material to the appeal are given on a date subsequent to that on which the award itself has been published the period of 21 days runs from that subsequent date.[51] Time for appeal may be extended even if it has expired at the time of the application.[52] Such extension of time will probably be required in many cases where the other party to the arbitration is outside the jurisdiction of the English Court and it is therefore necessary before service can be effected to obtain an order for leave to serve the notice of motion outside the jurisdiction.[53] The notice

---

51. RSC Order 73, rule 5(2). The extension of the period of 21 days after the award has been made is needed, particularly in those cases where an arbitrator or umpire has omitted to give reasons or sufficient reasons for his award and an order is made under section 1(5) that he should do so.

52. RSC Order 3, rule 5.

53. Application for leave should be made *ex parte* to the commercial judge under RSC Order 73, rule 7. In such an application an affidavit must be produced stating the grounds on which the application is made, in particular stating that the arbitration to which the appeal relates is governed by English Law or has been held within the jurisdiction of the English Courts. It will be observed that leave may be granted to serve proceedings outside the jurisdiction where the arbitration has been held abroad but is subject to English procedural law. The procedure is otherwise substantially the same as that for *ex parte* applications under RSC Order 11, rule 1.

of originating motion must state the grounds of appeal and this should be done with sufficient clarity to enable the other party to know the precise case which is being made against the award.[54] Where the appeal is made with the consent of the other party to the arbitration, a copy of the consent must be served with the notice of appeal. In those cases where the appeal is founded on evidence by affidavit, a copy of the affidavit must also be served with the notice of appeal.[55] The notice of motion, together with any affidavit to be used at the hearing, must be served at least two clear days before the date named for the hearing.[56] The originating motion for leave to appeal, if any, should be combined in one document with the motion for the appeal itself[57] and must be set down for hearing, with the return date left blank or with a nominal return date inserted, at the Crown Office, Room 478, Royal Courts of Justice, Strand, WC2A 2LL, in the Arbitration Case List.[58] The Crown Office will then automatically transmit the motion to the Commercial Court Office. The solicitors for the parties should then liaise with the Commercial Court Listing Officer[59] and counsels' clerks in order to fix a date for the hearing. If it is necessary to obtain leave to appeal under section 1(3) of the Arbitration Act 1979 the motion applying for leave will be heard in open Court by a commercial judge regardless of whether the arbitration from which the application arises is or is not of a commercial character. If leave to appeal is granted the commercial judge trying the application will then decide whether, having regard to RSC Order 73, rule 6, it is appropriate that the appeal itself should be heard by a commercial judge or by a Queen's Bench Division judge outside the Commercial Court.[60] If it is not necessary to obtain leave to appeal because the parties consent to the appeal, the solicitors for the parties should contact the Commercial Court Listing Officer before fixing a hearing date for the appeal to ascertain whether the commercial judge, having regard to RSC Order 73, rule 6, regards the appeal as appropriate for hearing in the Commercial Court or by a Queen's Bench Division judge outside the Commercial Court. If the appeal is to proceed in the Commercial Court a date for hearing can then be arranged through counsel's clerks. The hearing of the appeal takes place in open Court.

---

54. RSC Order 73, rule 5(5).
55. RSC Order 73, rule 5(5).
56. RSC Order 8, rule 2(2).
57. For a precedent see p. 155 below.
58. Directions for London given by the Lord Chief Justice on 31st July 1981, [1981] 1 W.L.R. 1296, para. 14, set out at p. 168 below.
59. Room 198, Royal Courts of Justice, Strand, London WC2A 2LL, Tel. No. 01-405-7641, Ext. 3826; Telex 296983 COMM-G.
60. This changes the previous practice adopted until 1982 and accords with the judgment of the Court of Appeal in *F.G. Whitley & Sons Co. Ltd.* v. *Clwyd CC, The Times,* 6th August 1982.

Principles on which leave to appeal will be granted

The principles which should be applied by the commercial judge in deciding whether to grant leave to appeal were recently considered by the House of Lords in *Pioneer Shipping Ltd.* v. *B.T.P. Tioxide (The Nema).*[61] These are set out in the speech of Lord Diplock who played a major part in the passage of the Bill through the House of Lords. As expressed by Lord Diplock, these principles may be summarised as follows:—

(1) Leave to appeal should never be granted unless the judge considers that, having regard to all the circumstances, the determination of the question of law concerned could substantially affect the rights of one or more of the parties to the arbitration agreement.[62]

(2) Where the question of law involved is the construction of a "one-off" clause, that is to say, a clause which is not found in standard form or widely-used mercantile contracts, the application of which to the particular facts of the case is an issue in the arbitration, leave to appeal should not normally be given unless it is apparent to the judge upon a mere perusal of the reasoned award itself, without the benefit of adversarial argument, that the meaning ascribed to the clause by the arbitrator is obviously wrong.[63]

(3) If, on a mere perusal of the award without the benefit of adversarial argument, it appears to the judge that it is possible that argument might persuade him, despite his first impression to the contrary, that the arbitrator might be right, he should refuse leave to appeal.[63]

In *B.V.S. S.A.* v. *Kerman Shipping Co. S.A.*[64] Parker, J., having expressed the view that the House of Lords could not have intended that applications for leave would normally be dealt with on the papers alone, stated that the combined effect of Lord Diplock's speech and the decision of the Court of Appeal in *Italmare Shipping Co.* v. *Ocean Tanker Co. Inc.*[65] was as follows:—

> "(a) that in a 'one-off' case, in the absence of special circumstances, leave should not be given unless on the conclusion of argument on the application for leave the Court has formed the provisional view that the arbitrator was wrong and considers that it would need a great deal of convincing that he was right,
>
> "(b) that if the Court does form such a view then, again in the absence of special circumstances, leave should be granted".

---

61. [1981] 2 Lloyd's Rep. 239.
62. Arbitration Act 1979, section 1(4).
63. *The Nema* [1981] 2 Lloyd's Rep. 239, at p. 247.
64. [1982] 1 W.L.R. 166, at p. 171. See also *National Rumour Compania S.A.* v. *Lloyd-Libra Navegacao S.A.* [1982] 1 Lloyd's Rep. 472; *Jamil Line for Trading and Shipping Ltd.* v. *Atlantic Handelsgesellschaft Harder & Co.* [1982] 1 Lloyd's Rep. 481.
65. [1982] 1 W.L.R. 158.

In *International Sea Tankers Inc.* v. *Hemisphere Shipping Co. Ltd.*[66] Lord Denning, M.R., said that in such a case

> "the judge should not give leave to appeal from the arbitrator if he thinks the arbitrator was right or probably right or may have been right. He should only give leave to appeal if he forms the provisional view that the arbitrator was wrong on a point of law . . .".

(4) Where **(a)** a question of law involved is the construction of a clause which is *not* a one-off clause in the sense that it is to be found in standard form or widely-used mercantile contracts the application of which clause to the particular facts of the case is an issue in the arbitration and **(b)** the facts are such that it is not unlikely that they will be repeated in similar transactions between other parties engaged in the same trade, i.e. they are not "one-off" events, and **(c)** the decision on the question of construction in the circumstances of the particular case would add significantly to the clarity and certainty of English commercial law, bearing in mind that a super-abundance of citable judicial decisions arising out of slightly different facts is calculated to hinder rather than promote clarity in settled principles of commercial law, and **(d)** the judge considers that a strong *prima facie* case has been made out that the arbitrator has been wrong in his construction, it would be proper to give leave to appeal.[67] In *International Sea Tankers Inc.* v. *Hemisphere Shipping Co. Ltd.*[68] Lord Denning, M.R., stated:

> "When the case is not 'one-off' . . . but it gives rise to a question of construction of a standard form with facts which may occur repeatedly or from time to time, then the judge shall give leave if he thinks that the arbitrator may have gone wrong on the construction of the standard form: but not if he thinks the arbitrator was right".

(5) Where the matters for consideration on application for leave to appeal included those factors set out in **(4)(a)** and **(c)** above but the facts to which the clause had to be applied were "one-off" events, the same stricter criteria should be applied as are set out in **(2)** and **(3)** above.[67]

(6) Where the matter for decision by the arbitrator is whether the contract has been discharged by frustration or fundamental breach and particularly where the

---

66. [1982] 1 Lloyd's Rep. 128, at p. 131.

67. ibid., p. 248. And see *Italmare Shipping Co.* v. *Ocean Tanker Co. Inc., The Rio Sun, (supra).* See also the approach of Parker, J., in *B.V.S. S.A.* v. *Kerman Shipping, supra*: a strong *prima facie* case involved a stricter test than that applicable in deciding whether to order a special case under section 21 of the Arbitration Act 1950 (see p. 124 above). For an example of the strong *prima facie* case test where the clause (in a charter-party) was a hybrid—neither a truly "one-off" clause nor a standard clause: see *Phoenix Shipping Corporation* v. *Apex Shipping Corporation* [1982] 1 Lloyd's Rep. 476.

68. [1982] 1 Lloyd's Rep. 128, at p. 131. See also *Tor Line A.B.* v. *Alltrans Group of Canada Ltd.* [1982] 1 Lloyd's Rep. 617.

facts involved are "one-off" events, what the judge should normally ask himself is not simply whether he agrees with the arbitrator's conclusion but whether it appears upon perusal of the award[69] either that the arbitrator misdirected himself in law or that his decision was such that no reasonable arbitrator could reach.[67] In *B.V.S. S.A.* v. *Kerman Shipping Co. S.A.*[70] Parker, J., stated that the effect of Lord Diplock's speech was that leave should not be given unless the Court on the conclusion of argument, **(a)** reaches a provisional view that the arbitrator has applied the wrong test, or if no test is disclosed, that no reasonable arbitrator applying the right test could have reached such a conclusion and **(b)** is of the opinion that it would take a great deal of convincing to the contrary.

(7) Where **(a)** the matter for decision by the arbitrator is whether the contract has been discharged by frustration and the events relied upon as amounting to frustration are *not* "one-off" events affecting only the particular parties to the abritration, but events of a general character that affect similar transactions between many other persons engaged in the same kind of commercial activity[71] and **(b)** it is in the interests of legal certainty that there should be some uniformity in the decisions of arbitrators as to the effect of such an event upon similar transactions in order that other traders may be sufficiently certain where they stand as to be able to close their own transactions without recourse to arbitration, and **(c)** the judge thinks that in the particular case the conclusion reached by the arbitrator, although not one which no reasonable arbitrator could have reached, was not right[72] it might, in the absence of a consent appeal under section 1(3)(a), be a proper exercise of the judge's discretion to give leave to appeal in order to express a conclusion as to the frustrating effect of the event so as to afford

---

69. Presumably without the benefit of adversarial argument, adopting the same approach as in (2) above, but see also Parker, J., in *B.V.S. S.A.* v. *Kerman Shipping, supra,* at p. 172 to the effect that the House of Lords did not intend that applications for leave to appeal should normally be dealt with on the papers alone.

70. *Supra,* at p. 172. In *L'Office National du Thè et du Sucre* v. *Philippine Sugar Trading (London) Ltd.* [1983] 1 Lloyd's Rep. 89, Lloyd, J., applied to a frustration case where the facts appear to have been "one-off" the test of asking whether the award was "obviously wrong", which probably is not substantially different from that of Lord Diplock stated in the text and explained by Parker, J.

71. Lord Diplock cited as examples the closing of the Suez Canal, the United States soya bean embargo and the war between Iraq and Iran; ibid; p. 248. See also *International Sea Tankers Inc.* v. *Hemisphere Shipping Co., The Wenjaing* [1982] 1 Lloyd's Rep. 128, in which the Court of Appeal applied this approach to an award in relation to the blocking and trapping of a vessel in the Shatt-al-Arab in 1981, in the course of the Iran-Iraq war.

72. It does not appear that in such a case it is necessary that it should be apparent to the judge without the benefit of adversarial argument that the arbitrator is obviously wrong. In *B.V.S. S.A.* v. *Kerman Shipping, supra,* at p. 173 Parker, J. considered that it was intended by the House of Lords that a strong *prima facie* case should be made out in argument that the arbitrator was wrong.

guidance binding[73] upon the arbitrators in other arbitrations arising out of the same events.

(8) There may be cases where, notwithstanding that having regard to the above seven factors, it would be a proper exercise of the judicial discretion to give leave to appeal, it would nevertheless be wrong to grant leave because the parties had in the circumstances of the case set up the arbitration as a matter of urgency to obtain a quick decision, arriving at finality in the dispute as early as possible.[74]

Where the dispute arises out of the construction of a one-off contract relating to a particular trade and the parties selected an arbitrator for his experience and knowledge of the commercial background and usages of that trade, that is a factor which will count on the side of refusing leave to appeal.[75]

The criteria to be applied in deciding whether to give leave to appeal are in ordinary cases intended to be much stricter than those formerly used in deciding whether to order a special case to be stated under section 21(1) of the Arbitration Act 1950 as laid down in *Halfdan Grieg & Co. A/S* v. *Sterling Coal & Navigation Corporation, The Lysland*[76] and therefore if nothing more can be shown than those features of the award leave will normally be refused.[77] This will be true even in those cases not falling within the categories listed above but, in principle, the more far-reaching the effects of the point of law involved, the less strict the criteria for deciding whether to grant leave to appeal should be. If the point of law is one which can affect not only persons within a particular trade but persons in other trades as well and persons not in commerce or trade at all, it would be proper to grant leave on the basis of little more than its being shown that the point is capable of serious argument.[77] In those cases where the point of law is an entirely new one on which there is no authority this may be a special factor making it proper to grant leave on no more strict a test than that laid down in *The*

---

73. Lord Diplock, at p. 248, uses the wording "binding". It may well be the case that the evidence of the same relevant events in subsequent arbitrations may differ from the evidence before the arbitration in question and in such cases the arbitrators in the subsequent arbitration would not be bound by the judge's decision.

74. This, it is suggested, is the effect of the statements at pp. 243 and 248 in the speech of Lord Diplock with regard to the special circumstances in which the arbitration in *The Nema* was set up. See also *B.V.S. S.A.* v. *Kerman Shipping Co. S.A.* [1982] 1 W.L.R. 166 *per* Parker, J., at pp. 169–170. Where one or both parties have at the hearing requested the arbitrator to give a reasoned award, that may be a factor to be taken into account in favour of leave to appeal being granted: see Parker, J., at p. 170 and *Italmare Shipping Co.* v. *Ocean Tanker Co. Inc.* [1982] 1 W.L.R. 158.

75. *B.V.S. S.A.* v. *Kerman Shipping Co. S.A.*, *supra*, at p. 170.

76. [1973] Q.B. 843. See p. 124 above.

77. *B.V.S. S.A.* v. *Kerman Shipping Co. S.A.*, *supra*, *per* Parker, J., at p. 173. See also *The Alaskan Trader* [1983] 1 Lloyd's Rep. 310 in which Bingham, J., expressed the view that a less strict test than the "strong *prima facie* case" test might be applicable in that case which raised a fundamental question of contract law.

Lysland[76] on the grounds that it is of importance that authoritative guidance be given at the earliest possible moment.[77] Where, however, the arbitration is in substance a disciplinary procedure, such as that provided for under section 20 of the Lloyd's Act 1871, it is not appropriate to apply the principles laid down in *Pioneer Shipping Ltd.* v. *B.T.P. Tioxide Ltd.* and leave to appeal should not be given unless there is a clear-cut question of law which can substantially affect the applicant's rights and on which he can make out a *prima facie* case that the award is wrong.[77a]

In some cases it may be appropriate, having regard to all the circumstances of the case, that leave to appeal should be made conditional on the applicants' putting up security for a claim against them. In *Clea Shipping Corporation* v. *Bulk Oil International*[78] Bingham, J., held that it was appropriate to impose on the applicants for leave to appeal the condition that they must lodge security for a part of the claim against them within a specified period. The practice on this point remains to be developed. It may well not be appropriate, when deciding whether to make leave to appeal conditional, to take into account the apparent strength of the applicant's case. It is submitted that the dominant considerations, although not the only ones, should be the conduct of the applicants prior to the application and their present and prospective financial standing.

Appeals to the Court of Appeal

Appeals to the Court of Appeal against decisions of the judge on appeals against awards under section 1 of the Arbitration Act 1979 are not permitted unless (1) the judges of the Court of Appeal give leave and (2) the judge has certified that the question of law to which the decision of the Court relates either is one of general public importance or is one which for some other special reason should be considered by the Court of Appeal.[79] The principles to be applied by the Court of Appeal in deciding whether to grant leave to appeal were recently considered in *Babanaft International Co. S.A.* v. *Avant Petroleum Inc.*[80] The Court of Appeal ought to consider the judgment under appeal and ask similar questions which the House of Lords in *Pioneer Shipping Ltd.* v. *B.T.P. Tioxide Ltd.*[81] had ruled should be asked by the judges in deciding whether to grant leave to appeal against an award.

Although in its original form, the Arbitration Act 1979 made no special provision in relation to appeals from the judge's orders granting or refusing leave to appeal against awards the Act has subsequently been amended by the addition

---

77a. *Moran* v. *Lloyd's* [1983] 1 Lloyd's Rep. 51.
78. *The Alaskan Trader* [1983] 1 Lloyd's Rep. 310, at p. 319.
79. Arbitration Act 1979, section 1(7).
80. [1982] 2 Lloyd's Rep. 99.
81. [1981] 2 Lloyd's Rep. 239.

of subsection 6A of section 1, the effect of which is that no appeal lies to the Court of Appeal from a judge's decision to grant or refuse leave to appeal unless the judge gives leave to appeal against the decision.[82] In some cases it may be appropriate for the judge hearing an application for leave to appeal to the Court of Appeal against an order by him granting or refusing leave to appeal against an award to confine leave to appeal to particular questions of law and to decline leave in respect of others.[83]

In *The Antaios No. 2*,[83a] Staughton, J., having refused leave to appeal against the award under section 1(3) in a case where he considered that the award was probably right held that there were three classes of case in which the problem of deciding whether to grant leave to appeal to the Court of Appeal under section 1(6A) might arise:

> (1) Where the judge had laid down guidelines as to the operation of the 1979 Act, in which case the judge should give leave to appeal to the Court of Appeal so that there could be an opportunity for the Court of Appeal to review the guidelines; (2) where the judge had decided the matter as one of discretion, in which case leave to appeal to the Court of Appeal should be refused; (3) where the judge had concluded that the arbitrators were probably right even if on a substantial and arguable point of law, in which case leave to appeal to the Court of Appeal should be refused.

Applications for orders that arbitrators give reasons for their awards

The introduction by the Arbitration Act 1979 of reasoned awards was a necessary prerequisite if the system of judicial review described above was to replace the special case procedure and the power to set aside for error of fact or law on the face of the award. The Act contains no requirement that every award should contain reasons but it is desirable that reasons should be given as a matter of course and it is understood that this practice is now being followed in most maritime arbitrations in London.[84] Guidance on the degree of formality or informality of reasoning which ought to be given by arbitrators as part of their awards was given by Donaldson, L.J., in *Bremer Handelsgesellschaft m.b.H.* v. *Westzucker G.m.b.H.*[85]:

> "Yet another feature of the old special case procedure which made for delay was the form of the award. This was necessarily stylized, being divided into four parts—preamble, findings of fact, submissions of the parties and conclusions. It was not something which most arbitrators felt that they could draft without professional assistance and those who provided such assistance had other clients and commitments to consider. This produced still further delay.

---

82. Supreme Court Act 1981, section 148(2).
83. *F.G. Whitley & Sons Co. Ltd.* v. *Clwyd County Council. (The Times*, 6th August 1982).
83a. (19th November 1982) 87 LMLN.
84. See lectures by Donaldson, L.J., at Arbitration, Vol. 45, No. 3, p. 147 and by Lloyd, J., at Arbitration, Vol. 47, No. 1, p. 55.
85. [1981] 2 Lloyd's Rep. 130, at pp. 132–133.

"It is of the greatest importance that trade arbitrators working under the 1979 Act should realize that their whole approach should now be different. At the end of the hearing they will be in a position to give a decision and the reasons for that decision. They should do so at the earliest possible moment. The parties will have made their submissions as to what actually happened and what is the result in terms of their respective rights and liabilities. All this will be fresh in the arbitrators' minds and there will be no need for further written submissions by the parties. No particular form of award is required. Certainly no one wants a formal 'Special Case'. All that is necessary is that the arbitrators should set out what, on their view of the evidence, did or did not happen and should explain succinctly why, in the light of what happened, they have reached their decision and what that decision is. This is all that is meant by a 'reasoned award'.

"For example, it may be convenient to begin by explaining briefly how the arbitration came about—'X sold to Y 200 tons of soyabean meal on the terms of GAFTA Contract 100 at US.$Z per ton c.i.f. Bremen. X claimed damages for non-delivery and we were appointed arbitrators'. The award could then briefly tell the factual story as the arbitrators saw it. Much would be common ground and would need no elaboration. But when the award comes to matters in controversy, it would be helpful if the arbitrators not only gave their view of what occurred, but also made it clear that they have considered any alternative version and have rejected it, e.g. 'The shippers claimed that they shipped 100 tons at the end of June. We are not satisfied that this is so', or as the case may be, 'We are satisfied that this was not the case'. The arbitrators should end with their conclusion as to the resulting rights and liabilities of the parties. There is nothing about this which is remotely technical, difficult or time consuming.

"It is sometimes said that this involves arbitrators in delivering judgments and that this is something which requires legal skills. This is something of a half truth. Much of the art of giving a judgment lies in telling a story logically, coherently and accurately. This is something which requires skill, but it is not a legal skill and it is not necessarily advanced by legal training. It is certainly a judicial skill, but arbitrators for this purpose are judges and will have no difficulty in acquiring it. Where a 1979 Act award differs from a judgment is in the fact that the arbitrators will not be expected to analyse the law and the authorities. It will be quite sufficient that they should explain how they reached their conclusion, e.g., 'We regarded the conduct of the buyers, as we have described it, as constituting a repudiation of their obligations under the contract and the subsequent conduct of the sellers, also as described, as amounting to an acceptance of that repudiatory conduct putting an end to the contract'. It can be left to others to argue that this is wrong in law and to a professional judge, if leave to appeal is given, to analyse the authorities. This is not to say that where arbitrators are content to set out their reasoning on questions of law in the same way as judges, this will be unwelcome to the Courts. Far from it. The point which I am seeking to make is that a reasoned award, in accordance with the 1979 Act, is wholly different from an award in the form of a special case. It is not technical, it is not difficult to draw and above all it is something which can and should be produced promptly and quickly at the conclusion of the hearing. That is the time when it is easiest to produce an award with all the issues in mind".

In *Hayn Roman & Co. S.A.* v. *Cominter (U.K.) Ltd.*[86] Goff, J., stated that:

"it is incumbent upon arbitrators, in giving their reasons, to explain on what basis they have rejected contentions that have been advanced before them. They are not being asked to go into great detail; they are simply being asked to deal with submissions which have been advanced before them because this is just the kind of matter which the parties, if their contentions are rejected, may wish to pursue on appeal".

The Arbitration Act 1979 makes special provision for cases where arbitrators do not give any reasons after having been asked to do so by one or other of the parties and for cases where, having given reasons, these are in insufficient detail to enable the Court to consider any question of law that may arise on the award should an appeal be brought.[87] There may be cases where it would be appropriate for an application for leave to be adjourned until the Court has before it the arbitrator's reasons or further reasons.[88]

Section 1 of the Arbitration Act 1979 provides:

"(5) Subject to subsection (6) below, if an award is made and, on an application made by any of the parties to the reference,—
      (a) with the consent of all the other parties to the reference, or
      (b) subject to section 3 below,[89] with the leave of the Court,
it appears to the High Court that the award does not or does not sufficiently set out the reasons for the award, the Court may order the arbitrator or umpire concerned to state the reasons for his award in sufficient detail[90] to enable the Court, should an appeal be brought under this section, to consider any question of law arising out of the award.

      "(6) In any case where an award is made without any reason being given,[91] the High Court shall not make an order under subsection (5) above unless it is satisfied—

---

86. [1982] 2 Lloyd's Rep. 458, at p. 464.

87. For examples of the exercise of the power to order further reasons under section 1(5) see: *Italmare Shipping Co.* v. *Tropwood A.G.* [1982] 2 Lloyd's Rep. 441; *Stinnes Interoil* v. *A. Halcoussis & Co.* [1982] 2 Lloyd's Rep. 445; *Hayn Roman & Co. S.A.* v. *Cominter (U.K.) Ltd.* [1982] 2 Lloyd's Rep. 458; *Vermala Shipping Enterprises Ltd.* v. *The Minerals and Metals Trading Corporation of India* [1982] 1 Lloyd's Rep. 469.

88. *Vermala Shipping Enterprises Ltd.* v. *The Minerals and Metals Trading Corporation of India*, *supra*.

89. Section 3 provides that if the parties to the reference have entered into an exclusion agreement which excludes the right of appeal in relation to that award the High Court shall not grant leave to make an application for reasons for such award.

90. If, on an application for leave to appeal, the arbitrators' reasoning in the award is too obscure for the judge to take a view on the application, the Court may of its own motion remit the award for clarification: *Kaffeehandelsgesellschaft K.G.* v. *Plagefim Commercial S.A.* [1981] 2 Lloyd's Rep. 190.

91. It appears that where some reasons are given but they are insufficiently explicit it is unnecessary to satisfy the Court of the subsection (6) matters in order to apply for an order under subsection (5).

(a) that before the award was made one of the parties to the reference gave notice to the arbitrator or umpire concerned that a reasoned award would be required; or

(b) that there is some special reason why such a notice was not given".

Application by originating summons

Applications for leave to apply for reasons and applications for reasons must be made to a commercial judge, unless he otherwise orders.[92] Such applications must be made by originating summons in the form set out in Appendix A No. 10 of the Supreme Court Practice 1982 unless there is a pending action on foot when the applications are to be made by summons in the action.[93] A precedent of an originating summons is set out at page 163 below. In cases where it is relevant to the determination of the application for the Court to know what questions of law were argued before the arbitrators, it may be necessary for the applicant to provide a brief affidavit stating what questions of law were argued in the arbitration and such an affidavit will be necessary if evidence as to what was submitted at the arbitration is in the form of documents.[93a] The summons must be served both on the arbitrator or umpire and on any other party to the reference.[94] The application must be made and the summons served within 21 days after the award has been made and published to the parties.[95] Application for an extension of time can be made before or after time has expired[96] and this may well be necessary where one or more parties to the arbitration are not within the jurisdiction of the English Courts, as is frequently the position and have not instructed London solicitors to accept service. In such cases it will be necessary for the party making the application for leave to apply for an order for reasons to apply for leave to serve the summons outside the jurisdiction.[97] The summons must state the grounds upon which the application for leave and for an order for reasons is made and where the application is founded on evidence by affidavit a copy of the affidavit must be

---

92. RSC Order 73, rules 3(2) and 6. For a discussion of the circumstances in which a commercial judge might order that such an application should be heard outside the Commercial Court by a High Court judge see p. 122 above.

93. RSC Order 73, rule 3(3).

93a. *Vermala Shipping Enterprises Ltd.* v. *The Minerals and Metals Corporation of India Ltd. (The Gay Fidelity)* [1982] 1 Lloyd's Rep. 469, at pp. 470–1.

94. RSC Order 73, rule 3(4).

95. RSC Order 73, rule 5(1).

96. RSC Order 3, rule 5.

97. Application for leave should be made *ex parte* to the commercial judge under RSC Order 73, rule 6. On such an application an affidavit must be produced stating the grounds on which the application is made, in particular stating that the arbitration to which the application relates is governed by English Law or has been held within the jurisdiction of the English Courts. The procedure is otherwise substantially the same as that for *ex parte* applications under RSC Order 11, rule 1.

served with the summons.[98] If the arbitrator or umpire or the other party consents to the application for reasons a copy of the consent in writing must be served with the summons.[98]

Appeals to the Court of Appeal

No appeal lies to the Court of Appeal from a decision of the High Court to grant or refuse leave to make an application under subsection 5(6) or to make or refuse to make an order for reasons under that subsection unless the High Court gives leave.[99]

Preliminary points of law—the consultative case

Under section 21(1) of the Arbitration Act 1950 it was provided that an arbitrator or umpire might state in the form of a special case for the decision of the High Court any question of law arising in the course of the reference. The Court had a discretion to order an arbitrator or umpire to state such a special case if he declined to do so at the request of one or other of the parties. This procedure, which is not frequently used, is still available where the arbitration is not one to which the Arbitration Act 1979 applies.[100] Applications to the Court for orders requiring arbitrators to state a special case on a preliminary question of law are very rare indeed but, if necessary, can be made in the same manner as the application for an order that the arbitrator should state his award in the form of a special case for the opinion of the Court, namely by originating summons.[101]

Section 2 of the Arbitration Act 1979

For arbitrations to which the Arbitration Act 1979 applies[100] the old consultative case procedure has been abolished and replaced by a procedure more consonant with the system of judicial review of awards described above.[102] Section 2 of the 1979 Act gives the Court jurisdiction, unless the parties to the arbitration have entered into a valid exclusion agreement as defined by section 3 of the Act, to determine any question of law arising in the course of the reference provided that *either*

> **(a)** consent has been given by the arbitrator or umpire who has entered on the reference *or*
> **(b)** all the parties to the arbitration have consented.[103]

---

98. RSC Order 73, rule 5(5).
99. The Supreme Court Act 1981, section 148(2), has amended the Arbitration Act 1979 by adding to section 1 a further subsection (6A) to this effect.
100. See, for the application of the 1979 Act, fn. 44, p. 131 above.
101. RSC Order 73, rule 3 in the form in force up to 1st August 1979: see *Compania Maritima Zorroza S.A.* v. *Maritime Bulk Carriers Corporation* [1980] 2 Lloyd's Rep. 186. For the special case procedure, see p. 124 above.
102. Page 130.
103. Section 2(1).

The Court's discretion

If these conditions are satisfied the Court then has a discretion whether to entertain an application to determine the preliminary point of law. Before acceding to such an application the Court must be satisfied of two matters, namely:

(a) that the determination of the application might produce substantial savings in costs to the parties *and*

(b) that the question of law is one in respect of which leave to appeal would be likely to be given if the question of law were raised on application for leave to appeal against a reasoned award under section 1(3)(b) of the Act.[104]

It was held by Parker, J., in *Gebr. Broere B.V. v. Saras Chimica S.p.A.*[104a] that where all parties to the arbitration consent to the determination of a question of law section 2 (2) has no application and the Court does not have to exercise its discretion in respect of (a) or (b) above.

It is to be observed that the Arbitration Act 1979 makes no provision for the arbitrator or umpire to provide the Court with any findings of fact for the purpose of enabling the Court to evaluate the materiality of the question of law to the matters in dispute or to satisfy itself of requirements (a) and (b) above. The commercial judges will probably have to work out some procedural machinery for dealing with this problem if and when it arises. In cases where the question of law arises out of particularly complex facts it may be appropriate for the arbitrator or umpire to make an interim award in respect of the relevant facts under section 14 of the Arbitration Act 1950. Nevertheless, the onus of putting before the judge agreed or at least undisputed facts relevant to the exercise of his discretion under section 2(2) must lie on the party or parties requesting that he should accede to the application.

Application by originating motion

All applications for the determination of a preliminary point of law must be made by originating motion to a commercial judge in Court who will hear the application even if the arbitration from which the application arises is not of a commercial character.[105] A precedent is set out at page 161 below. The motion

---

104. Section 2(2). For the principles upon which the judge should exercise his discretion in deciding whether to give leave to appeal under section 1(3)(b) of the 1979 Act, see p. 135 above and *Pioneer Shipping Ltd.* v. *B.T.P. Tioxide* (*The Nema*) [1981] 2 Lloyd's Rep. 239.

104a. *The Times*, 27th July 1982.

105. RSC Order 73, rule 2(1). This is in accordance with the judgment of the Court of Appeal in *F. G. Whitley & Sons Co. Ltd.* v. *Clwyd C.C.* (*The Times*, 6th August 1982) and alters the previous practice.

must be set down in the Arbitration Case List[106] at the Crown Office, Room 458, with the return date left blank or with a nominal return date inserted. The Crown Office then transmits the motion to the Commercial Court Office, Room 244A, Royal Courts of Justice, and a date for hearing can then be arranged by liaison with the Commercial Court Listing Officer[107] and counsels' clerks. Where necessary, the preliminary application for leave that a preliminary point should be determined should be included in a summons to fix a date for hearing of argument on the main application and no date will be fixed for such hearing unless and until the Court is satisfied that the requirements of section 2(2) are fulfilled.[107a] If leave for the determination of a question of law is given, the commercial judge will then consider whether, having regard to RSC Order 73, rule 6, the hearing of the preliminary point of law should take place in the Commercial Court or before a Queen's Bench judge outside the Commercial Court.[108] If the hearing is to take place in the Commercial Court the solicitors should liaise with the Commercial Court Listing Officer and counsels' clerks so that a date for hearing can be fixed. The hearing of the preliminary point of law takes place in open Court.

The application must be made and notice of it served within 14 days after the arbitrator or umpire has given his consent to the application being made or after the other parties have given their consent.[109]

The notice of originating motion must be served at least two clear days before the date fixed for the hearing of the motion.[110] It must state the grounds for the application and if evidence is to be relied on it must be put on affidavit and served with the notice. So also must copies of the consent of the arbitrator or umpire or the other parties if given in writing.[111] If the other parties to the arbitration do not consent to the application to the Court to determine a preliminary point of law it may be necessary to obtain leave to serve notice of originating motion outside the jurisdiction of the English Courts. For this purpose application must be made *ex parte* to the commercial judge,[112] supported by an affidavit stating the grounds on which application is made, in particular that the arbitration is governed by English Law or is being held within the jurisdiction, also in what place or country the other party or parties are or probably may be

---

106. Directions for London, 31st July 1981, [1981] 1 W.L.R. 1296.
107. Telephone No. 01-405 7641, Ext. 3826; Telex 296983 COMM-G.
107a. *Gebr. Broere B.V.* v. *Saras Chimica S.p.A.* (*The Times*, 27th July 1982.)
108. For a discussion of the way in which the commercial judges may apply RSC Order 73, rule 6, see p. 122 above.
109. RSC Order 73, rule 5(3). The Court has a discretion to extend time upon application before or after the period has expired: RSC Order 3, rule 5.
110. RSC Order 8, rule 2(2).
111. RSC Order 73, rule 5(5).
112. RSC Order 73, rule 7.

found. Otherwise the procedure is the same as for applications under RSC Order 11, rule 1.[112]

Appeals to the Court of Appeal

Appeals against the judge's decision to entertain or not to entertain applications for a preliminary point of law lie to the Court of Appeal, but only if the judge gives leave to appeal.[113]

A decision of the Court on a preliminary point of law under section 2(1) can be appealed to the Court of Appeal but only if two preconditions are satisfied:

> (1) the High Court or the Court of Appeal gives leave *and*
> (2) it is certified by the High Court that the question of law to which its decision relates *either* is one of general public importance *or* is one which for some other special reason should be considered by the Court of Appeal.[114]

The principles to be applied by the Court of Appeal in deciding whether to grant leave to appeal were recently considered in *Babanaft International Co. S.A. v. Avant Petroleum Inc.*[115] The Court of Appeal ought to consider the judgment under appeal and ask similar questions to those which the House of Lords in *Pioneer Shipping Ltd. v. B.T.P. Tioxide Ltd.*[116] had ruled should be asked by the judges in deciding whether to grant leave to appeal against an award. Leave to appeal is less readily given under section 2 than under section 1 because section 2 has the purpose of enabling the parties to interrupt the arbitration to get a decision of the Court and if it were used to obtain definitive decisions of the Court of Appeal or the House of Lords that would create unacceptable interruptions in the conduct of arbitrations, but there may be cases where the preliminary question of law, if rightly decided, determines the whole dispute between the parties and in such a case leave to appeal should be no less readily given than if it were an application for leave under section 1.

Extension of arbitrators' powers under the Arbitration Act 1979

A serious defect in the powers of arbitrators was their lack of power to enforce prompt compliance with their interlocutory orders and their lack of power to strike out claims for want of prosecution.[117] One consequence was that those who

---

112. RSC Order 73, rule 7.
113. Arbitration Act 1950, section 2A, introduced by the Supreme Court Act 1981, section 148(3).
114. Arbitration Act 1979, section 2(3).
115. [1982] 2 Lloyd's Rep. 99.
116. [1981] 2 Lloyd's Rep. 239.
117. See *Bremer Vulkan Schiffbau und Maschinenfabrik v. South India Shipping Corporation Ltd.* [1981] A.C. 909.

set out to avoid satisfying their contractual liabilities for as long as possible had ample opportunity for doing so. The arbitrators could do very little in practice to avoid this abuse. This defect seriously weakened the attraction of London as an international arbitration centre. Section 5 of the Arbitration Act 1979 is an attempt to remedy this aspect of the law.

Its effect is as follows. If there has been a failure by any party to the reference to comply with an order made by an arbitrator or umpire within the time specified in the order or, if no time is specified, within a reasonable time, the arbitrator or umpire or any party to the reference can apply to the High Court to make and the Court can make an order extending the powers of the arbitrator or umpire in the following respects: "the arbitrator or umpire shall have power, to the extent and subject to any conditions specified in that order, to continue with the reference in default of appearance or of any other act by one of the parties in like manner as a judge of the High Court might continue with proceedings in that Court where a party fails to comply with an order of that Court or a requirement of the rules of Court."[118]

The importance of this provision is that it enables the Court, on the application of the arbitrator or umpire, to clothe the latter with the power which a High Court judge would have, were he trying the arbitration as an action in Court, to make peremptory orders to enforce compliance with the interlocutory timetable and rules of Court.

> "Thus the Court may order that if the claimant does not deliver his points of claim within a specified time, the claim will be dismissed. And a respondent may be told that in default of delivering a defence, he will be debarred from defending and the claimant will be free to prove his claim without opposition. Similarly, default in complying with orders for discovery may lead to orders that the claim or part of it be dismissed or the defence or part of it be struck out".[119]

It is not open to the parties to the reference effectively to contract out of this power.[120]

Application for an extension of the powers of an arbitrator or umpire must be made by an originating summons in Form No. 10 in Appendix A of the Rules of the Supreme Court or, in the unlikely event that an action is pending, by a summons in the action.[121] A precedent of an originating summons is set out at page 165 below. Order 72 makes no provision as to the parties to be served with

---

118. Section 5 of the Arbitration Act 1979.
119. *Per* Donaldson, L.J., an address to the Chartered Institute of Arbitrators, 22nd August 1979, Abritration, Vol. 45, No. 3, p. 147.
120. Section 5(5) of the 1979 Act.
121. RSC Order 73, rule 3. For the appropriate form see p. 165 below.

the summons, but in most cases, it is suggested, it would be appropriate for all parties to the arbitration to be served, including the arbitrator or umpire where the summons is issued by one of the parties. Where the summons is taken out by the arbitrator or umpire himself all the other parties to the arbitration probably ought to be served or at least given notice of the summons. The application must be made to a commercial judge and heard by him unless he otherwise orders.[122] If any of the parties to be served are outside the jurisdiction and have not appointed solicitors with instructions to accept service within the jurisdiction it will be necessary to apply for leave to serve the originating summons outside the jurisdiction. Application should be made to the commercial judge *ex parte*.[123] It should be accompanied by an affidavit stating the grounds on which the application is made, in particular showing in what place or country the person to be served is or may probably be found, that the arbitration in question is governed by English Law or has been, is being, or is to be held within the jurisdiction of the English Courts.

Commercial judges as arbitrators

Since the coming into force of the Administration of Justice Act 1970 commercial judges have been empowered to accept appointments as sole arbitrators or as umpires in commercial arbitrations. This important and convenient change in the law was introduced as a result of the recommendations set out in the Report of the Commercial Court Users' Conference 1962.[124] The Report recognised that many foreign trading organisations preferred to refer their disputes to arbitration, rather than to litigation, that the commercial community had an "inherent dislike of publicity and especially of the system of oral examination and cross-examination", and that in many countries it was considerably more difficult to enforce a *judgment* of the Commercial Court than to enforce an arbitral award by reason of the Geneva Convention on the Execution of Foreign Arbitral Awards, 1927, which provides for the reciprocal enforcement of awards, having been signed by many more States than allowed enforcement within their territory of *judgments* of the English Courts. It therefore recommended that the commercial judges should have power to sit in private as an arbitrator in appropriate cases.

Section 4(1) of the Administration of Justice Act 1970 provides:

> "A judge of the Commercial Court may, if in all the circumstances he thinks fit, accept appointment as sole arbitrator, or as umpire, by or by virtue of an

---

122. RSC Order 73, rules 3(2) and 6. For a discussion as to the circumstances when it would be appropriate for a commercial judge to decline to hear an application and to adjourn the summons to a High Court judge outside the Commercial Court, see p. 122 above.

123. RSC Order 73, rule 7.

124. Cmnd. 1616, p. 19.

arbitration agreement within the meaning of the Arbitration Act 1950, where the dispute appears to him to be of a commercial character".

There are three matters which have to be satisfied before a commercial judge can accept an appointment to sit as an arbitrator or umpire.

(1) The dispute must appear to him to be of a commercial character. In effect, this means that appointments will not be accepted in relation to disputes of a kind which would not have a sufficiently commercial flavour to admit of their being tried in an action in the Commercial Court.[125]

(2) The commercial judge must "in all the circumstances" think that it is fit that he should accept the appointment. This gives the judge a wide discretion to pick and choose for there are certain types of dispute which would not be appropriate for judicial arbitration, such as run-of-the-mill damage to cargo disputes, or disputes as to time-charter hire statements or disputes which substantially turn on complex issues of fact but do not involve considerable amounts of money. It has become the practice to appoint judicial arbitrators in relation to disputes which raise undecided questions of commercial law or which involve exceptionally large sums in issue or which raise issues of fact or law, the decision as to which is likely to be accepted in a particular market, such as the recent judicial arbitration relating to the application of marine war risks policies to the vessels trapped in the Shatt-al-Arab as a result of the Iran-Iraq war.[126] It is, however, impossible and inappropriate to define where the line should be drawn between what will and what will not be a dispute suitable for judicial arbitration.

(3) The judge is not permitted to accept appointment as sole arbitrator or umpire unless the Lord Chief Justice has informed him that, having regard to the state of business in the High Court and in the Crown Court, he can be made available to do so.[127] This provision is in order to ensure that the commercial judges' time does not become unduly pre-committed to commercial arbitrations. Although the number of appointments of judge-arbitrators has been growing since 1970 it has not yet reached the point where appointments are making significantly large inroads into the time of the commercial judges.[128]

---

125. See p. 23 above for a discussion as to what disputes are commercial and RSC Order 72, rule 1.
126. *The Bamburi* [1982] 1 Lloyd's Rep. 312.
127. Administration of Justice Act 1970, section 4(2),
128. For a discussion of the small extent to which the facility of judicial arbitration has been used, see p. 13 above.

Judge-arbitrators or umpires are not subject to supervisory control by the High Court as are other arbitrators. Control and supervision by the Court of Appeal is substituted for that of the High Court under the Arbitration Act 1950 in several important respects by Schedule 3 to the 1970 Act,[129] although some of the supervisory powers are not exercisable at all in relation to judge-arbitrators. Schedule 3 has been amended by the Arbitration Act 1979[130] to exclude provisions dealing with cases stated by judge-arbitrators under section 21 of the Arbitration Act 1950 which was repealed by the 1979 Act.

The principal provisions of Schedule 3 in respect of judge-arbitrators and umpires are as follows. The Court of Appeal in substitution for the High Court is given certain supervisory powers:

> **(1)** Under section 1 of the 1950 Act leave must be obtained from the Court of Appeal for the revocation of authority of a judge-arbitrator or umpire.[131]
>
> **(2)** Applications for remission of a judge-arbitrator's or umpire's award under section 22 of the Arbitration Act 1950 must be made to the Court of Appeal.[132]
>
> **(3)** Applications for the removal of a judge-arbitrator or umpire (a fairly rare procedure) and for the setting aside of an award for misconduct under section 23 of the Arbitration Act 1950 must be made to the Court of Appeal.[132]

Certain other powers of the High Court are to be exercised by the judge-arbitrator or judge-umpire himself:

> **(1)** In place of section 8(3) of the Arbitration Act 1950 whereby the High Court is given power to order an umpire to enter immediately on the reference as sole arbitrator, a judge-umpire is given power, on the application if any party to the reference and notwithstanding terms to the contrary in the arbitration agreement, to enter on the reference in place of the arbitrators as if he were sole arbitrator.[133]
>
> **(2)** The judge-arbitrator or judge-umpire himself is to make any orders under section 12(4), (5) and (6) of the 1950 Act which relate to orders for writs of subpoena in respect of witnesses and documents and to the making of interlocutory orders as to security for costs,

---

129. Section 4(4) and (5). See p. 185 below.
130. Section 8(3)(c). Whether these provisions have survived the repeal, in so far as concerns arbitrations to which the 1979 Act does *not* apply, remains a matter of doubt.
131. Schedule 3, para. 2.
132. Schedule 3, para. 9(1).
133. Schedule 3, para. 4.

discovery of documents, interrogatories, giving of evidence by affidavit, the taking of evidence on commission, the preservation, interim custody or sale of any goods which are the subject-matter of the reference, the giving of security for the amount in dispute in the reference, the detention, preservation or inspection of any property or thing which is the subject of the reference or as to which any question may arise in the reference, authorising for such purposes the entry on to one of the party's premises, authorising the taking of samples, making of observations or experiments and interim injunctions, such as *Mareva* injunctions, and appointments of receivers.[134] Orders made on these matters are treated as made by the judge-arbitrator or umpire in his capacity as a judge of the High Court.[134]

(3) The provisions of section 13(2) and (3) of the 1950 Act in relation to time for making the award and the removal of arbitrators who are slow in conducting the reference do not apply to a judge-arbitrator or umpire but he is given power to enlarge any time limit for the making of an award.[135]

(4) The judge-arbitrator or umpire has power to make declarations and orders in relation to charging orders for solicitors' costs under section 18(5) of the 1950 Act,[136] but any such orders shall be treated as having been made in his capacity as a High Court judge.[137]

(5) The power of the High Court under section 24(2) of the 1950 Act to order the removal of an issue involving allegations of fraud into the High Court does not apply to an agreement under which a judge-arbitrator or umpire has been appointed, but where an allegation of fraud is made against one of the parties to the dispute the judge-arbitrator or umpire may "so far as may be necessary to enable that question to be determined by the High Court order that the agreement by or by virtue of which he was appointed shall cease to have effect and revoke his own authority as arbitrator or umpire".[138] Any such order has the effect of an order of the High Court.

(6) The judge-arbitrator or umpire is empowered to give leave under section 26 of the 1950 Act for the enforcement of his own awards.[139]

---

134. Schedule 3, para. 5(1) and (2).
135. Schedule 3, para. 6.
136. Schedule 3, para. 7(2).
137. Schedule 3, para. 7(3).
138. Schedule 3, para. 10(2).
139. Schedule 3, para. 12.

(7) Applications under section 5 of the Arbitration Act 1979 for the extension of the arbitrator's powers to deal with non-compliance with the interlocutory timetable or with failure to prosecute the claim or to appear to defend it cannot be made and indeed need not be made in the case of a judge-arbitrator or umpire. He himself, in his capacity as a High Court judge, can exercise that power by giving himself such powers as a High Court judge would have to deal with delay in the course of an action in court.[140]

Further special provisions applicable to judge-arbitrators and umpires will be found in Schedule 3 to the Administration of Justice Act 1970, reprinted at the end of this book.[141]

The jurisdiction exercisable by the High Court in relation to arbitrators and umpires *otherwise than* under the Arbitration Act 1950 is to be exercisable in relation to judge-arbitrators and umpires by the Court of Appeal.[142] Consequently the Court of Appeal is given jurisdiction in relation to all those matters which under the Arbitration Act 1979 must be referred to the High Court with the exception of applications to extend the powers of arbitrators under section 5.[143] Therefore, for example, the application for leave to appeal against a judge-arbitrator's award under section 1(3) must be made to the Court of Appeal which presumably must for this purpose apply the same principles as a judge would apply if he were considering an application, as indicated in *Pioneer Shipping Ltd. v. B.T.P. Tioxide (The Nema)*,[144] although the fact that the award is that of a judge-arbitrator or umpire will no doubt be regarded as a factor to be weighed in the exercise of the discretion by the Court of Appeal. Applications for reasons for an award and for a hearing of a preliminary point of law would also have to be made to the Court of Appeal in the unlikely event that they became necessary.[145]

Those who wish to appoint a judge-arbitrator or umpire should write a letter to the particular commercial judge through his own clerk, briefly describing the nature of the issues in dispute and setting out any matters relevant to the judge's decision whether to accept the appointment.[146] If the judge decides that it would be appropriate for him to accept the appointment, before doing so he must apply for the consent of the Lord Chief Justice under section 4(2) of the Administration

---

140. Arbitration Act 1979, section 5(3) and (4).
141. At p. 185 below.
142. Administration of Justice Act 1970, section 4(5).
143. See above and Arbitration Act 1979, section 5(3) and (4).
144. [1981] 2 Lloyd's Rep. 239. See p. 147 above.
145. Arbitration Act 1979, section 1(5) and section 2(2).
146. See p. 150 above. It is convenient where the appointment is as sole arbitrator for both parties through their solicitors to send a joint letter on the lines suggested.

of Justice Act 1970.[147] When this has been given he will inform the parties of his willingness to accept the appointment. In the event of the parties wishing to bring on for hearing a judicial arbitration with great urgency or at a particular date they should, instead of approaching one of the commercial judges, consult the Commercial Court Listing Officer at the Commercial Court Office, Room 198, Royal Courts of Justice, and he will be able to say which of the commercial judges might be available to accept the appointment.

Dates for the hearing of arbitrations by judge-arbitrators or umpires must be arranged through the Commercial Court Listing Officer. The allocation of dates for the hearing depends on the availability of judge-time in the Commercial List, the policy being that hearings of arbitrations normally have to take their turn in the List with the actions in Court.

The fees payable for the services of a judge as arbitrator or umpire are to be taken in the High Court[148] and are not paid to the judge. The fees presently fixed are at the rate of £500 on appointment, which is refunded in full if the arbitration does not proceed, and £500 for every day or part thereof after the first day.[149] There is no fee for the time taken in writing the award and in this respect the services of judge-arbitrators are certainly cheaper than commercial or other legal arbitrators.

---

147. See p. 150 above.
148. Administration of Justice Act 1970, section 4(3).
149. Supreme Court Fees Order 1980, S.I. 1980, No. 821, para. 5(2) and Schedule, section I, para. 25.

ARBITRATION DOCUMENTS

(1) Originating Motion for Leave to Appeal[1] and for the Appeal

IN THE HIGH COURT OF JUSTICE   19   B No.
QUEEN'S BENCH DIVISION
COMMERCIAL COURT
IN THE MATTER OF THE ARBITRATION ACTS 1950 TO 1979
AND
IN THE MATTER OF AN ARBITRATION

BETWEEN:

BLACK SHIPPING COMPANY LIMITED
Applicants
Owners

–and–

BROWN SUGAR COMPANY LIMITED
Respondents
Charterers

NOTICE OF ORIGINATING
MOTION AND OF APPEAL

TAKE NOTICE that the High Court of Justice Queen's Bench Division Commercial Court at the Royal Courts of Justice, Strand, London, WC2A 2LL, will be moved on the expiration of——clear days after the service of this notice or as soon thereafter as Counsel can be heard, by Counsel on behalf of the above

---

1. Application for leave to appeal and for the appeal itself under section 1(2) of the Arbitration Act 1979 must be made by originating motion and may be included in one application, see RSC Order 73, rule 2(2). As a matter of practice, however, it is not likely that if the Court grants leave it will go on to consider the substantive appeal in the same hearing. See *Tor Line A.B.* v. *Alltrans Group of Canada Limited, The TFL Prosperity* [1982] 1 Lloyd's Rep. 617, 626–627. The form of the originating motion must be in accordance with that set out in The Supreme Court Practice, Vol. 2, Appendix A, Form No. 13 (see Order 8, rule 3). See, generally, p. 132 above.

named Applicants (hereinafter referred to as "Owners") for an Order that Owners have leave to appeal to the High Court on the questions of law arising out of an Award dated 3rd September 1981 made by Frederick Ackroyd Haphazard as a sole Arbitrator in an arbitration between the Owners and the Respondents (hereinafter referred to as "Charterers") namely (I) whether on the facts found the Charterparty between the Owners and the Charterers dated November 24th, 1978 terminated at midnight on February 21st, 1979 by reason of the Charterers' repudiation thereof.
(II) Whether the Owners were obliged to accept the Charterers' repudiation of the said contract if the Charterers established that the Owners had "no legitimate interest" in keeping the contract in existence and
(III) if the answer to (I) is "yes", whether on the facts found the Owners had "no legitimate interest" in keeping the contract in existence.

AND if leave be granted, for an Order varying the said Award as hereinafter appears, alternatively remitting the Award to the said Arbitrator together with the Court's opinion on the said question of law.

AND for an order that the costs of and incidental to this application and appeal be paid by the Charterers.

AND FURTHER TAKE NOTICE that the grounds of this application[2] and appeal are as follows:—
(1) That the determination of the said questions of law would substantially affect the rights of the Owners and the Charterers.

(2) That the determination of the said questions of law is of general importance to the Owners and Charterers of all vessels which we chartered under Charterparties governed by English law in circumstances where either party repudiates or renounces the Charterparty.

(3) That the question (II) raises a question of general importance in English contract law, namely whether an innocent party is obliged to accept the repudiation by the guilty party of a contract in circumstances where the innocent party has "no legitimate interest" in keeping the contract alive.

---

2. It may be doubtful whether Order 73, rule 2(2) (or Order 8, rule 3) actually requires the inclusion of a statement of the ground for the application for leave to appeal (see *The TFL Prosperity (supra)* at p. 626) but as a matter of practice it is often done.

(4) That the said question (III) also raises questions of law of general importance, namely in the event that an innocent party is obliged to accept a repudiation if he has "no legitimate interest" as aforesaid, the matters which are relevant in determining whether such an interest exists.

(5) That on the facts found and as a matter of law the conclusions of the Arbitrator (as set out in the Award) are clearly wrong and/or are such that could not have been reached by a reasonable Arbitrator.

(6) That the Arbitrator having held that the Charterers repudiated the Charterparty by intimating their intention not to pay any further hire for the vessel erred in law in some or all of the following respects.

> (i) In concluding that the Charterers were entitled to a declaration that the Charterparty terminated automatically by reason of their own repudiation thereof.

> (ii) In holding that the Owners should have accepted the Charterers' repudiation by midnight on February 21st, 1979.

> (iii) In failing to apply the principles of law, established by the *ratio decidendi* of *White and Carter (Councils) Limited* v. *McGregor* [1962] A.C. 413, that an injured party is entitled to elect whether or not to accept repudiation by the other party or hold him to the contract.

> (iv) In failing to apply the principle of law that an unaccepted repudiation/remuneration of a contract is a "thing writ in water".

> (v) In holding that, notwithstanding that the Owners had no obligation to accept the Charterers' repudiation in February, 1979, the Owners had no legitimate interest in pursuing their claim for hire rather than a claim for damages.

> (vi) Having held that the vessel remained at Charterers' disposal at an anchorage off London until the expiry of the time charter period on 31st December 1979, in failing to hold that the Owners were entitled to a declaration that the Charterparty remained in force and that the vessel was on hire until the said date.

(7) That, in the premises, the Arbitrator should not have awarded the Charterers the declaration referred to in (6)(i) herein and their costs of the arbitration, but should have awarded the Owners:

> (i) $1,000,000, this being the unpaid hire due 1st February–31st December 1979

> (ii) Interest on the above sum at a rate of 17% per annum,

and the Arbitrator should have further ordered that the Charterers bear and pay their own and the Owners' costs of the arbitration and the costs of the Award.

DATED the   day of   19

(2) Originating Motion for Setting Aside or Remission of an Award for Misconduct[3]

IN THE HIGH COURT OF JUSTICE   19   B No.
QUEEN'S BENCH DIVISION
COMMERCIAL COURT
IN THE MATTER OF THE ARBITRATION ACTS 1950 TO 1979
AND
IN THE MATTER OF AN ARBITRATION

BETWEEN:

BLACK SHIPPING COMPANY LIMITED
Applicants
Owners

–and–

BROWN SUGAR COMPANY LIMITED
Respondents
Charterers

NOTICE OF ORIGINATING
MOTION AND OF APPEAL

TAKE NOTICE that the High Court of Justice Queen's Bench Division Commercial Court at the Royal Courts of Justice, Strand, London, WC2A 2LL, will be moved on the expiration of——clear days after the service of this notice or as soon thereafter as Counsel can be heard, by Counsel on behalf of the above named Applicants for an Order pursuant to s.22 and s.23(2) of the Arbitration Act 1950 that the arbitration award of Frederick Ackroyd Haphazard dated 20th January 1981, whereby it was awarded and adjudged that the Applicants should pay the Respondents the sum of £70,000 plus interest and costs be set aside or alternatively remitted to the said arbitrator.

AND THAT the costs of and incidental to this application be paid by the Respondent

---

3. The form prescribed by Order 73, rule 2(1)(a) and (c) and Order 73, rule 3 (the actual form being set out in The Supreme Court Practice, Vol. 2, Appendix A, Form No. 13. If the facts allegedly constituting misconduct are not agreed between the parties as having happened, then the applicant should also provide the Court with an affidavit briefly stating the facts relied upon.

AND FURTHER TAKE NOTICE that the grounds for this application are as follows:

That the arbitrator misconducted himself in that, by reason only of the Applicants' failure to serve a Points of Defence within a year from the date of service of the Points of Claim, he made the said Award without hearing any argument on the merits of the case, but merely at the Respondents' request, notwithstanding that no order, final or otherwise in relation to the service of the Points of Defence had been asked for at any time by the Respondents or made by the arbitrator.

DATED the   day of

(3) Originating Motion for the decision of a Preliminary Point of Law[4]

IN THE HIGH COURT OF JUSTICE   19   B No.
QUEEN'S BENCH DIVISION
COMMERCIAL COURT
IN THE MATTER OF THE ARBITRATION ACTS 1950 TO 1979
AND
IN THE MATTER OF AN ARBITRATION

BETWEEN:

BLACK SHIPPING COMPANY LIMITED
Applicants
Owners

–and–

BROWN SUGAR COMPANY LIMITED
Respondents
Charterers

NOTICE OF ORIGINATING
MOTION AND OF APPEAL

TAKE NOTICE that the High Court of Justice Queen's Bench Division Commercial Court at the Royal Courts of Justice, Strand, London, WC2A 2LL, will be moved on the expiration of——clear days after the service of this notice or as soon thereafter as Counsel can be heard, by Counsel on behalf of the above named Applicants for the determination by the High Court pursuant to s.2(1)(a)[5] of the Arbitration Act 1979 of the following question of law which has arisen in the course of an arbitration between the Applicants and the Respondents before Frederick Ackroyd Haphazard, namely:

Whether an agent acting within his actual or ostensible authority, made a statement which was untrue in circumstances where he had no reasonable grounds to believe

---

4. The form prescribed by Order 73, rule 2(1)(e).
5. If the application is made with the consent of the arbitrator or umpire; section 2(1)(b) if it is made with the consent of all other parties.

that it was true, could be held liable for that statement under the Misrepresentation Act 1967 s.2(1)?[6]

AND for an Order that the Respondents pay the costs of and incidental to this application.

DATED the   date of   19

---

6. For a preliminary question of law asked for and answered by the Court in a non-arbitration case, see *Resolute Maritime Inc.* v. *Nippon Kaiji Kyokai, The Times,* 7th December 1982.

(4) Originating Summons for an Order Directing the Arbitrator to State Further Reasons[7]

IN THE HIGH COURT OF JUSTICE   19   B No.
QUEEN'S BENCH DIVISION
COMMERCIAL COURT
IN THE MATTER OF THE ARBITRATION ACTS 1950 TO 1979
AND
IN THE MATTER OF AN ARBITRATION

BETWEEN:

> BLACK SHIPPING COMPANY   *Plaintiff*
> LIMITED
> –and–

> BROWN SUGAR COMPANY   *First Defendants*
> LIMITED
> –and–

> FREDERICK ACKROYD   *Second Defendant*
> HAPHAZARD[8]

LET ALL PARTIES attend the Judge in the Commercial Court, Royal Courts of Justice, Strand, London, on   day the   day of   19   , at   o'clock in the forenoon, on the hearing of an application by the above named Plaintiff pursuant to s.1(5) of the Arbitration Act 1979 that the arbitrator should state further reasons for his holding that "the Owners had no legitimate interest in pursuing their claim for hire rather than a claim for damages" and that the said reasons should include:

(1) The reason why the owners did not have a "legitimate interest" in continuing the charterparty at midnight on 21st February 1979, and

---

7. The form prescribed by RSC Order 73, rule 3. In cases where it is relevant to the determination of the application for the Court to know what questions of law were argued before the arbitrator, it may be necessary for the applicant to provide a brief affidavit stating what questions of law were argued in the arbitration and such an affidavit will be necessary if evidence as to what was submitted in the arbitration is in the form of documents (see *Vermala Shipping Enterprises Ltd.* v. *The Minerals and Metals Corporation of India Ltd.* (*The Gay Fidelity*) [1982] 1 Lloyd's Rep. 469, 470–471 (Staughton, J.).
8. The arbitrator must be served with the summons under RSC Order 73, rule 3(4).

(2) The submissions advanced at the hearing on the question of the Owners' legitimate interest by (a) the Plaintiffs and (b) the First Defendants, indicating which submissions he rejected and which he accepted.

AND let the Defendant etc. . . .[9]

---

9. The formal parts of Form No. 10 in RSC Vol. 2, Appendix A, should follow.

(5) Originating Summons for an Order Extending the Powers of an Arbitrator[10]

IN THE HIGH COURT OF JUSTICE   19   B No.
QUEEN'S BENCH DIVISION
COMMERCIAL COURT
IN THE MATTER OF THE ARBITRATION ACTS 1950 TO 1979
AND
IN THE MATTER OF AN ARBITRATION

BETWEEN:

        BLACK SHIPPING COMPANY   *Plaintiff*
        LIMITED
        –and–

        BROWN SUGAR COMPANY   *First Defendants*
        LIMITED
        –and–

        FREDERICK ACKROYD   *Second Defendant*
        HAPHAZARD[8]

LET all parties attend the Judge in Commercial Court, Royal Courts of Justice, Strand, London on   day of the   day of   19   , at   o'clock in the forenoon, on the hearing of an application by the above named Plaintiff pursuant to s.5 of the Arbitration Act 1979 that the arbitrator shall have the power to continue with the reference in default of the appearance of the Defendant (the Respondent in the Arbitration).

AND let the Defendant . . . etc"[11]

---

10. The form prescribed by Order 73, rule 3(2).
11. See fn. 9 *supra*.

APPENDIX A

Mr. Justice Kerr

PRACTICE DIRECTION
as to Hearings in September

March 1977

As part of the present scheme to provide an extended service to the public during the month of September one of the judges of the Commercial Court will be available to hear commercial actions and summonses covered by R.S.C., O.72 throughout September 1977. Applications for hearings in September will be dealt with in the same manner as fixtures during term time. As at present, dates for actions and Special Cases will be fixed by the judge in charge of the Commercial List (on a "not before" basis) and dates for summonses by his clerk. The scheme will apply equally to proceedings issued in the Commercial Court and to proceedings transferred to the court. Summonses will generally be heard on Tuesdays and Fridays, but there will be flexibility. To obtain a date for a hearing in September it will not be necessary to establish that the matter is "Long Vacation Business" within R.S.C., O.64, r.4, but the judge in charge of the list will exercise a discretion whether or not to accept fixtures for September. In exercising this discretion preference will be given to urgent matters (including in particular commercial matters which would otherwise come before one of the vacation judges), Special Cases and short cases. In cases of urgency and if time permits, the scheme will also apply to the judge sitting as sole arbitrator or umpire in short arbitrations pursuant to s.4 of the Administration of Justice Act 1970.

Applications for dates for hearings in September can in principle be made at any time from now. In practice, however, September fixtures are unlikely to be granted before Easter, but then increasingly as the summer progresses. The reason is to maintain flexibility and to keep dates available for urgent matters nearer the time. But an exception will be made for Special and Consultative Cases stated by arbitration tribunals which are only expected to take one to two days and which cannot be fitted in before the end of July. These are ready for trial, rarely settle, and should in principle be dealt with as soon as possible.

APPENDIX B

DIRECTIONS FOR LONDON

Given by the Lord Chief Justice on July 31, 1981

All proceedings in the Queen's Bench Division for hearing in London shall be set down in the appropriate list and administered as follows:

1. The Crown Office List
(a) Proceedings required to be heard by or applications required to be made to a Divisional Court of the Queen's Bench Division;
(b) Proceedings pursuant to R.S.C., O.53, O.54 and O.56 which may be heard by a single Judge;
(c) Actions directed to be set down in the Crown Office List;
(d) Proceedings pursuant to R.S.C., O.55, O.94 and O.111;
(e) Save as is otherwise expressly provided, any other special case or case stated under any statute or order.

2. Administrative Provisions in respect of the Crown Office List
Without prejudice to any party's right to apply for directions to a Judge for the time being hearing matters in the Crown Office List and the right of the Master of the Crown Office to refer such a matter to a Judge, the Crown Office List shall be administered by the Crown Office under the direction of the Master of the Crown Office.

3. The Jury List
Actions ordered to be tried by a Judge and jury.

4. The Non-Jury List
(a) Actions other than jury actions or short causes set down under the provisions of R.S.C., O.34, r.3;
(b) Preliminary questions or issues ordered to be tried under R.S.C., O.33, r.3 and 4(2);

(*c*) Motions to commit other than those required to be heard by a Divisional Court of the Queen's Bench Division;

(*d*) Motions for judgment.

5. The Short Cause List

Actions ordered to be tried by a Judge alone where the time estimated for the trial does not exceed four hours.

12. The Commercial List

(*a*) Actions for trial in the Commercial Court.

(*b*) Any matter in paragraph 4 hereof which appertains to a matter in the Commercial Court.

13. The Arbitration Case List

Proceedings under R.S.C., O.73, r.2

14. Administrative Provisions—Commercial and Arbitration Case Lists

Actions or other proceedings in the Commercial Court will be dealt with as follows:

(*a*) Any party to an action to be tried in the Commercial Court may at any stage in the proceedings apply to the Commercial Judge by summons to fix a date for the trial or to vary or vacate such a date.

(*b*) An order made by the Court fixing the date of hearing will normally also provide for a date by which the cause must be set down for trial in the Commercial List.

(*c*) When a party to an action who has set it down for trial notifies the other parties to the action that he has done so, he should also inform the Commercial Court Listing Officer to the same effect.

(*d*) If any action which has been set down for trial in the Commercial Court is settled or withdrawn, or if the estimate of length of trial is revised, it shall be the duty of all parties to notify the Court of the fact without delay.

(*e*)   (i) Any proceeding in the Arbitration Case List shall in the first instance be referred to the Judge in charge of the Commercial List for his consideration as to its suitability for retention in that list.

(ii) Where the Judge directs that such a matter shall be heard by a Commercial Judge any party may thereafter apply to fix a date for trial.

APPENDIX C

Mr. Justice Parker

PRACTICE DIRECTION
given on 9th November 1981

Statement on revised practice

As is stated in the Annual Practice the Commercial Court has always sought to adapt its procedure to the continually changing needs of the commercial community and there has for some time existed, as a means of communication between the Court and that community, the Commercial Court Committee.

One of the principal functions of the Court has been and still is to deal swiftly with urgent matters. This it has done by bringing on for trial swiftly, cases in which for one reason or another, justice requires such a course to be taken, and by disposing as quickly as possible of other urgent matters such as applications for summary judgment, for orders continuing or discharging interlocutory injunctions for interlocutory orders of various kinds, for orders to arbitrators to state a special case under the Arbitration Act, 1950, or, now, motions for leave to appeal under the Arbitration Act, 1979, and so on.

Recently the volume of such urgent matters requiring early disposal has very considerably increased. In 1978 for example, 1180 summonses occupying 115 judge days were heard while in the year to July, 1981, the comparative figures were 2106 summonses and 277 judge days.

The result has been that return dates for such urgent matters have had to be put further and further ahead. In order that earlier return dates may be given for such matters which are likely to occupy less than one day, it has been decided, after discussion in the Commercial Court Committee to introduce, initially for an experimental period only, a new system.

As from Friday Nov. 20 all five Commercial Judges will normally sit on Fridays solely for the purpose of dealing with summonses and other short but urgent matters, and Tuesdays will cease to be summons days.

I say normally for it is recognized:

(1) that such a practice might involve the parties to a case part heard on a Thursday in unjustifiable extra expense if the case were adjourned to Monday in order to enable the Judge to deal with short matters on Friday.

170

(2) that there may be short matters which for one reason or another cannot be heard on a Friday and must be heard on a Tuesday or some other day.

(3) that if all Judges are taking short matters on Fridays there may be insurmountable difficulties for both sides of the profession in having more than one matter in which they are involved coming on on the same day.

The new system will therefore be operated on a flexible basis so as to obviate, or at least to reduce to a minimum, the foregoing difficulties and any others which may be found to arise when it is in operation.

In order that the new system can operate efficiently two essential requirements must be fulfilled. They are:

(1) Parties must notify the Commercial Court Office of any change in the estimated lengths of their summonses or other matters immediately such changes become known.

(2) Where Counsel are involved in more than one summons listed for a particular date, notification of that fact may be made to such office by Counsel's Clerks not later than 9.30 a.m. on the day prior to the return date.

In anticipation of the possible introduction of this system, the number of matters listed for Tuesdays has recently been kept down to a minimum but there are some which are still so listed. The parties involved should, if they possibly can, apply for the matter to be refixed for a Friday. This need not involve any delay.

The new system will make it possible for some at least of matters which are presently fixed for dates more than two months in the future to be refixed for earlier dates. Parties with such late return dates, who wish their matters to be heard earlier, should make application to Mr. Bird for earlier dates.

In conclusion I should stress two points:

(1) The purpose of the system is to accelerate urgent matters. Applications for leave to appeal under the 1979 Act are normally regarded as being in this category. I should, however, mention that there are several hundred applications for leave to appeal or other matters arising out of arbitration awards which were issued more than a year ago but for which no return date has yet been sought. Such, and other, dormant applications, although coming within a category normally regarded as urgent, will, if hereafter proceeded with, not be regarded as urgent in the absence of some convincing argument for sudden urgency being shown. It may be that many of them are in fact dead. If they are it would be of the greatest assistance to the Court if that fact could be notified as soon as possible.

(2) It may be that the benefit to litigants which the new system is designed to produce will produce difficulties not presently envisaged.

It will be of the greatest assistance if the existence of, and any suggestions for dealing with, any such difficulties are promptly communicated to the Commercial Court Committee in accordance with the open invitation which appears at par. 72/8/3 of the Annual Practice.[1]

PARKER, J.

*   *   *   *

1. Suggestions concerning the Commercial Court

The Commercial Court was established at the end of the last century in order to meet the special problems of the commercial community. Since then it has sought periodically to adapt its procedure to the continually changing needs of that community. The success of this process depends in part upon a steady flow of information and constructive suggestions between the court and those who appear there either as litigants or as their professional advisers. The formation of the Commercial Court Users' Liaison Committee will greatly assist this process and it is hoped that all concerned will make the fullest use of this additional channel of communication.

APPENDIX D

Mr. Justice PARKER

STATEMENT
given on 15th March 1982

There has for some time been exhibited in the Commercial Court Office a notice stating that all documents relevant to a chambers application should be lodged by noon on the day before the hearing date and warning that a failure to comply may result in the application not being heard.

Despite this, there are very many cases in which, for no good reason, the documents are not lodged by the time indicated and in some cases documents are not handed in until the application is called on.

This places a severe and unnecessary burden on Mr. Bird and his staff who have to spend time trying to chase up documents by telephone. It also leads to hearing times being unnecessarily prolonged because the Court has been unable to read the documents in advance.

With the steadily increasing numbers of applications and the concentration of applications into Friday's list it has become necessary for documents to be lodged two days instead of one day before the hearing and for cases in which there is a failure to comply with this requirement to be stood out at the expense of the party in default unless good cause for the failure is shown and the failure will not unduly prolong the hearing time for the application.

In addition, in order that the Court should have an early opportunity to consider whether a case is suitable for retention in the commercial list the main pleadings should always be lodged at the time of the first inter partes application in any action. Many cases are launched in the commercial list for no better reason than that one or other or both parties are banks, or shipping companies, or insurers, or commodity traders, or that the action is for breach of contract for sale of goods. If the issues in the case are not commercial issues at all but, for example a quality dispute in a sale of goods case, or a conversion or fraud, the resolution of which involves no commercial expertise, the case will normally be transferred to the Q.B. List.

Accordingly, the existing notice will be replaced as from 22nd March 1982 by the following notice:

173

It is the responsibility of both parties to an application to the Commercial Judge-in-Chambers to lodge all documents relevant to the application in Room 198 by noon two days before the date fixed for the hearing. Any affidavits already filed should be bespoken and the exhibits, if any, lodged. On the first occasion when any inter-partes application is made in an action the documents should always include the main pleadings and the parties should be prepared, if necessary, to justify the retention of the action in the Commercial List.

Failure to comply with this direction will normally result in the application not being heard on the date fixed at the expense of the party in default.

A copy of this notice should be attached to the copy application served on the parties.

Copies will be available in the office and it is the responsibility of the applicant to attach a copy to the summons served on the opposite party.

In order that this change may be as widely known as possible, Mr. Bird will be sending copies of the new notice to those firms of solicitors who most frequently use the Court with a request that it be drawn to the attention of all concerned.

The co-operation which will enable the Court to deal with its business without unnecessary delays will, I hope, make it unnecessary to make frequent use of the sanction of standing cases out.

APPENDIX E

ORDER 72

COMMERCIAL ACTIONS

Application and interpretation (O.72, r.1).

1.—(1) This Order applies to commercial actions in the Queen's Bench Division, and the other provisions of these Rules apply to those actions subject to the provisions of this Order.

(2) In this Order "commercial action" includes any cause arising out of the ordinary transactions of merchants and traders and, without prejudice to the generality of the foregoing words, any cause relating to the construction of a mercantile document, the export or import of merchandise, affreightment, insurance, banking, mercantile agency and mercantile usage.

The Commercial List (O.72, r.2).

2.—(1) There shall be a list, which shall be called "The commercial list", in which commercial actions in the Queen's Bench Division may be entered in accordance with the provisions of this Order, for trial in the Commercial Court and one of the Commercial Judges shall be in charge of that list.

(2) In this Order references to the judge shall be construed as references to the judge for the time being in charge of the commercial list.

(3) The judge shall have control of the actions in the commercial list and, subject to the provisions of this Order and to any directions of the judge, the powers of a judge in chambers (including those exercisable by a master or registrar) shall, in relation to any proceedings [in such action (including any appeal from any judgment, order or decision of a master or registrar, given or made prior to transfer of the action to the commercial list), be exercisable by the judge.]^A

(4) Paragraph (3) shall not be construed as preventing the powers of the judge being exercised by some other judge.

A. The words in square brackets were substituted with effect from 1st January 1983 by 1982 S.I. No. 1786, para. 19.

Powers, etc., of Liverpool and Manchester district registrars (O.72, r.3).

3.—(1) All interlocutory applications in an action in the commercial list proceeding in the district registry of Liverpool or the district registry of Manchester, other than an application under rule 6, must be made to the registrar of that registry notwithstanding that the action is in the commercial list, and the registrar may make such order on any such application as he thinks fit or may adjourn the application to be heard by the judge:

Provided that if any party to any such application requests the registrar to adjourn the application to the judge for hearing by him the registrar shall adjourn it accordingly.

(2) It shall be the duty of the registrar of each of the said registries to keep the judge's clerk informed of the progress of actions in the commercial list proceeding in that registry and, in particular, to inform him of the making of an order that such an action shall be tried at Liverpool or Manchester, as the case may be, and of the date fixed for the trial.

Entry of action in commercial list when action begun (O.72, r.4).

4.—(1) Before a writ or originating summons by which a commercial action in the Queen's Bench Division is to be begun is issued out of the central office, the district registry of Liverpool or the district registry of Manchester, it may be marked in the top left-hand corner with the words "Commercial Court," and on the issue of a writ or summons so marked the action begun thereby shall be entered in the commercial list.

(2) If the plaintiff intends to issue the writ or originating summons by which a commercial action in the Queen's Bench Division is to be begun out of the Central Office and to mark it in accordance with paragraph (1), and the writ or the originating summons, as the case may be, is to be served out of the jurisdiction, an application for leave to issue the writ or summons and to serve the writ or the summons out of the jurisdiction may be made to the judge.

(3) The affidavit in support of an application made to the judge by virtue of paragraph (2) must, in addition to the matters required by Order 11, rule 4(1) to be stated, state that the plaintiff intends to mark the writ or originating summons in accordance with paragraph (1) of this rule.

(4) If the judge hearing an application made to him by virtue of paragraph (2) is of opinion that the action in question should not be entered in the commercial list, he may adjourn the application to be heard by a master.

Transfer of action to commercial list after action begun (O.72, r.5).

5.—(1) At any stage of the proceedings in a commercial action in the Queen's Bench Division[B] any party to the action may apply by summons to the judge or, if the action is proceeding in the district registry of Liverpool or the district registry of Manchester, to the registrar of that registry to transfer the action to the commercial list.

(2) When an application under paragraph (1) is made to the registrar of either of the said registries, the registrar may either order the action to be transferred to the commercial list or adjourn the summons to be heard by the Judge.

(3) If, [at any stage of the proceedings][C] in a commercial action in the Queen's Bench Division, it appears to the Court that the action may be one suitable for trial in the Commercial Court and any party wishes the action to be transferred to the commercial list, then, subject to paragraph (4), the Court may [adjourn any hearing so that it can proceed before the judge and be treated][C] by him as a summons to transfer the action to that list.

(4) The registrar of the district registry of Liverpool or the district registry of Manchester may, instead of adjourning a summons under paragraph (3), order the action to be transferred to the commercial list; and if on the hearing of any summons in a commercial action in the Queen's Bench Division by the registrar of any district registry any party requests the registrar to adjourn the summons under paragraph (3) so that it can be heard by the judge, the registrar shall adjourn the summons accordingly, and the adjourned summons shall be treated by the judge as a summons to transfer the action to the commercial list.

(5) Where the judge orders a commercial action in the Queen's Bench Division proceeding in a district registry to be transferred to the commercial list he may also order the action to be transferred to the Royal Courts of Justice.

Removal of action from commercial list (O.72, r.6).

6.—(1) The judge may, of his own motion or on the application of any party, order an action in the commercial list to be removed from that list.

(2) Where an action is in the commercial list by virtue of rule 4, an application by a defendant or third party for an order under this rule must be made within 7 days after giving notice of intention to defend.

Pleadings in commercial list actions (O.72, r.7).

7.—(1) The pleadings in an action in the commercial list must be in the form of points of claim, or of defence, counterclaim, defence to counterclaim or reply, as the case may be and must be as brief as possible.

B. The words "before trial" have been deleted with effect from 1st January 1983 by 1982 S.I. No. 1786, para. 19.
C. The words in square brackets have been substituted by the above statutory instrument.

(2) Without prejudice to Order 18, rule 12(1), no particulars shall be applied for or ordered in an action in the commercial list except such particulars as are necessary to enable the party applying to be informed of the case he has to meet or as are for some other reason necessary to secure the just, expeditious and economical disposal of any question at issue in the action.

(3) The foregoing provisions are without prejudice to the power of the judge or of the district registrar of Liverpool or the district registrar of Manchester to order that an action in the commercial list shall be tried without pleadings or further pleadings, as the case may be.

Directions in commercial list actions (O.72, r.8).

8.—(1) Notwithstanding anything in Order 25, rule 1(1), any party to an action in the commercial list may take out a summons for directions in the action before the pleadings in the action are deemed to be closed.

(2) Where an application is made to transfer an action to the commercial list, Order 25, rules 2 to 7, shall, with the omission of so much of rule 7(1) as requires the parties to serve a notice specifying the orders and directions which they desire and with any other necessary modifications, apply as if the application were a summons for directions.

Trial with City of London special jury (O.72, r.9).

9.—[*Revoked by R.S.C. (Amendment No. 5) 1971 (S.I. 1971 No. 1955), at the same time as the abolition of City of London special juries by section 4 of the Courts Act 1971.*]

Production of certain documents in marine insurance actions (O.72, r.10).

10.—(1) Where in an action in the commercial list relating to a marine insurance policy an application for an order under Order 24, rule 3, is made by the insurer, then, without prejudice to its powers under that rule, the Court, if satisfied that the circumstances of the case are such that it is necessary or expedient to do so, may make an order, either in Form No. 94 in Appendix A or in such other form as it thinks fit, for the production of such documents as are therein specified or described.

(2) An order under this rule may be made on such terms, if any, as to staying proceedings in the action or otherwise, as the Court thinks fit.

(3) In this rule "the Court" means the judge, the district registrar of Liverpool or the district registrar of Manchester, as the case may be.

APPENDIX F

ORDER 73

ARBITRATION PROCEEDINGS

Arbitration proceedings not to be assigned to Chancery Division (O.73, r.1).

1. A cause or matter consisting of an application to the High Court or a judge thereof under Part I of the Arbitration Act 1950 or an appeal or application under the Arbitration Act 1979 shall not be assigned to the Chancery Division.

The foregoing provision shall not apply in relation to an application under section 4 of the said Act of 1950 made in proceedings assigned to the Chancery Division.

Matters for a judge in court (O.73, r.2).

2.—(1) Every application to the Court—
   (*a*) to remit an award under section 22 of the Arbitration Act 1950, or
   (*b*) to remove an arbitrator or umpire under section 23(1) of that Act, or
   (*c*) to set aside an award under section 23(2) thereof, or
   (*d*) for leave to appeal under section 1(2) of the Arbitration Act 1979, or
   (*e*) to determine, under section 2(1) of that Act, any question of law arising in the course of a reference,
must be made by originating motion to a single judge in court.

(2) Any appeal to the High Court under section 1(2) of the Arbitration Act 1979 shall be made by originating motion to a single judge in court and notice thereof may be included in the notice of application for leave to appeal, where leave is required.

(3) An application for a declaration that an award made by an arbitrator or umpire is not binding on a party to the award on the ground that it was made without jurisdiction may be made by originating motion to a single judge in court, but the foregoing provision shall not be taken as affecting the judge's power to refuse to make such a declaration in proceedings begun by motion.

Matters for judge in chambers or master (O.73, r.3).

3.—(1) Subject to the foregoing provisions of this Order and the provisions of this rule, the jurisdiction of the High Court or a judge thereof under the

Arbitration Act 1950 and the jurisdiction of the High Court under the Arbitration Act 1975 and the Arbitration Act 1979 may be exercised by a judge in chambers, a master or the Admiralty Registrar.

(2) Any application under section 1(5) of the Arbitration Act 1979 (including any application for leave), or under section 5 of that Act, shall be made to a judge.

(3) Any application to which this rule applies shall, where an action is pending, be made by summons in the action, and in any other case by an originating summons which shall be in Form No. 10 in Appendix A.

(4) Where an application is made under section 1(5) of the Arbitration Act 1979) including any application for leave), the summons must be served on the arbitrator or umpire and on any other party to the reference.

Applications in district registries (O.73, r.4).

4. An application under section 12(4) of the Arbitration Act 1950 for an order that a writ of subpoena ad testificandum or of subpoena duces tecum shall issue to compel the attendance before an arbitrator or umpire of a witness may, if the attendance of the witness is required within the district of any district registry, be made at that registry, instead of at the Central Office, at the option of the applicant.

Time-limits and other special provisions as to appeals and applications under the Arbitration Acts (O.73, r.5).

5.—(1) An application to the Court—
   (a) to remit an award under section 22 of the Arbitration Act 1950, or
   (b) to set aside an award under section 23(2) of that Act or otherwise, or
   (c) to direct an arbitrator or umpire to state the reasons for an award under section 1(5) of the Arbitration Act 1979
must be made, and the summons or notice must be served, within 21 days after the award has been made and published to the parties.

(2) In the case of an appeal to the Court under section 1(2) of the Arbitration Act 1979, the notice must be served, and the appeal entered, within 21 days after the award has been made and published to the parties:

Provided that, where reasons material to the appeal are given on a date subsequent to the publication of the award, the period of 21 days shall run from the date on which the reasons are given.

(3) An application, under section 2(1) of the Arbitration Act 1979, to determine any question of law arising in the course of a reference, must be made, and notice thereof served, within 14 days after the arbitrator or umpire has consented to the application being made, or the other parties have so consented.

(4) For the purpose of paragraph (2) the consent must be given in writing.

(5) In the case of every appeal or application to which this rule applies, the notice of originating motion or, as the case may be, the originating summons, must state the grounds of the appeal of application and, where the appeal or application is founded on evidence by affidavit, or is made with the consent of the arbitrator or umpire or of the other parties, a copy of every affidavit intended to be used, or, as the case may be, of every consent given in writing, must be served with that notice.

Applications and appeals to be heard by Commercial Judges

6.—(1) Any matter which is required, by rule 2 or 3, to be heard by a judge, shall be heard by a Commercial Judge, unless any such judge otherwise directs.

(2) Nothing in the foregoing paragraph shall be construed as preventing the powers of a Commercial Judge from being expressed by any judge of the High Court.

Service out of the jurisdiction of summons, notice, etc. (O.73, r.7).

7.—(1) Service out of the jurisdiction—

    (a) of an originating summons for the appointment of an arbitrator or umpire or for leave to enforce an award, or

    (b) of notice of an originating motion to remove an arbitrator or umpire or to remit or set aside an award, or

    (c) of an originating summons or notice of an originating motion under the Arbitration Act 1979, or

    (d) of any order made on such a summons or motion as aforesaid,

is permissible with the leave of the Court provided that the arbitration to which the summons, motion or order relates is governed by English law or has been, is being, or is to be held, within the jurisdiction.

(2) An application for the grant of leave under this rule must be supported by an affidavit stating the grounds on which the application is made and showing in what place or country the person to be served is, or probably may be found; and no such leave shall be granted unless it shall be made sufficiently to appear to the Court that the case is a proper one for service out of the jurisdiction under this rule.

(3) Order 11, rules 5, 6 and 8, shall apply in relation to any such summons, notice or order as is referred to in paragraph (1) as they apply in relation to a writ.

Registration in High Court of foreign awards (O.73, r.8).

8. Where an award is made in proceedings on an arbitration in any part of Her Majesty's dominions or other territory to which Part I of the Foreign Judgments (Reciprocal Enforcement) Act 1933 extends, being a part to which Part II of the Administration of Justice Act 1920 extended immediately before the said Part I was extended thereto, then, if the award has, in pursuance of the law in force in the place where it was made, become enforceable in the same manner as a judgment given by a court in that place, Order 71 shall apply in relation to the award as it applies in relation to a judgment given by that court, subject however, to the following modifications:—

(a) for references to the country of the original court there shall be substituted references to the place where the award was made; and

(b) the affidavit required by rule 3 of the said Order must state (in addition to the other matters required by that rule) that to the best of the information or belief of the deponent the award has, in pursuance of the law in force in the place where it was made, become enforceable in the same manner as a judgment given by a court in that place.

Registration of awards under Arbitration (International Investment Disputes) Act 1966 (O.73, r.9).

9.—(1) In this rule and in any provision of these rules as applied by this rule—

"the Act of 1966" means the Arbitration (International Investment Disputes) Act 1966;

"award" means an award rendered pursuant to the Convention;

"the Convention" means the Convention referred to in section 1(1) of the Act of 1966;

"judgment creditor" and "judgment debtor" means respectively the person seeking recognition or enforcement of an award and the other party to the award.

(2) Subject to the provisions of this rule, the following provisions of Order 71, namely, rules 1, 3 (1) (except sub-paragraphs (c) (iv) and (d) thereof), 7 (except paragraph (3)(c) and (d) thereof), and 10(3), shall apply with the necessary modifications in relation to an award as they apply in relation to a judgment to which Part II of the Foreign Judgments (Reciprocal Enforcement) Act 1933 applies.

(3) An application to have an award registered in the High Court under section 1 of the Act of 1966 shall be made by originating summons which shall be in Form No. 10 in Appendix A.

(4) The affidavit required by Order 71, rule 3, in support of an application for registration shall—

    (a) in lieu of exhibiting the judgment or a copy thereof, exhibit a copy of the award certified pursuant to the Convention, and

    (b) in addition to stating the matters mentioned in paragraph 3(1)(c)(i) and (ii) of the said rule 3, state whether at the date of the application the enforcement of the award has been stayed (provisionally or otherwise) pursuant to the Convention and whether any, and if so what, application has been made pursuant to the Convention which, if granted, might result in a stay of the enforcement of the award.

(5) There shall be kept in the Central Office under the direction of the senior master a register of the awards ordered to be registered under the Act of 1966 and particulars shall be entered in the register of any execution issued on such an award.

(6) Where it appears to the court on granting leave to register an award or on an application made by the judgment debtor after an award has been registered—

    (a) that the enforcement of the award has been stayed (whether provisionally or otherwise) pursuant to the Convention, or

    (b) that an application has been made pursuant to the Convention which, if granted, might result in a stay of the enforcement of the award,

the court shall, or, in the case referred to in sub-paragraph (b), may, stay execution of the award for such time as it considers appropriate in the circumstances.

(7) An application by the judgment debtor under paragraph (6) shall be made by summons and supported by affidavit.

Enforcement of arbitration awards (O.73, r.10).

10.—(1) An application for leave under section 26 of the Arbitration Act 1950 or under section 3(1)(a) of the Arbitration Act 1975 to enforce an award on an arbitration agreement in the same manner as a judgment or order may be made ex parte but the Court hearing the application may direct a summons to be issued.

(2) If the Court directs a summons to be issued, the summons shall be an originating summons which shall be in Form No. 10 in Appendix A.

(3) An application for leave must be supported by affidavit—

    (a) exhibiting

        (i) where the application is under section 26 of the Arbitration Act 1950, the arbitration agreement and the original award or, in either case, a copy thereof;

      (ii) where the application is under section 3(1)(*a*) of the Arbitration Act 1975, the documents required to be produced by section 4 of that Act,

  (*b*) stating the name and the usual or last known place of abode or business of the applicant (hereinafter referred to as "the creditor") and the person against whom it is sought to enforce the award (hereinafter referred to as "the debtor") respectively,

  (*c*) as the case may require, either that the award has not been complied with or the extent to which it has not been complied with at the date of the application.

(4) An order giving leave must be drawn up by or on behalf of the creditor and must be served on the debtor by delivering a copy to him personally or by sending a copy to him at his usual or last known place of abode or business or in such other manner as the Court may direct.

(5) Service of the order out of the jurisdiction is permissible without leave, and Order 11, rules 5, 6 and 8, shall apply in relation to such an order as they apply in relation to a writ.

(6) Within 14 days after service of the order or, if the order is to be served out of the jurisdiction, within such other period as the Court may fix, the debtor may apply to set aside the order and the award shall not be enforced until after the expiration of that period or, if the debtor applies within that period to set aside the order, until after the application is finally disposed of.

(7) The copy of that order served on the debtor shall state the effect of paragraph (6).

(8) In relation to a body corporate this rule shall have effect as if for any reference to the place of abode or business of the creditor or the debtor there were substituted a reference to the registered or principal address of the body corporate; so, however, that nothing in this rule shall affect any enactment which provides for the manner in which a document may be served on a body corporate.

APPENDIX G

ADMINISTRATION OF JUSTICE ACT 1970

4 Power of judges of Commercial Court to take arbitrations (1) A judge of the Commercial Court may, if in all the circumstances he thinks fit, accept appointment as sole arbitrator, or as umpire, by or by virtue of an arbitration agreement within the meaning of the Arbitration Act 1950, where the dispute appears to him to be of a commercial character.

(2) A judge of the Commercial Court shall not accept appointment as arbitrator or umpire unless the Lord Chief Justice has informed him that, having regard to the state of business in the High Court and [in the Crown Court],[1] he can be made available to do so.

(3) The fees payable for the services of a judge as arbitrator or umpire shall be taken in the High Court.

(4) Schedule 3 to this Act shall have effect for modifying, and in certain cases replacing, provisions of the Arbitration Act 1950 in relation to arbitration by judges and, in particular, for substituting the Court of Appeal for the High Court in provisions of that Act whereby arbitrators and umpires, their proceedings and awards, are subject to control and review by the court.

(5) Any jurisdiction which is exercisable by the High Court in relation to arbitrators and umpires otherwise than under the Arbitration Act 1950 shall, in relation to a judge of the Commercial Court appointed as arbitrator or umpire, be exercisable instead by the Court of Appeal.

★   ★   ★   ★

SCHEDULE 3

Application of Arbitration Act 1950 to Judge-Arbitrators
1 In this Schedule —
    (a) 'the Act' means the Arbitration Act 1950;
    (b) 'arbitration agreement' has the same meaning as in the Act; and

---

1. The words in square brackets were introduced by the Courts Act 1971, s.56(1) and Schedule 8, para. 60.

(c) 'judge-arbitrator' and 'judge-umpire' mean a judge of the Commercial Court appointed as arbitrator or, as the case may be, as umpire by or by virtue of an arbitration agreement.

2 In section 1 of the Act (authority of arbitrator to be irrevocable except by leave of the court), in its application to a judge-arbitrator or judge-umpire, the Court of Appeal shall be substituted for the High Court.

3 The power of the High Court under section 7 of the Act (vacancy among arbitrators supplied by parties) to set aside the appointment of an arbitrator shall not be exercisable in the case of the appointment of a judge-arbitrator.

4 Section 8(3) of the Act (power of High Court to order umpire to enter immediately on reference as sole arbitrator) shall not apply to a judge-umpire; but a judge-umpire may, on the application of any party to the reference and notwithstanding anything to the contrary in the arbitration agreement, enter on the reference in lieu of the arbitrators and as if he were the sole arbitrator.

5 (1) The powers conferred on the High Court or a judge thereof by section 12(4), (5) and (6) of the Act (summoning of witnesses, interlocutory orders, etc.) shall be exercisable in the case of a reference to a judge-arbitrator or judge-umpire as in the case of any other reference to arbitration, but shall in any such case be exercisable also by the judge-arbitrator or judge-umpire himself.

(2) Anything done by an arbitrator or umpire in the exercise of powers conferred by this paragraph shall be done by him in his capacity as judge of the High Court and have effect as if done by that court; but nothing in this paragraph prejudices any power vested in the arbitrator or umpire in his capacity as such.

6 Section 13(2) and (3) of the Act (extension of time for making award; provision for ensuring that reference is conducted with reasonable dispatch) shall not apply to a reference to a judge-arbitrator or judge-umpire; but a judge-arbitrator or judge-umpire may enlarge any time limited for making his award (whether under the Act or otherwise), whether that time has expired or not.

7 (1) Section 18(4) of the Act (provision enabling a party in an arbitration to obtain an order for costs) shall apply, in the case of a reference to a judge-arbitrator, with the omission of the words from 'within fourteen days' to 'may direct'.

(2) The power of the High Court to make declarations and orders for the purposes of section 18(5) of the Act (charging order for solicitor's costs) shall be exercisable in the case of an arbitration by a judge-arbitrator or judge-umpire as in the case of any other arbitration, but shall in any such case be exercisable also by the judge-arbitrator or judge-umpire himself.

(3) A declaration or order made by an arbitrator or umpire in the exercise of the power conferred by the last foregoing sub-paragraph shall be made by him in his capacity as judge of the High Court and have effect as if made by that court.

8 (1) Section 19 of the Act (power of High Court to order delivery of award on payment of arbitrators' fees into court) shall not apply with respect to the award of a judge-arbitrator or judge-umpire.

(2) A judge-umpire may withhold his award until the fees payable to the arbitrators have been paid into the High Court.

(3) Arbitrators' fees paid into court under this paragraph shall be paid out in accordance with rules of court, subject to the right of any party to the reference to apply (in accordance with the rules) for any fee to be taxed, not being a fee which has been fixed by written agreement between him and the arbitrator.

(4) A taxation under this paragraph may be reviewed in the same manner as a taxation of the costs of an award.

(5) On a taxation under this paragraph, or on a review thereof, an arbitrator shall be entitled to appear and be heard.

9 (1) In sections [21(1) and (2)]² 22 and 23 of the Act (special case, remission and setting aside of awards, etc.), in their application to a judge-arbitrator or judge-umpire, and to a reference to him and to his award thereon, the Court of Appeal shall be substituted for the High Court.

[(2) A decision of the Court of Appeal on a case stated by a judge-arbitrator or judge-umpire under section 21 of the Act (as amended by this paragraph) shall be deemed to be a judgment of that court for the purposes of section 3 of the Appellate Jurisdiction Act 1876 (appeal to House of Lords); but no appeal shall lie from any such decision without the leave of the Court of Appeal or the House of Lords.]²

10 (1) Section 24(2) of the Act (removal of issue of fraud for trial in the High Court) shall not apply to an agreement under or by virtue of which a judge-arbitrator or judge-umpire has been appointed; nor shall leave be given by the High Court under that subsection to revoke the authority of a judge-arbitrator or judge-umpire.

(2) Where, on a reference of a dispute to a judge-arbitrator or judge-umpire, it appears to the judge that the dispute involves the question whether a party to the dispute has been guilty of fraud, he may, so far as may be necessary to enable that question to be determined by the High Court, order that the agreement by or by virtue of which he was appointed shall cease to have effect and revoke his authority as arbitrator or umpire.

(3) An order made by a judge-arbitrator or judge-umpire under this paragraph shall have effect as if made by the High Court.

---

2. Repealed by the Arbitration Act 1979, s.8(3)(c). Whether these provisions have survived the repeal in so far as concerns arbitrations to which the 1979 Act does not apply remains a matter of doubt.

11 Section 25 of the Act (powers of court on removal of arbitrator or revocation of arbitration agreement) shall be amended as follows:—

    (a) after the words 'the High Court' where they first occur in subsection (1), where they occur for the first and second time in subsection (2), and in subsections (3) and (4), there shall be inserted the words 'or the Court of Appeal'; and

    (b) after those words where they occur for the second time in subsection (1) and for the third time in subsection (2) there shall be inserted the words 'or the Court of Appeal, as the case may be'.

12. The leave required by section 26 of the Act (enforcement in High Court) for an award on an arbitration agreement to be enforced as mentioned in that section may, in the case of an award by a judge-arbitrator or a judge-umpire, be given by the judge-arbitrator or judge-umpire himself.

INDEX

A

AGENTS. *See* "MAREVA" INJUNCTIONS.

APPEAL. *See also* ARBITRATION.
Court of Appeal, to, when will lie, 31–32
order for transfer to Commercial Court, against, 51

ARBITRATION. *See also* ARBITRATION AWARD; ARBITRATOR; "MAREVA" INJUNCTIONS; ORIGINATING SUMMONS PROCEDURE.
appeal,
  applications for leave to, 14, 15, 30
  Court of Appeal, to, 139–140
  question of law, on, 122
applications,
  concerning important general principles of arbitration law, 30
  determine any question of law to, 15, 30
  set aside award, to, 30
Arbitration Act 1950, under, 122–124
Commercial Court and, 121 *et seq.*
Commercial Court Committee report on, 130
consultative case, the, 144
disputes not necessarily commercial actions (prior to 1979), 30
documents,
  originating motion,
    decision of preliminary point of law, 161–162
    leave to appeal, for, and for the appeal, 155–158
    setting aside or remission of award, 159–160
  originating summons,
    order extending powers of arbitrator, 165
    order for arbitrator to state further reasons, 163–164
hazardous, 5

ARBITRATION—*cont.*
judicial,
  introduction of, 12
  not widely used, 13
"*Mareva*" injunctions to secure claims under, 97
maritime, 121
non-commercial, 30, 122
Order 73, r.6, 30
originating summons procedure, and, 35
preliminary points of law, 122, 144
  Arbitration Act 1950, s.21(1), 144
  Arbitration Act 1979, s.2, 144
  Court of Appeal, appeals to, 147
  Court's discretion, 145
  originating motion, application by, 145–147
proceedings,
  Arbitration Act 1950, under, 122–123
  Arbitration Act 1979, in relation to, 130
  Commercial Court, and, 121 *et seq.*
  in relation to all arbitrations, 127
special case procedure, 124–125
two-tier, 121

ARBITRATION AWARDS. *See also* ARBITRATION; ARBITRATOR.
applications,
  arbitrators to give reasons, for, 122, 140–142
    originating summons, by, 143–144
  leave to appeal against, for, 130–134
    principles on which granted, 135–139
  remit, to, 15, 30, 127
  set aside, to,
    error of law or fact, for, 125–127
    misconduct, for, 15, 129

ARBITRATOR. *See also* ARBITRATION; ARBITRATION AWARD.
applications,
  extended powers, for, 15
  give reasons, to, 15, 30, 122, 140–142

189

PRINTED IN GREAT BRITAIN BY
The Eastern Press Limited
SPECIALIST LAW BOOK
AND JOURNAL PRINTERS
LONDON AND READING